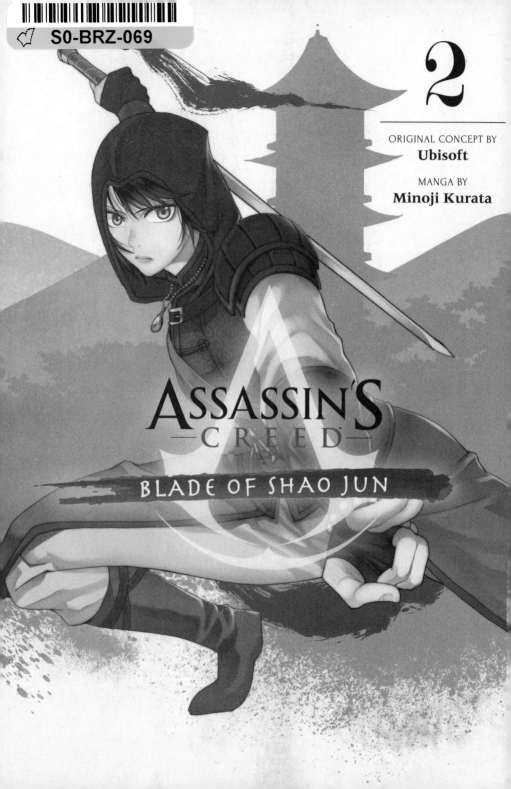

# 2

ORIGINAL CONCEPT BY
**Ubisoft**

MANGA BY
**Minoji Kurata**

# ASSASSIN'S
## —C R E E D—

### BLADE OF SHAO JUN

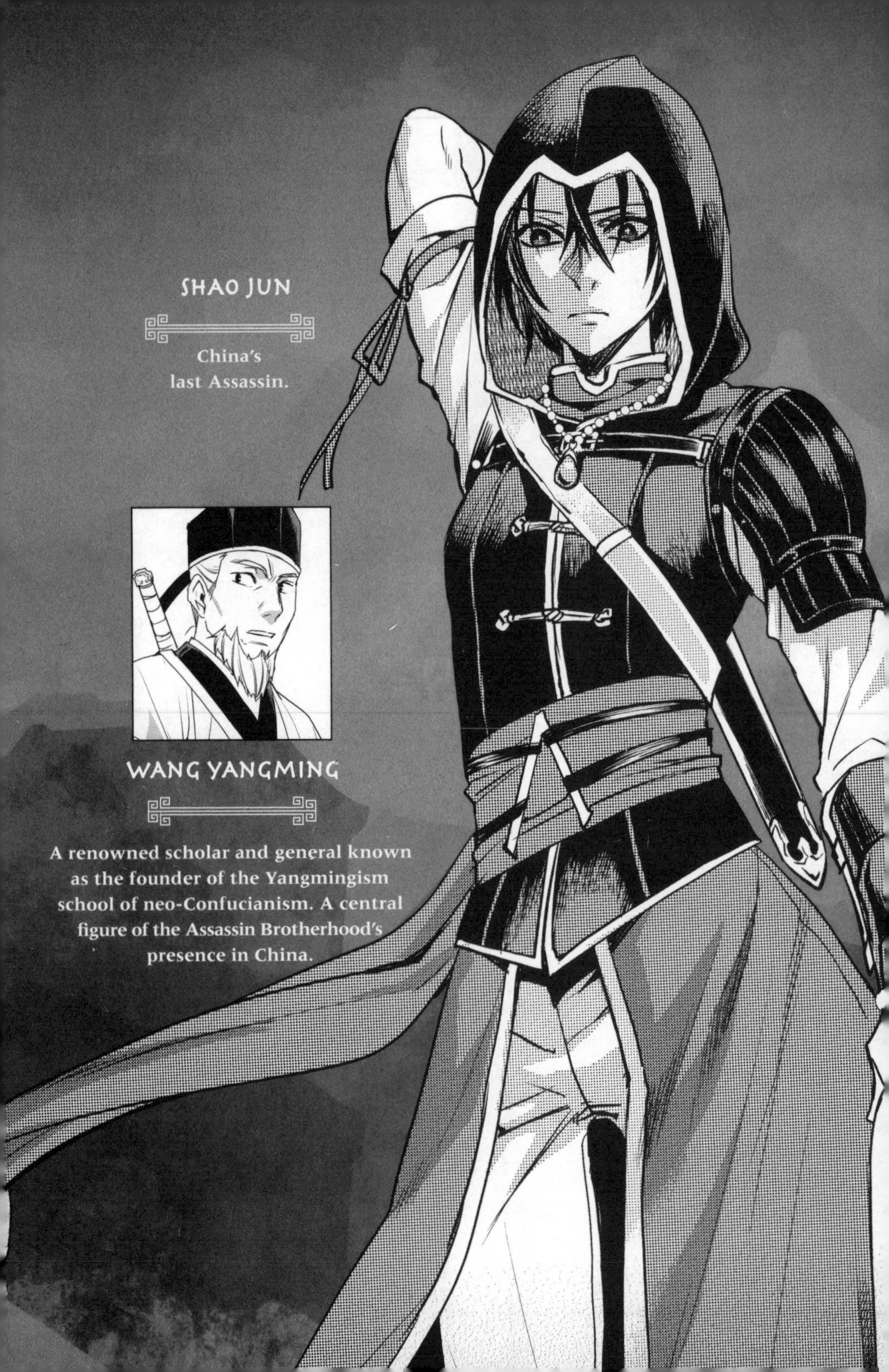
SHAO JUN
China's last Assassin.
WANG YANGMING
A renowned scholar and general known as the founder of the Yangmingism school of neo-Confucianism. A central figure of the Assassin Brotherhood's presence in China.

## The Ming Dynasty ruled in 16th century China.

During the chaos created by the emperor's political purge, eunuchs aligned with the Order of the Knights Templar took the opportunity to slay the allies of Shao Jun, leaving her as China's last remaining Assassin. The young woman fled to Europe and underwent grueling training, but now she's returned to her homeland seeking revenge.

The memories of this quest are carved into the very DNA of Lisa—a young woman in modern-day Yokohama who is Shao Jun's descendant! Now, Dr. Kagami is helping Lisa explore these memories and calling it "therapy" for the violent impulses that plague her—but it seems the doctor has ulterior motives!

### DR. KAGAMI

Claims that helping Lisa explore her ancestor's memories will serve as effective therapy.

### LISA

A young woman in modern-day Yokohama who worries about the violent impulses she harbors. She is Shao Jun's distant descendant.

### THE EIGHT TIGERS

A gang of tyrannical eunuchs backed by the emperor's patronage. In truth, they serve the Templar Order, which has spread its roots into China.

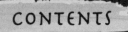

# CONTENTS

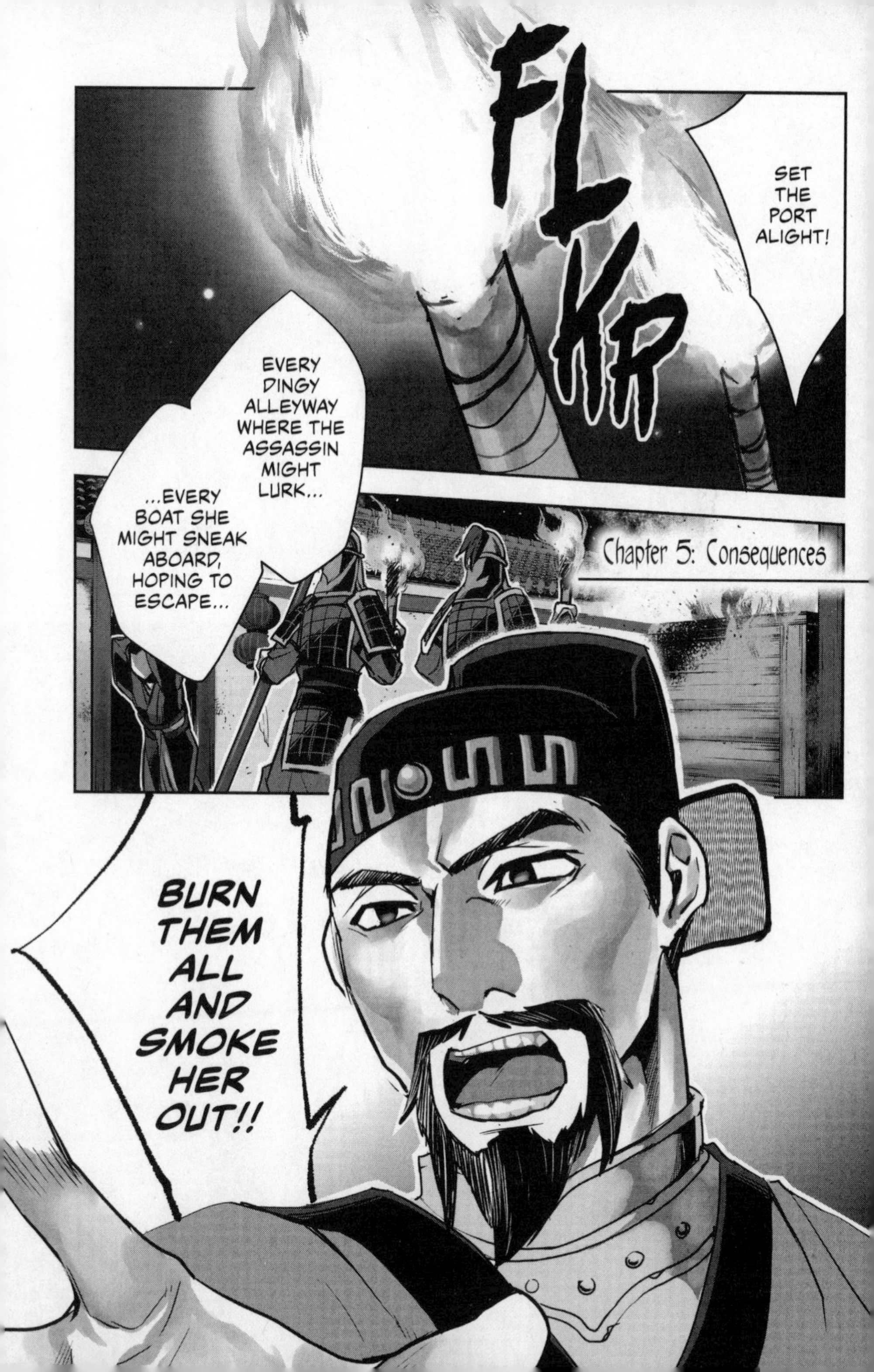
SET THE PORT ALIGHT!
FLKR
EVERY DINGY ALLEYWAY WHERE THE ASSASSIN MIGHT LURK...
...EVERY BOAT SHE MIGHT SNEAK ABOARD, HOPING TO ESCAPE...
Chapter 5: Consequences
BURN THEM ALL AND SMOKE HER OUT!!

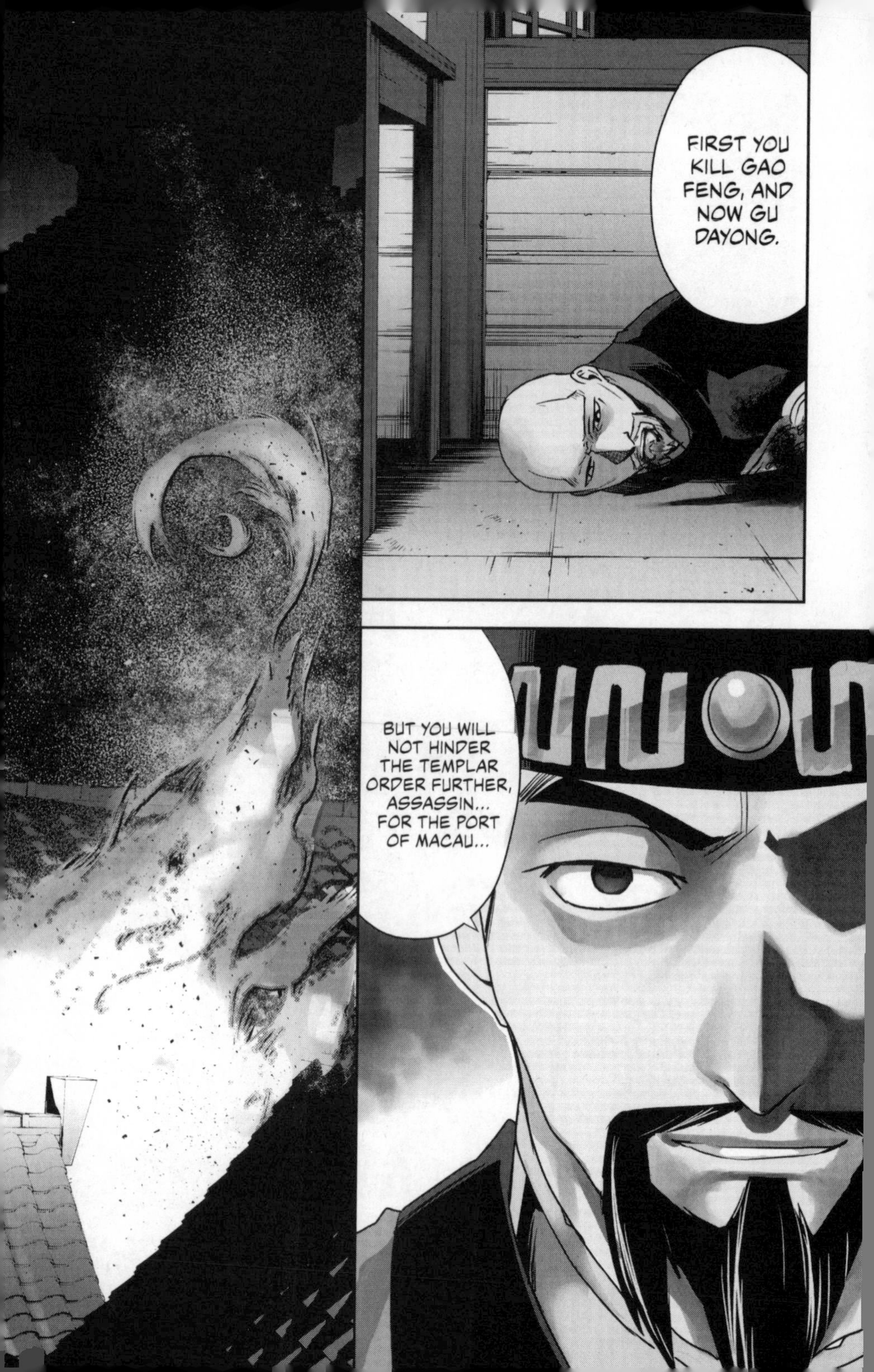
FIRST YOU KILL GAO FENG, AND NOW GU DAYONG.
BUT YOU WILL NOT HINDER THE TEMPLAR ORDER FURTHER, ASSASSIN... FOR THE PORT OF MACAU...

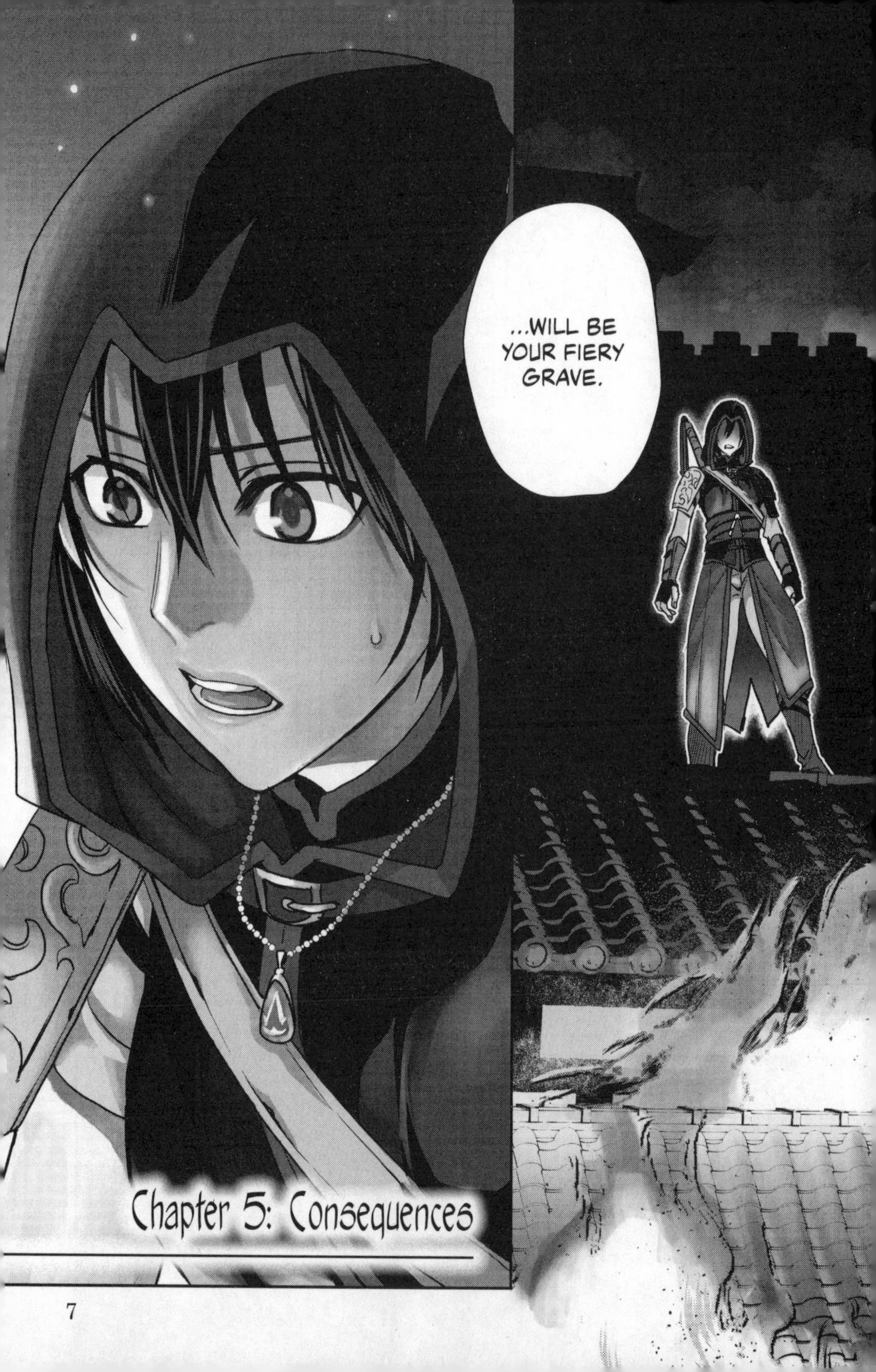
...WILL BE YOUR FIERY GRAVE.
Chapter 5: Consequences

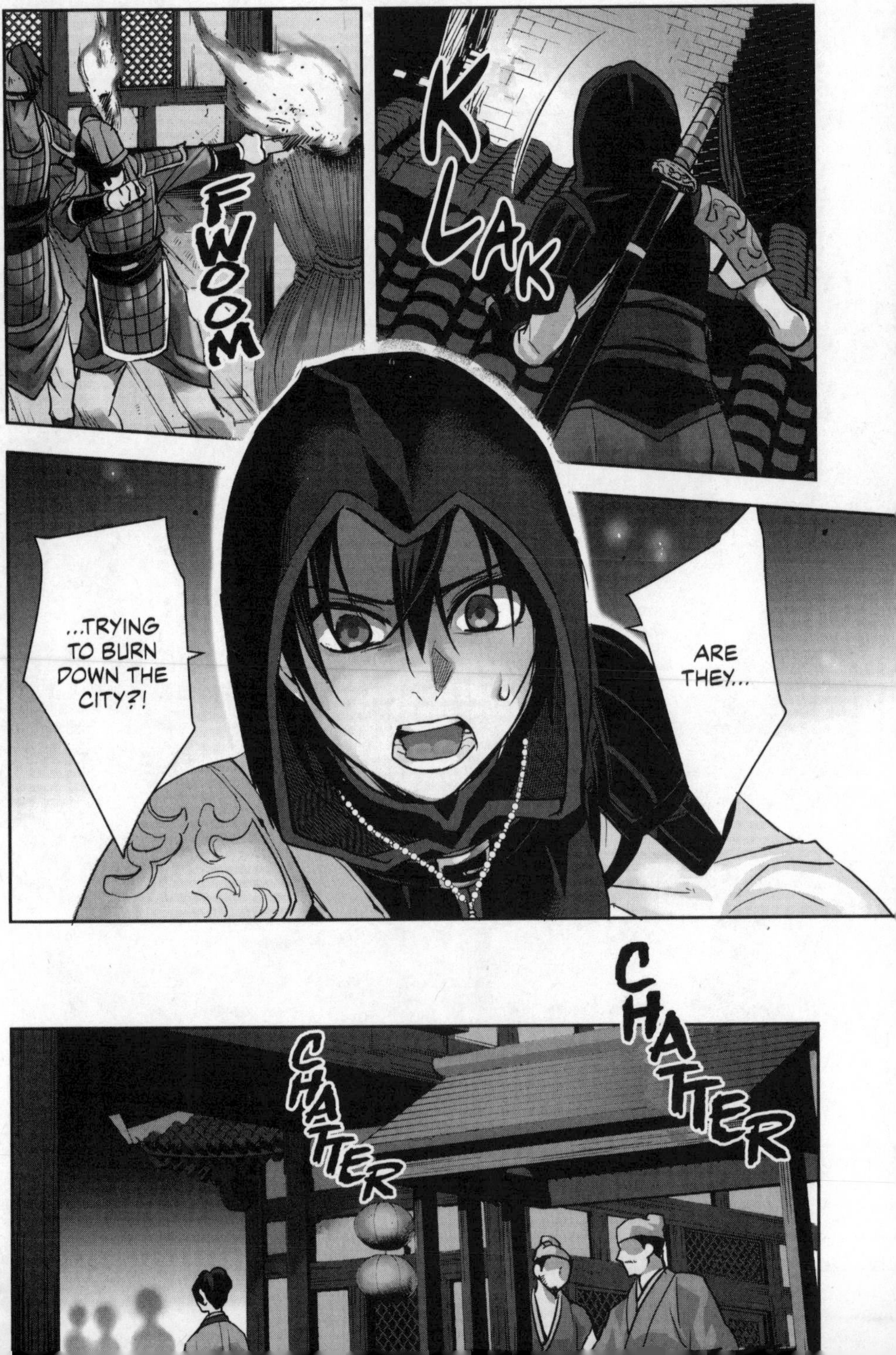
KLAK
FWOOM
ARE THEY...
...TRYING TO BURN DOWN THE CITY?!
CHATTER
CHATTER

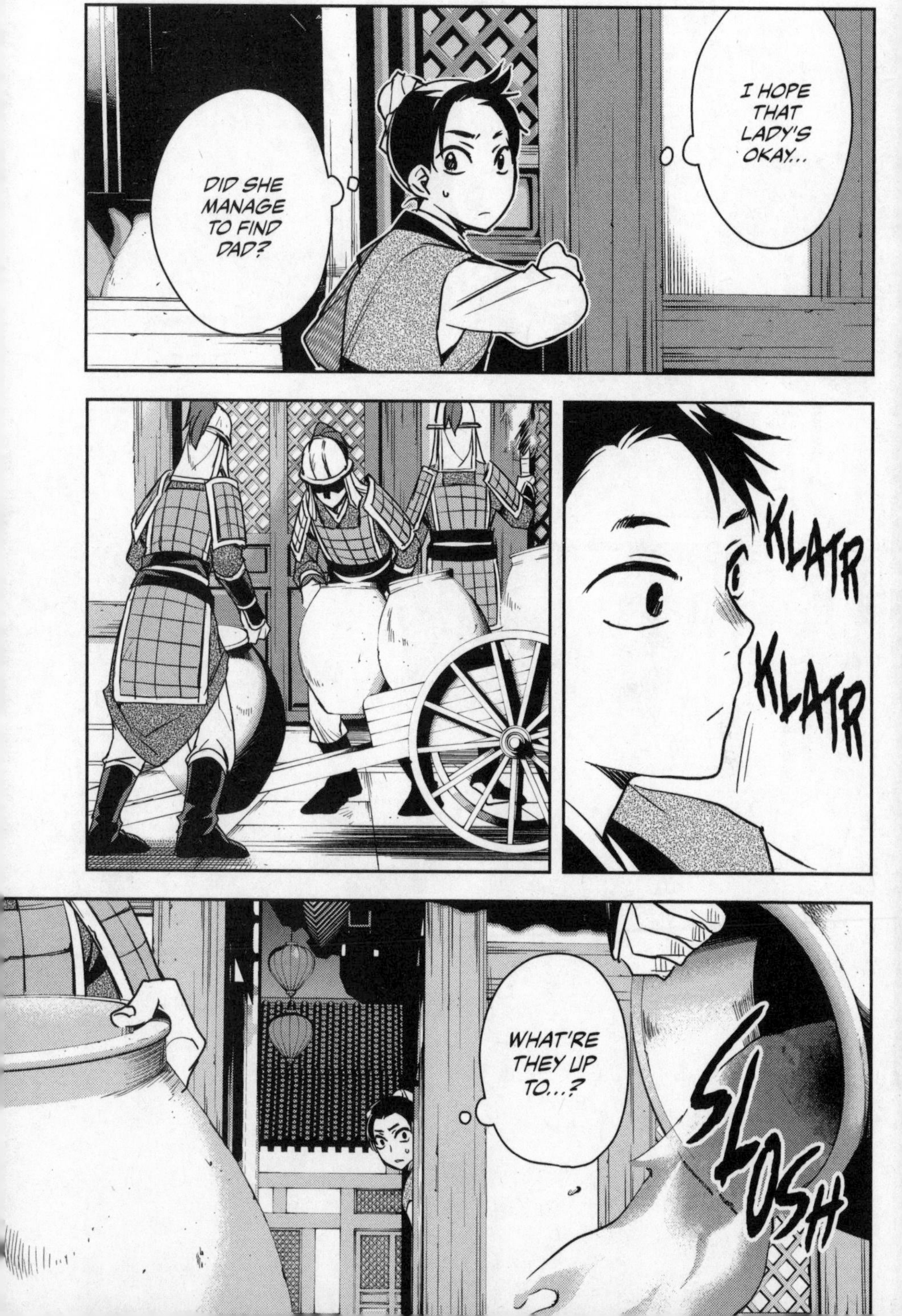
I HOPE THAT LADY'S OKAY...
DID SHE MANAGE TO FIND DAD?
KLATR
KLATR
WHAT'RE THEY UP TO...?
SLOSH

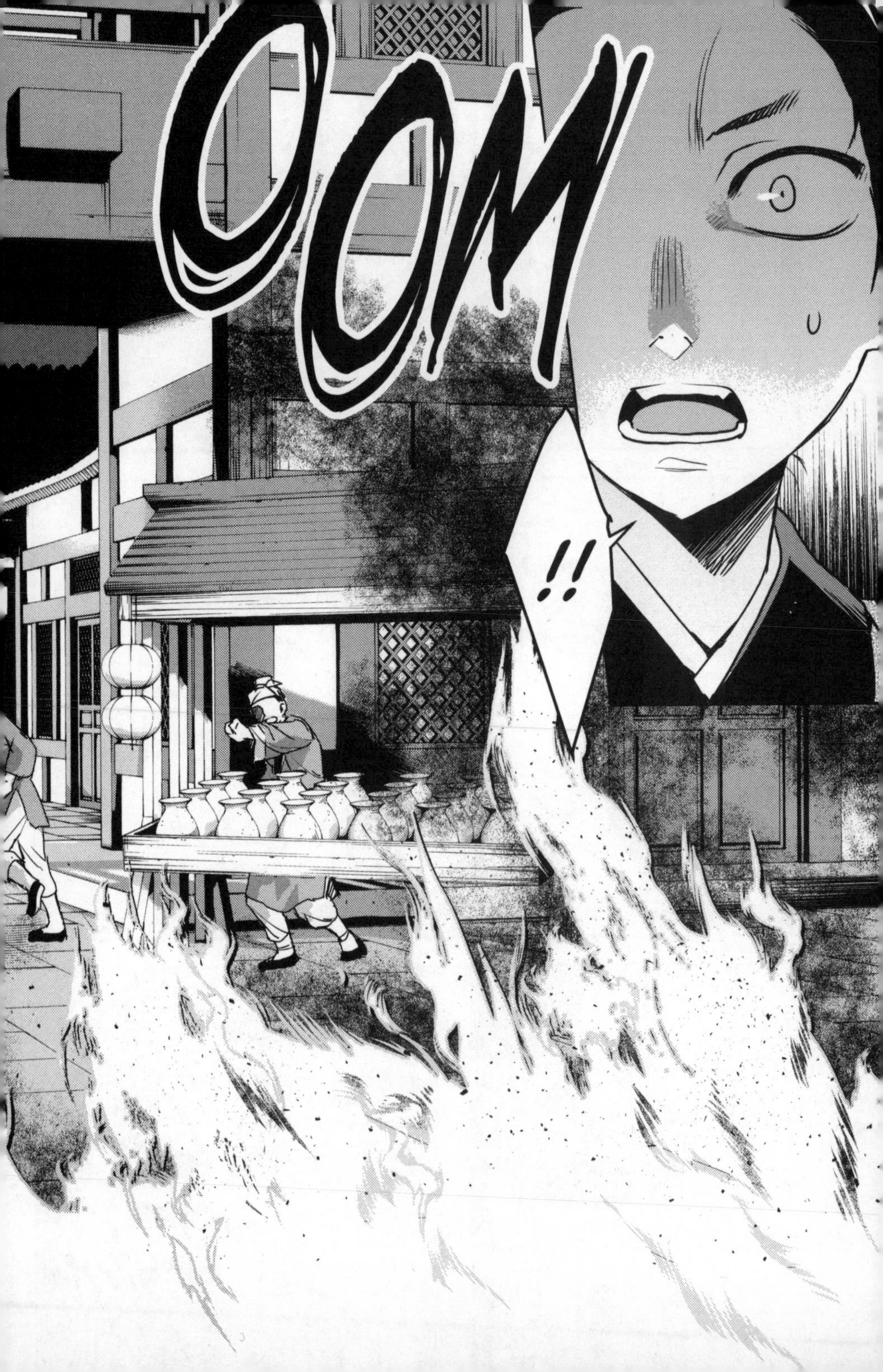
OOM
!!

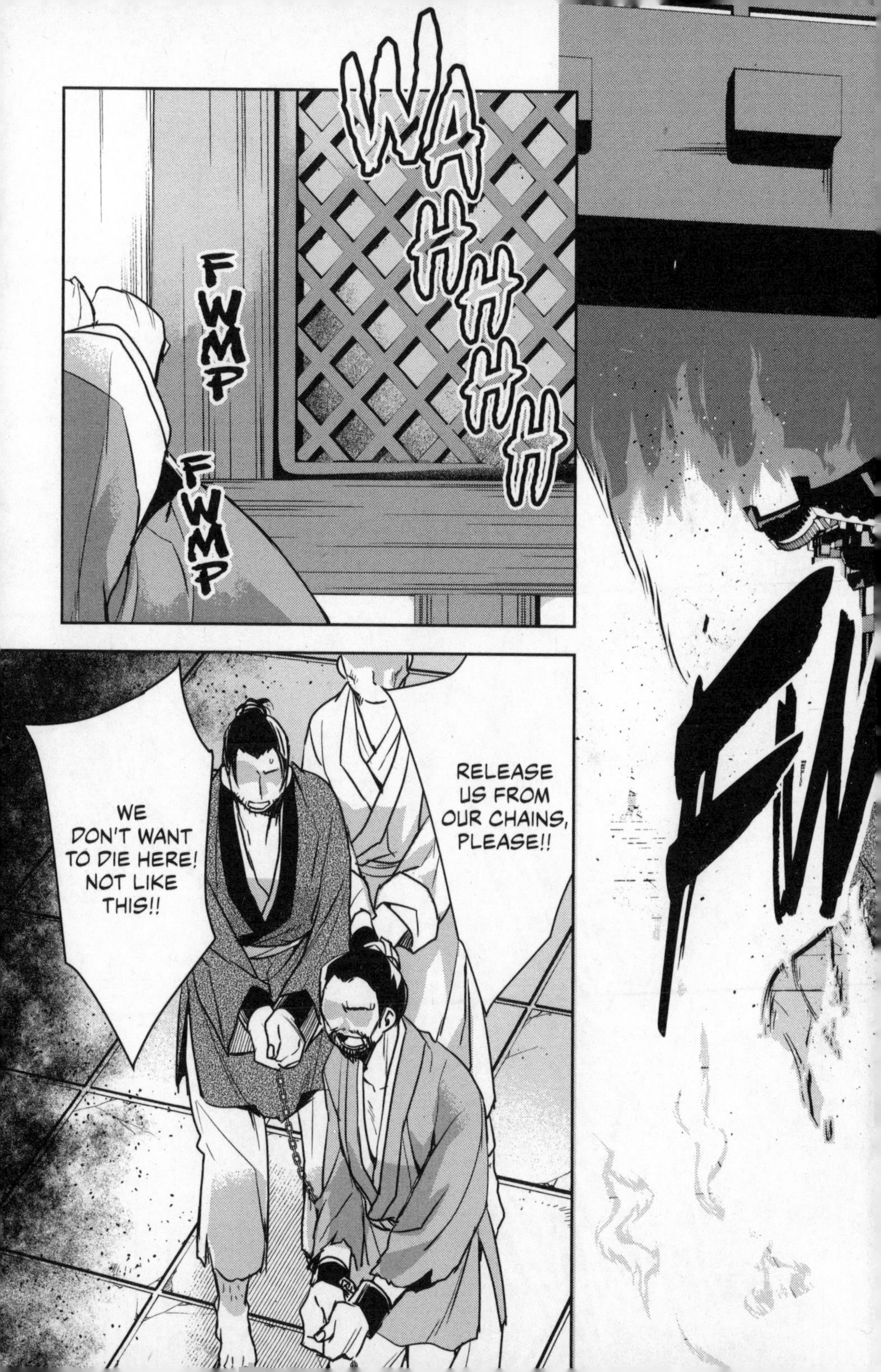
WAHHHHH
FWMP
FWMP
RELEASE US FROM OUR CHAINS, PLEASE!!
WE DON'T WANT TO DIE HERE! NOT LIKE THIS!!

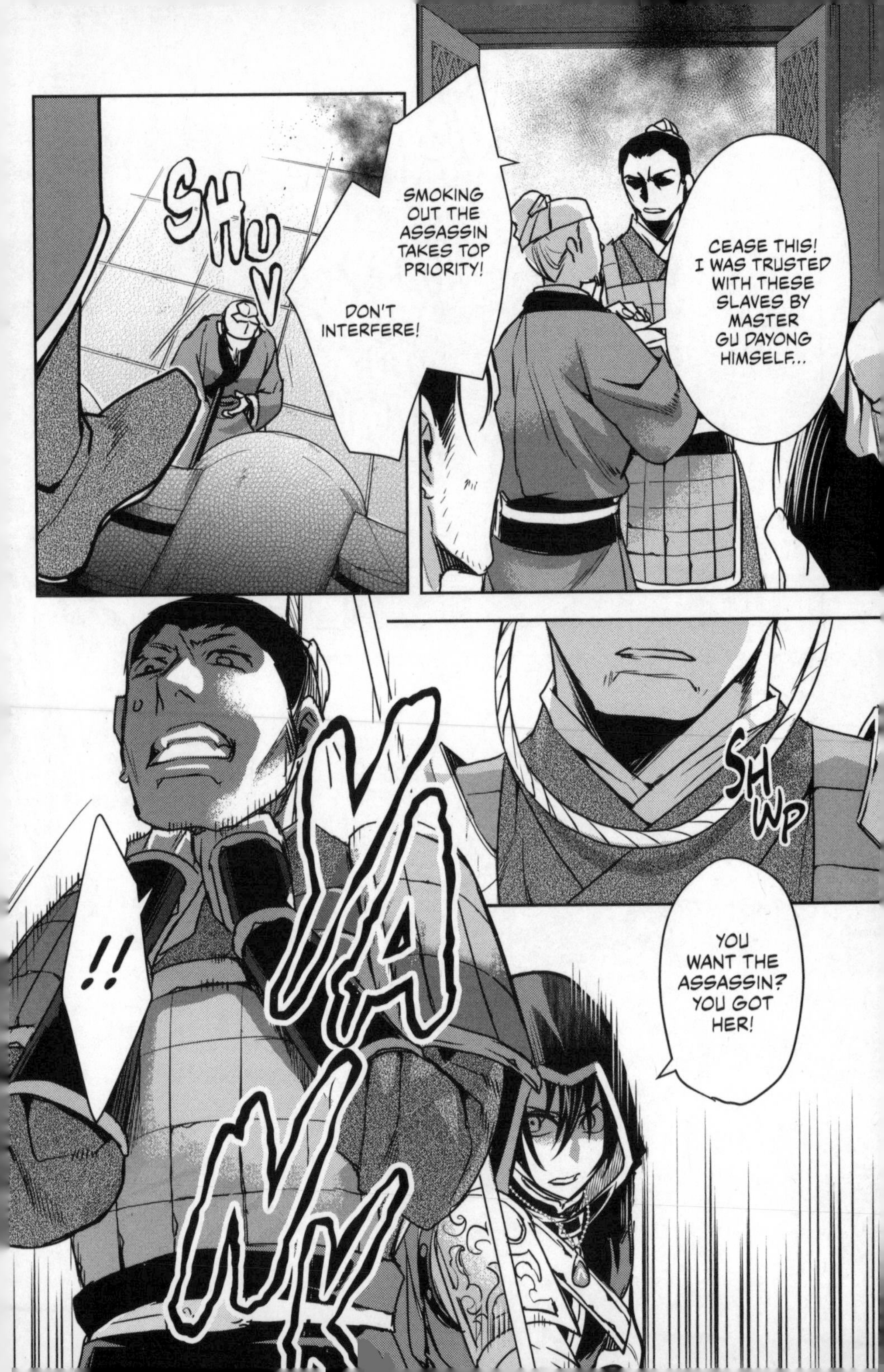
CEASE THIS! I WAS TRUSTED WITH THESE SLAVES BY MASTER GU DAYONG HIMSELF...
SMOKING OUT THE ASSASSIN TAKES TOP PRIORITY!
DON'T INTERFERE!
SHUV
SHWP
YOU WANT THE ASSASSIN? YOU GOT HER!
!!

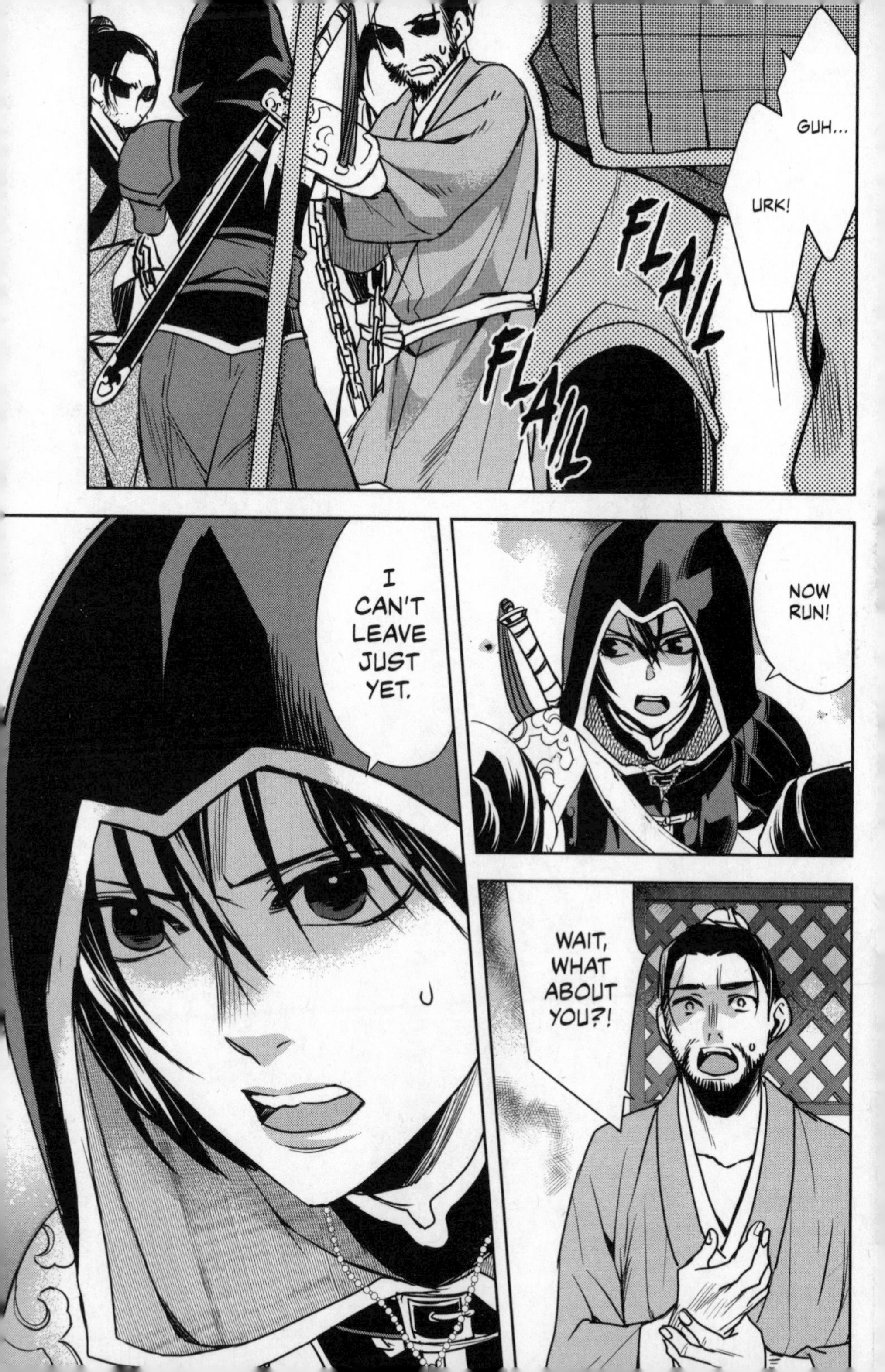
GUH...
URK!
FLAIL
FLAIL
NOW RUN!
WAIT, WHAT ABOUT YOU?!
I CAN'T LEAVE JUST YET.

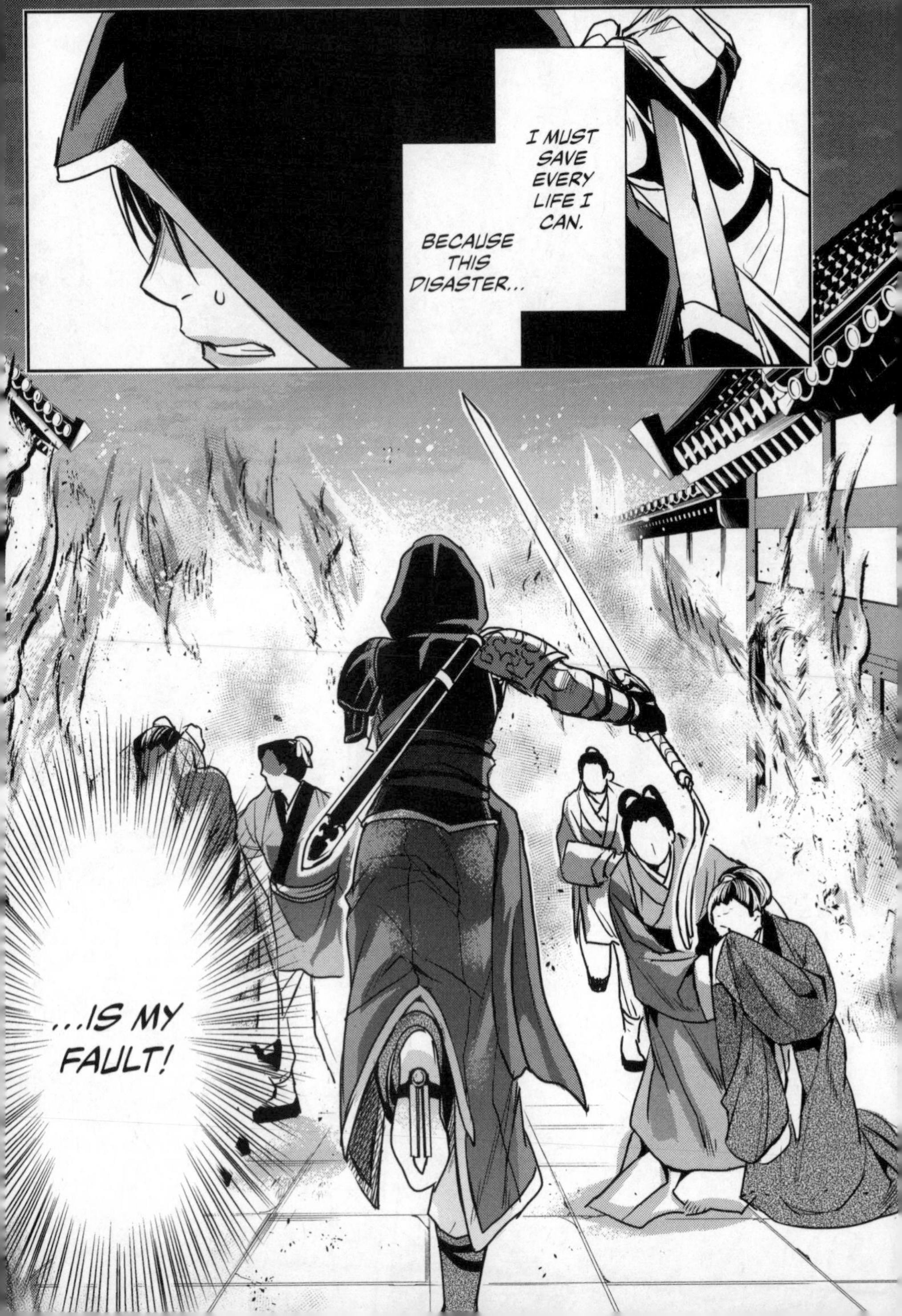
I MUST SAVE EVERY LIFE I CAN.
BECAUSE THIS DISASTER...
...IS MY FAULT!

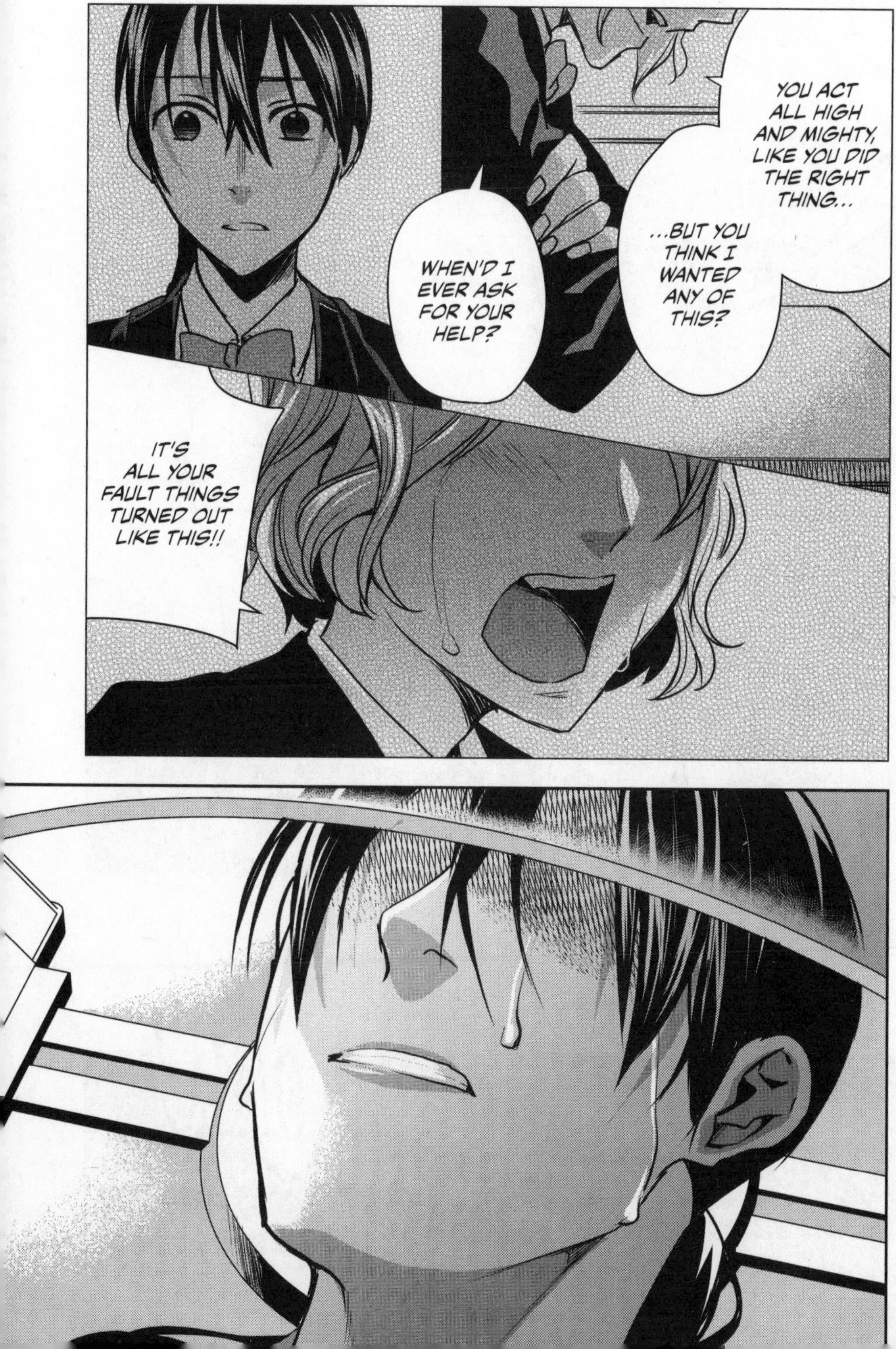
YOU ACT ALL HIGH AND MIGHTY, LIKE YOU DID THE RIGHT THING...
...BUT YOU THINK I WANTED ANY OF THIS?
WHEN'D I EVER ASK FOR YOUR HELP?
IT'S ALL YOUR FAULT THINGS TURNED OUT LIKE THIS!!

SHE'S CRYING?

AS I THOUGHT, SHE HAS A POWERFUL CONNECTION TO SHAO JUN'S EMOTIONS.

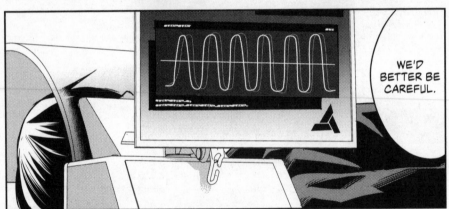

WE'D BETTER BE CAREFUL.

WAHHH!

FWOOOM

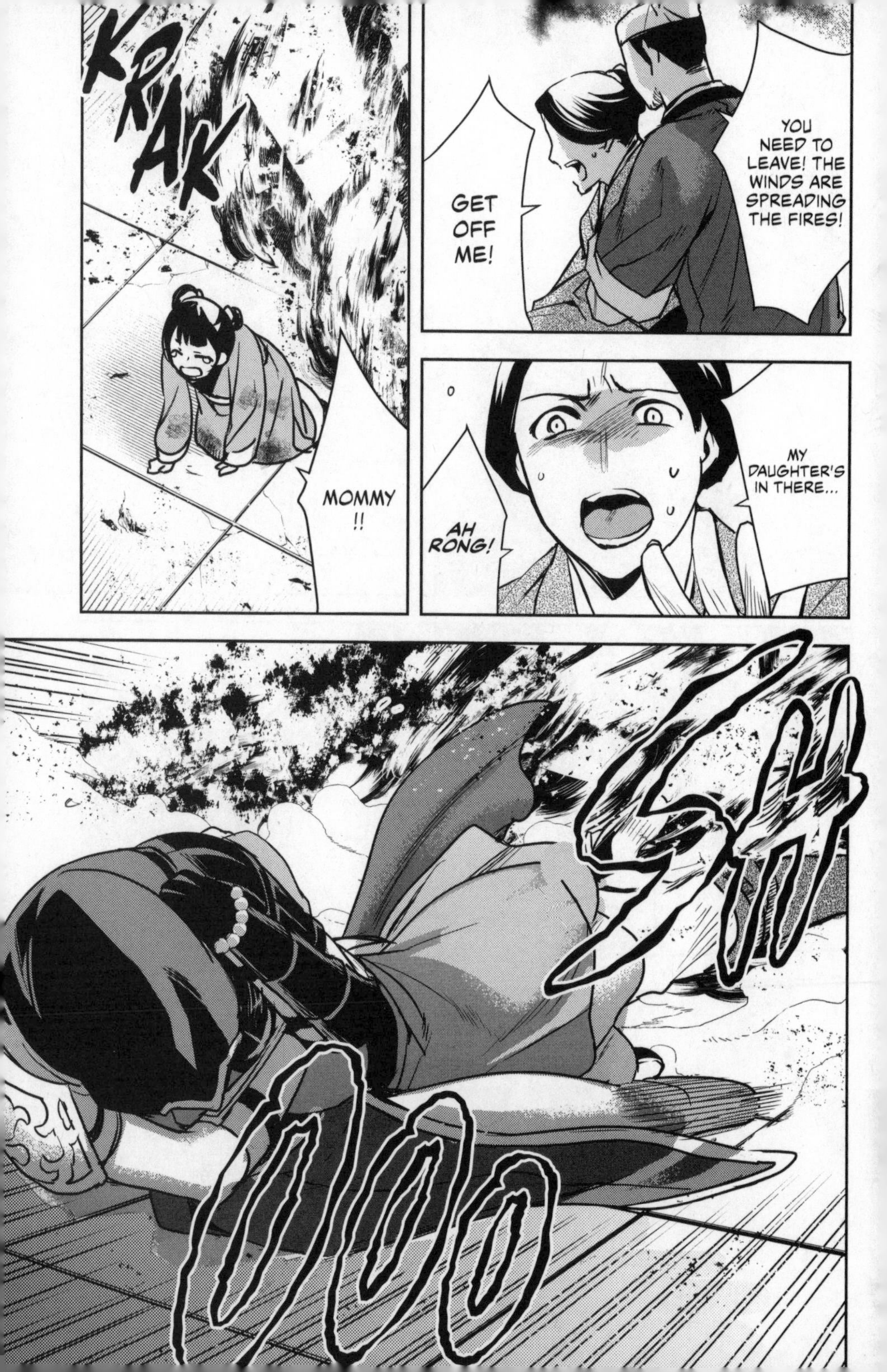
YOU NEED TO LEAVE! THE WINDS ARE SPREADING THE FIRES!
GET OFF ME!
MY DAUGHTER'S IN THERE...
O
AH RONG!
KRAK
MOMMY !!
SH
OOOO

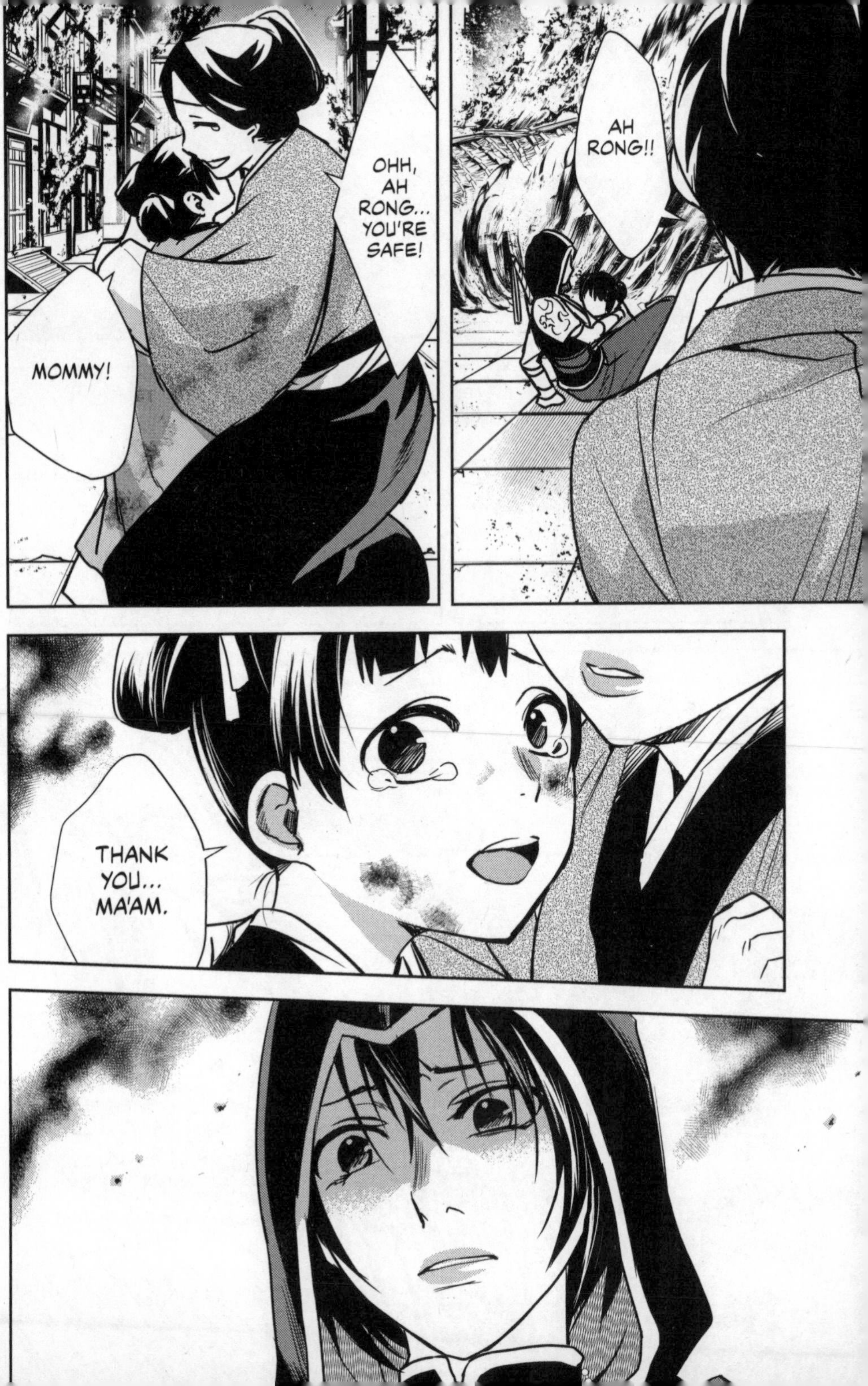
AH RONG!!
OHH, AH RONG... YOU'RE SAFE!
MOMMY!
THANK YOU... MA'AM.

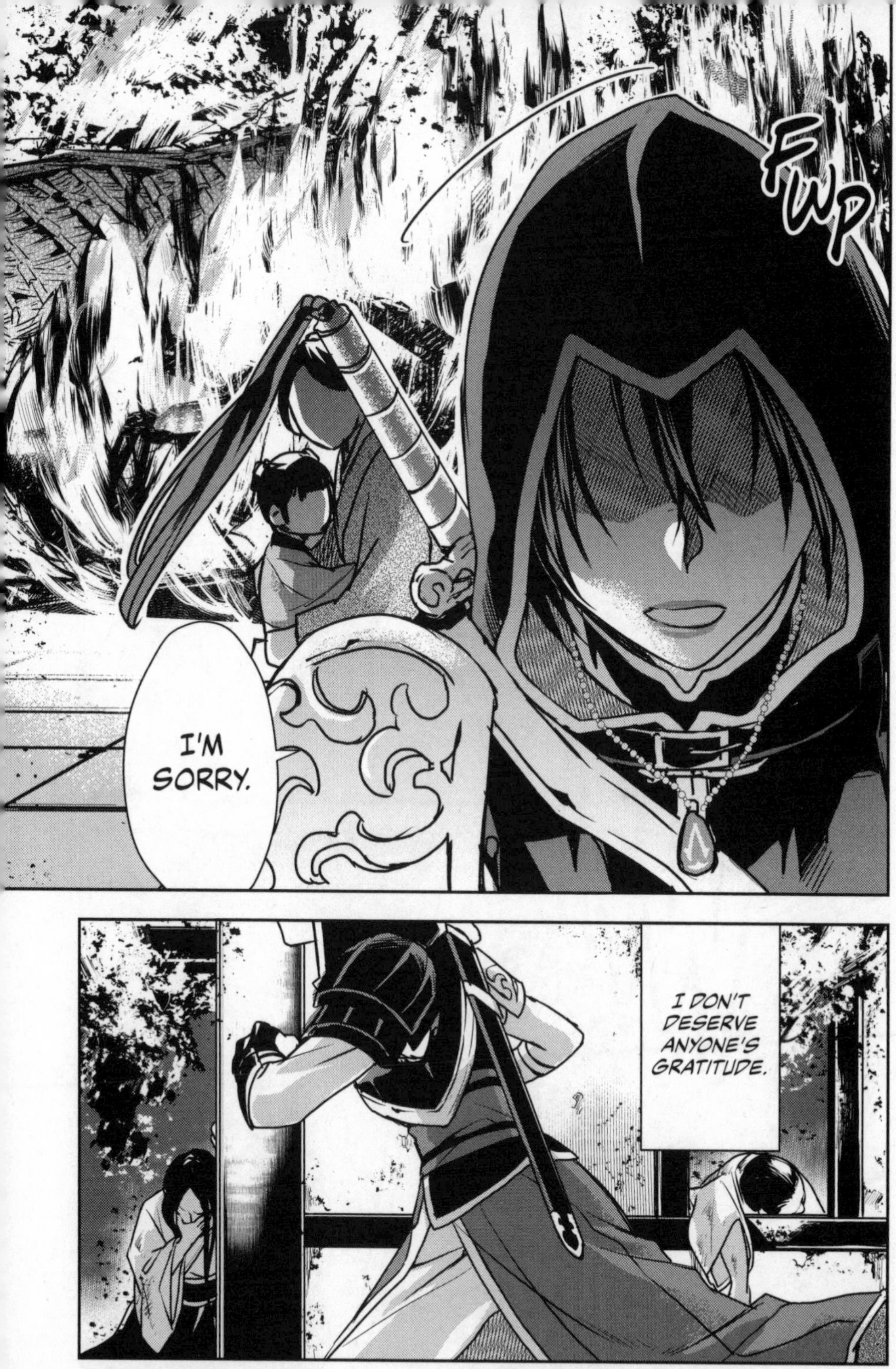
FWP
I'M SORRY.
I DON'T DESERVE ANYONE'S GRATITUDE.

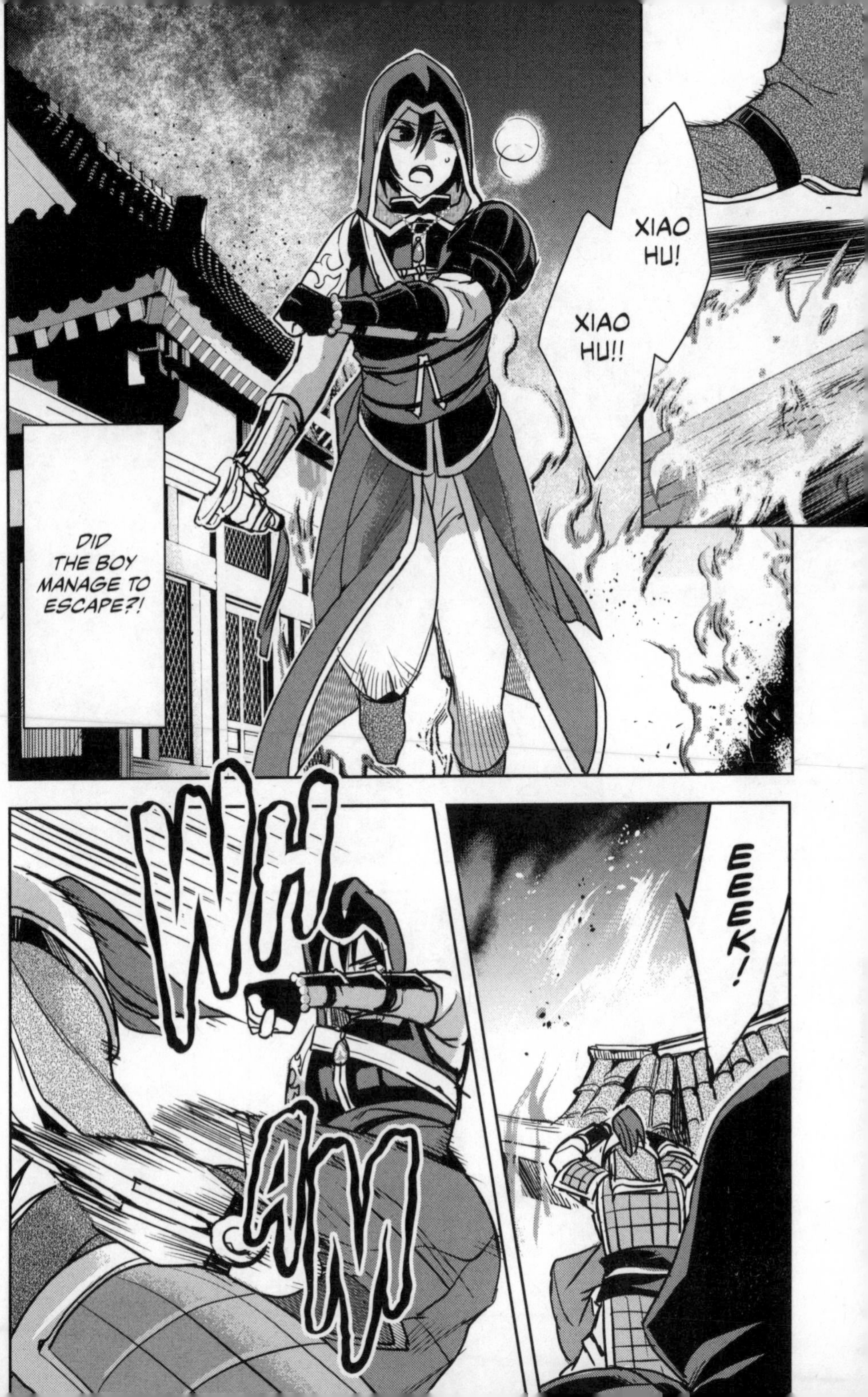
XIAO HU!
XIAO HU!!
DID THE BOY MANAGE TO ESCAPE?!
EEEEK!
WHAM

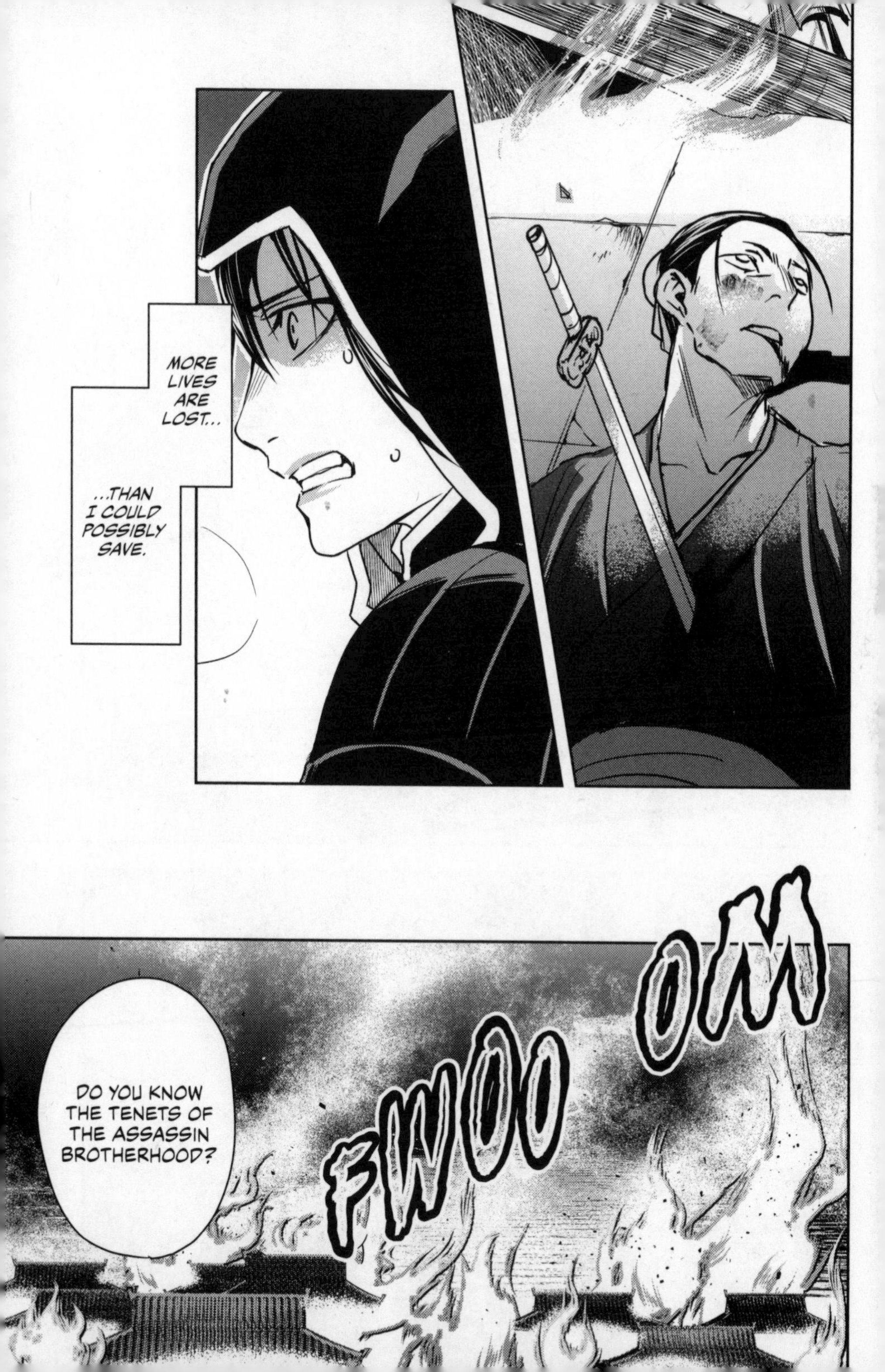
MORE LIVES ARE LOST...
...THAN I COULD POSSIBLY SAVE.
FWOO OM
DO YOU KNOW THE TENETS OF THE ASSASSIN BROTHERHOOD?

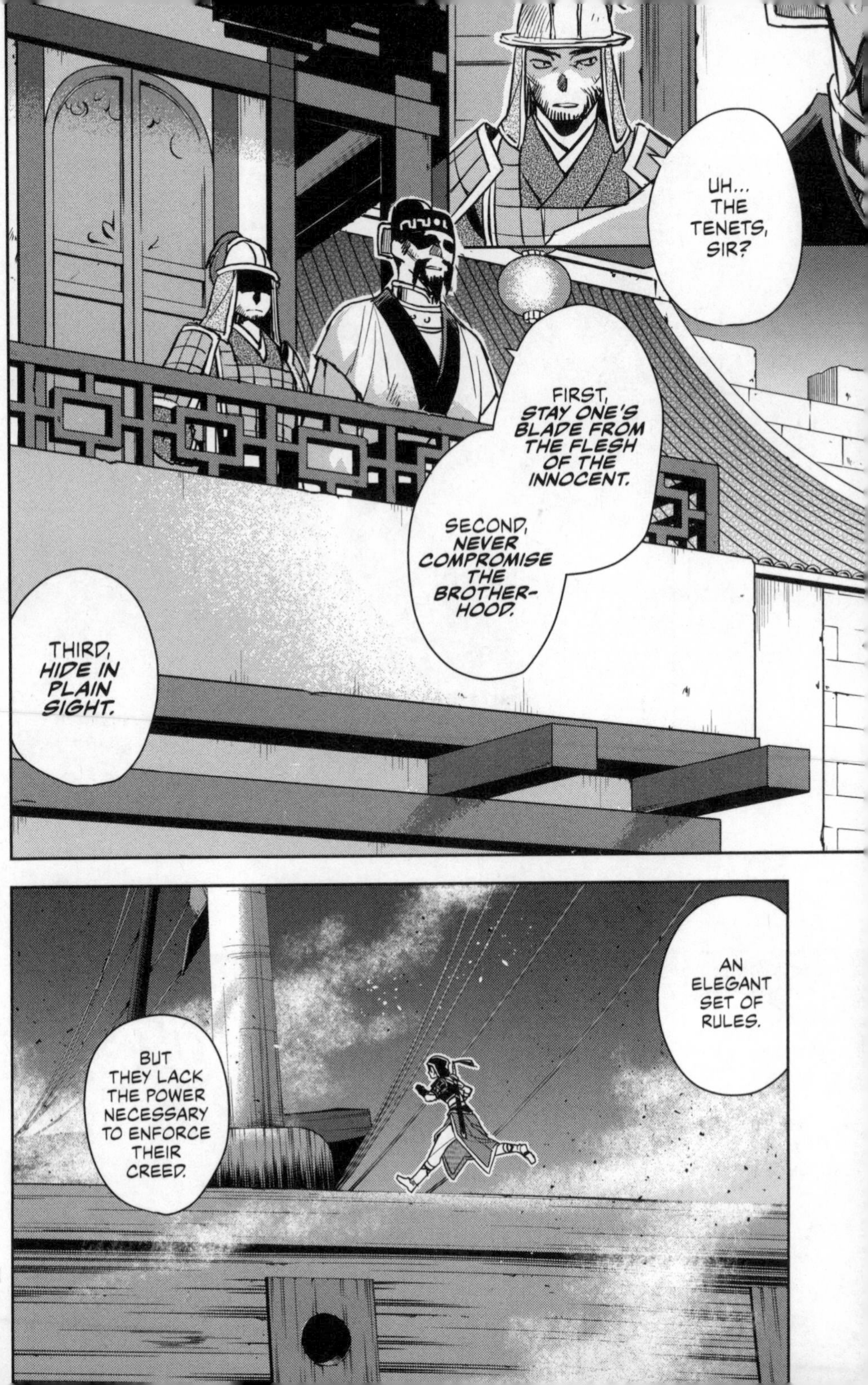
UH... THE TENETS, SIR?
FIRST, STAY ONE'S BLADE FROM THE FLESH OF THE INNOCENT.
SECOND, NEVER COMPROMISE THE BROTHERHOOD.
THIRD, HIDE IN PLAIN SIGHT.
AN ELEGANT SET OF RULES.
BUT THEY LACK THE POWER NECESSARY TO ENFORCE THEIR CREED.

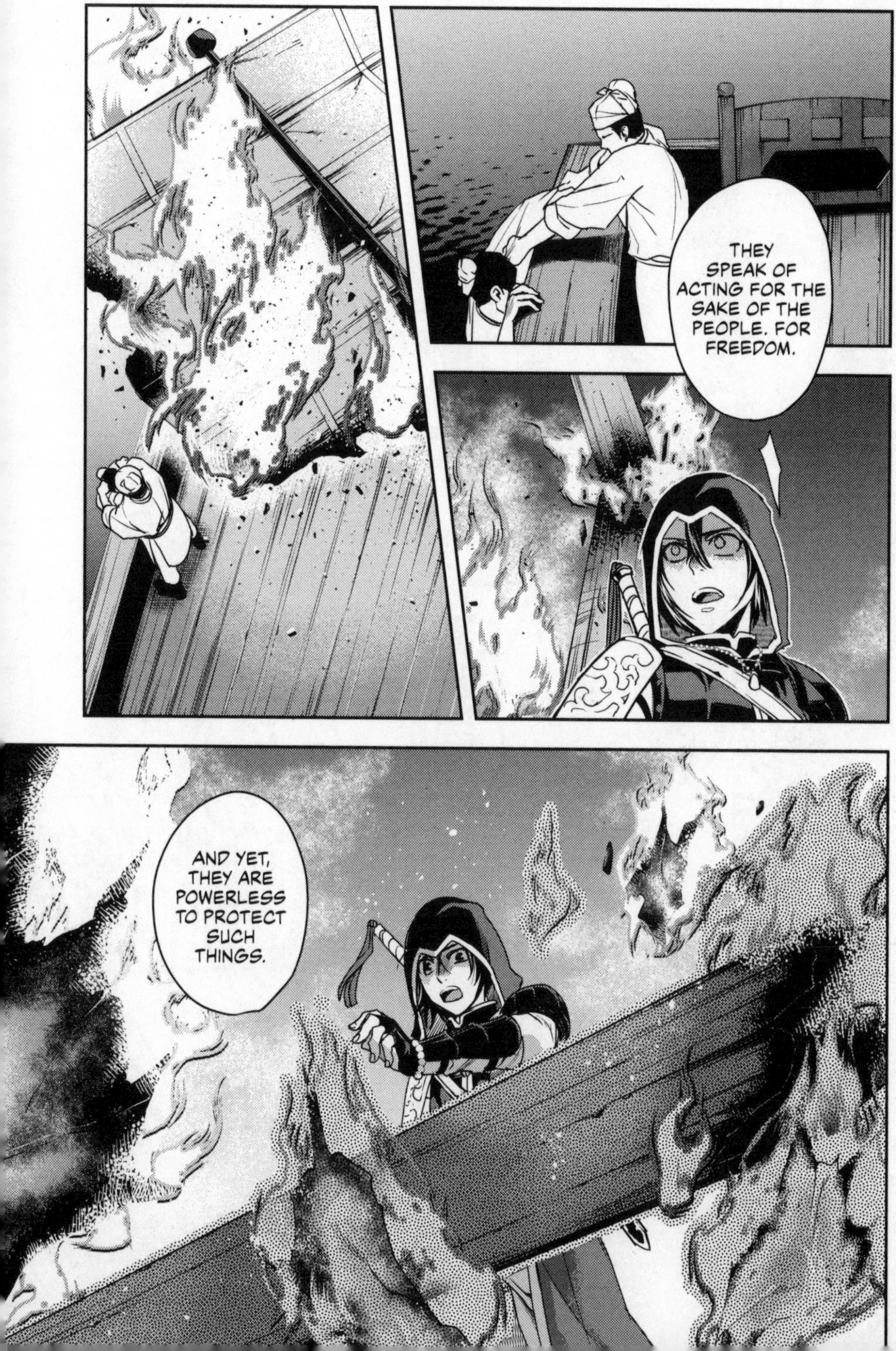
THEY SPEAK OF ACTING FOR THE SAKE OF THE PEOPLE. FOR FREEDOM.
AND YET, THEY ARE POWERLESS TO PROTECT SUCH THINGS.

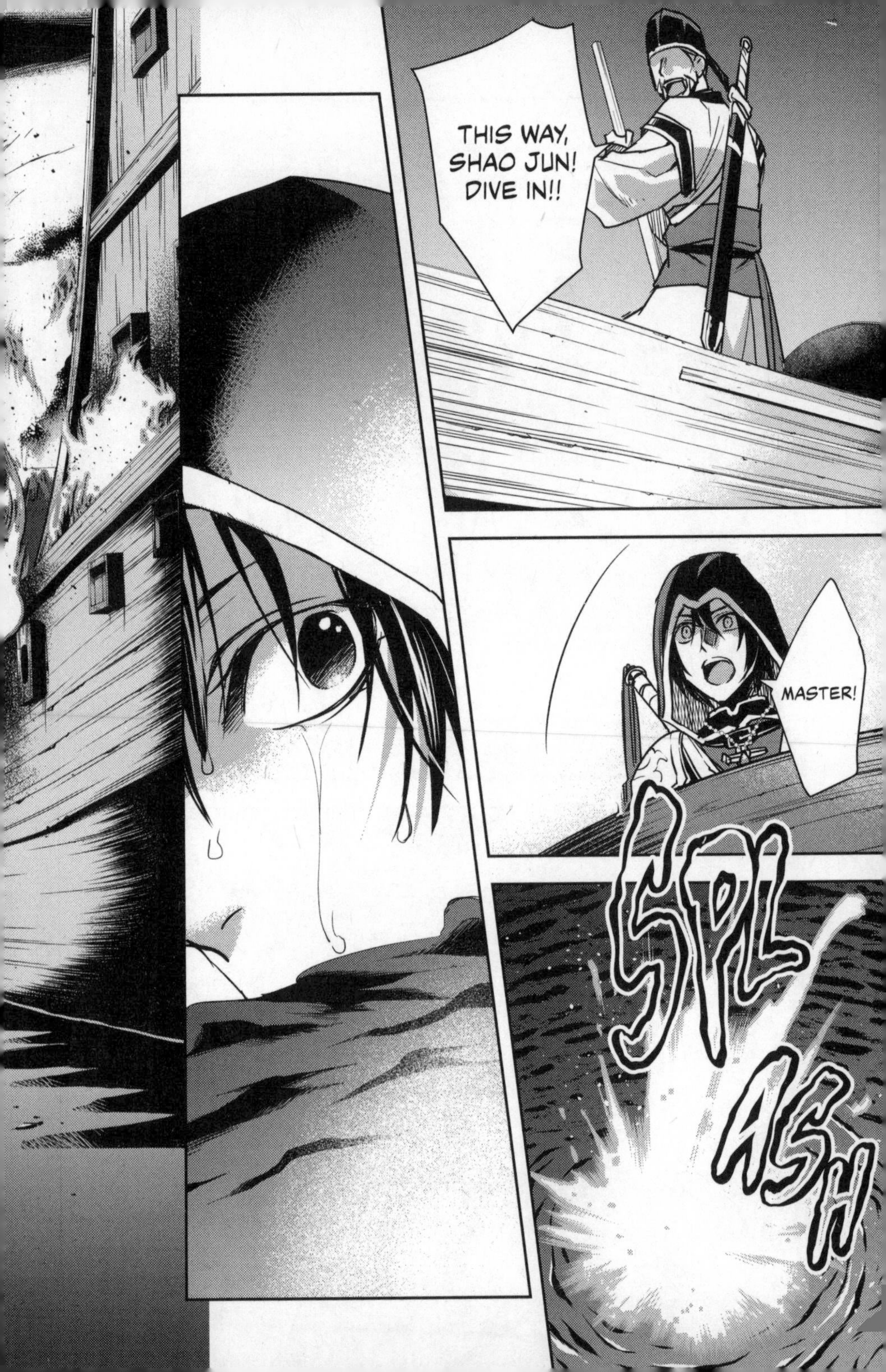
THIS WAY, SHAO JUN! DIVE IN!!
MASTER!
SPLASH

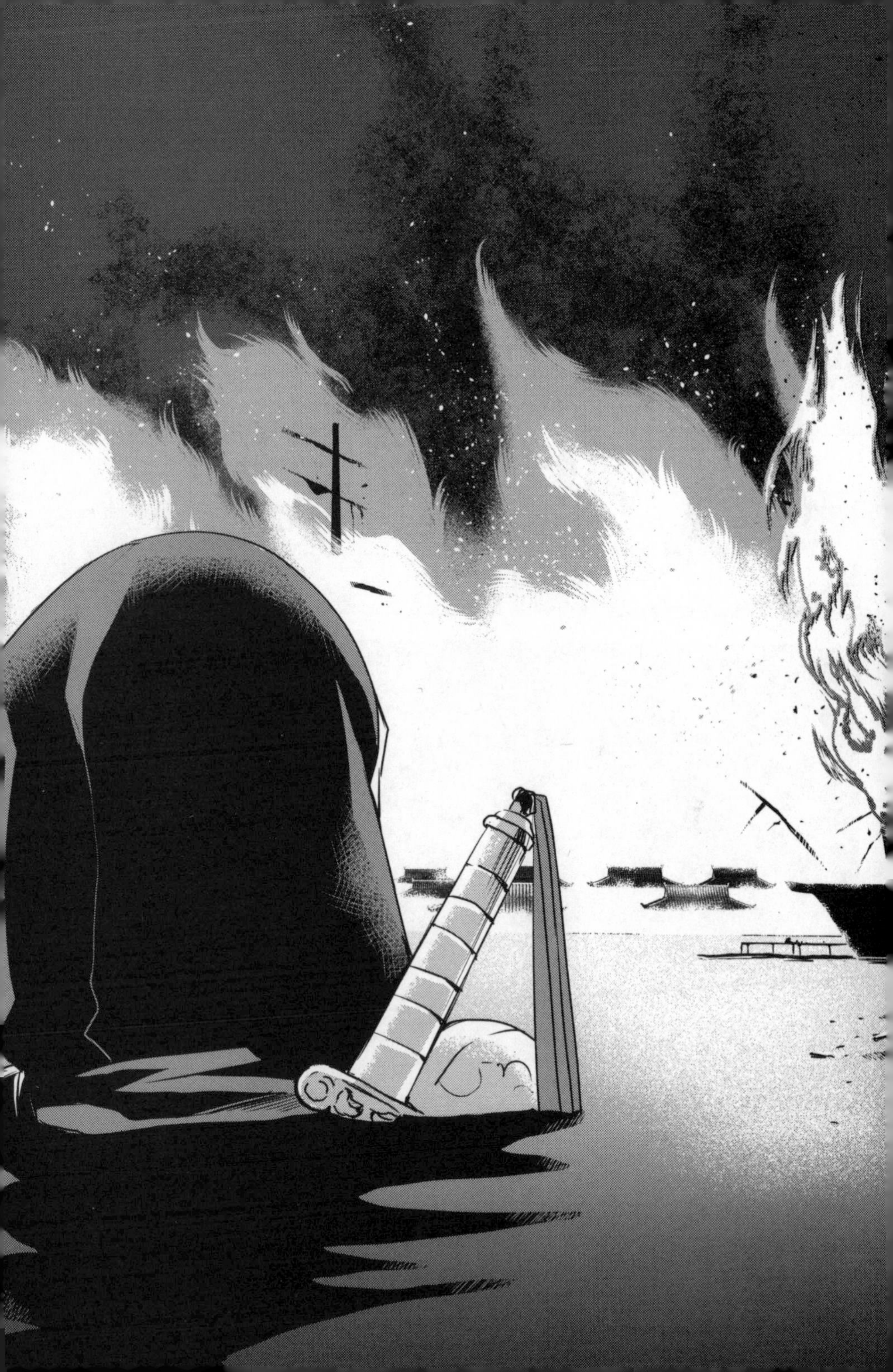

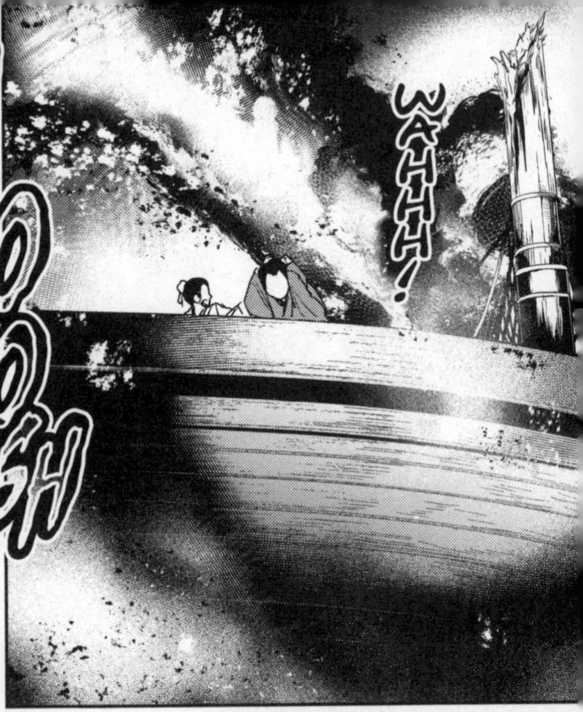
WAHHHH!
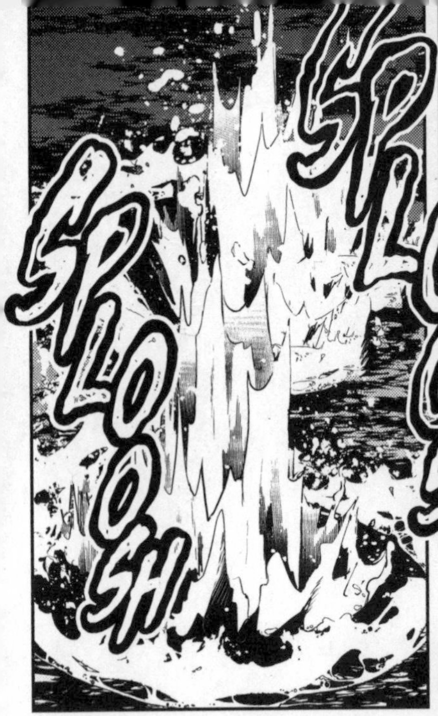
SPLOOSH
SPLOOSH
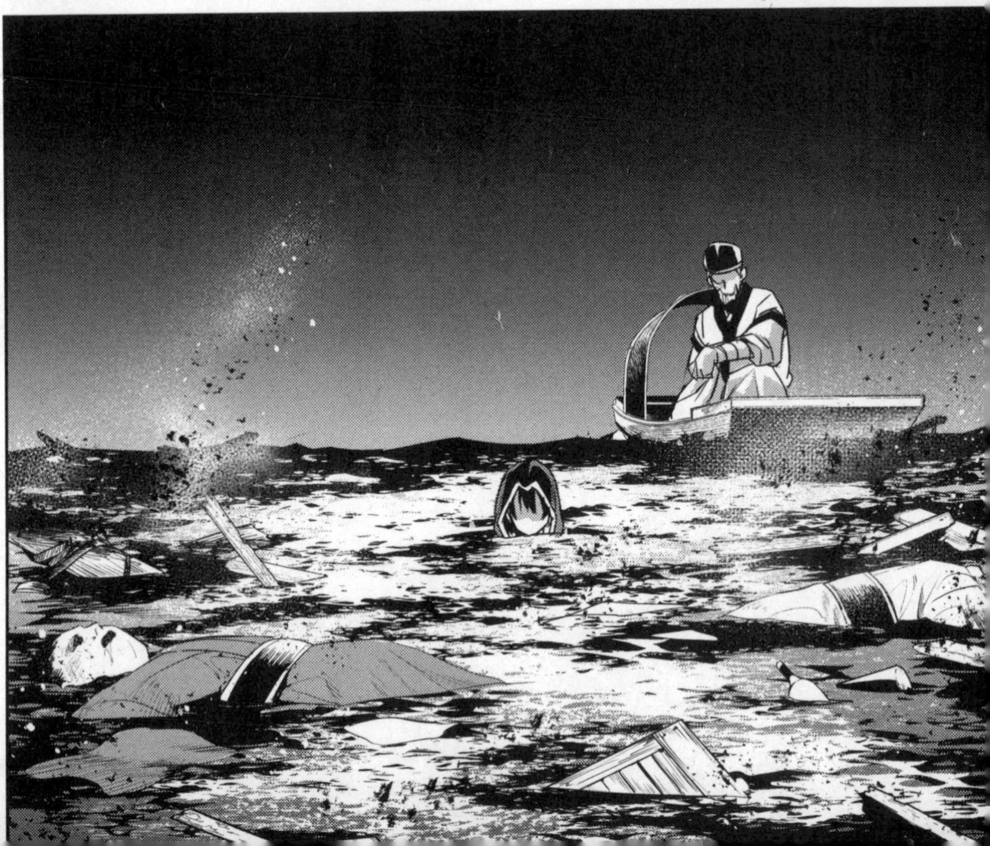

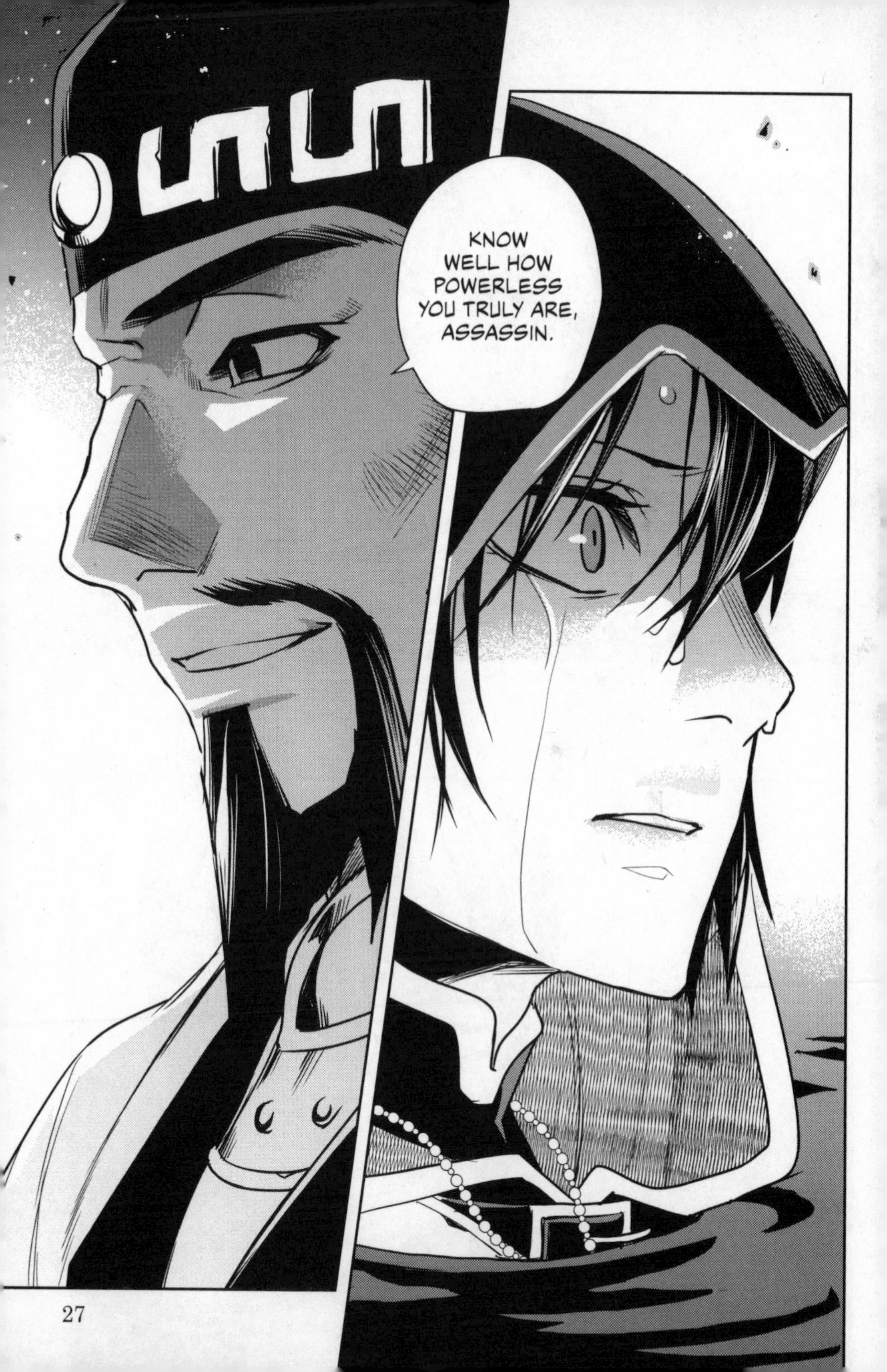
KNOW WELL HOW POWERLESS YOU TRULY ARE, ASSASSIN.

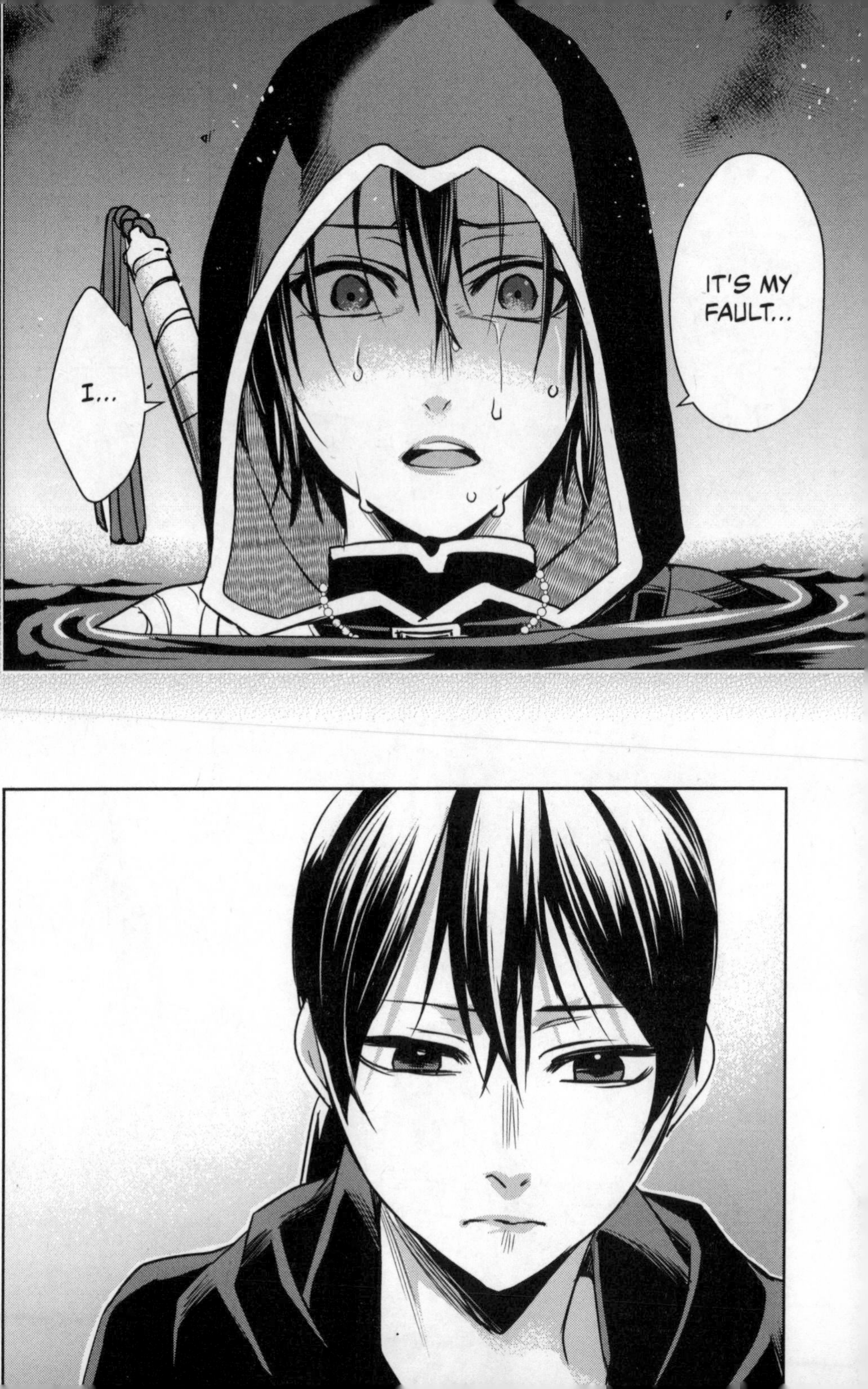
IT'S MY FAULT...
I...

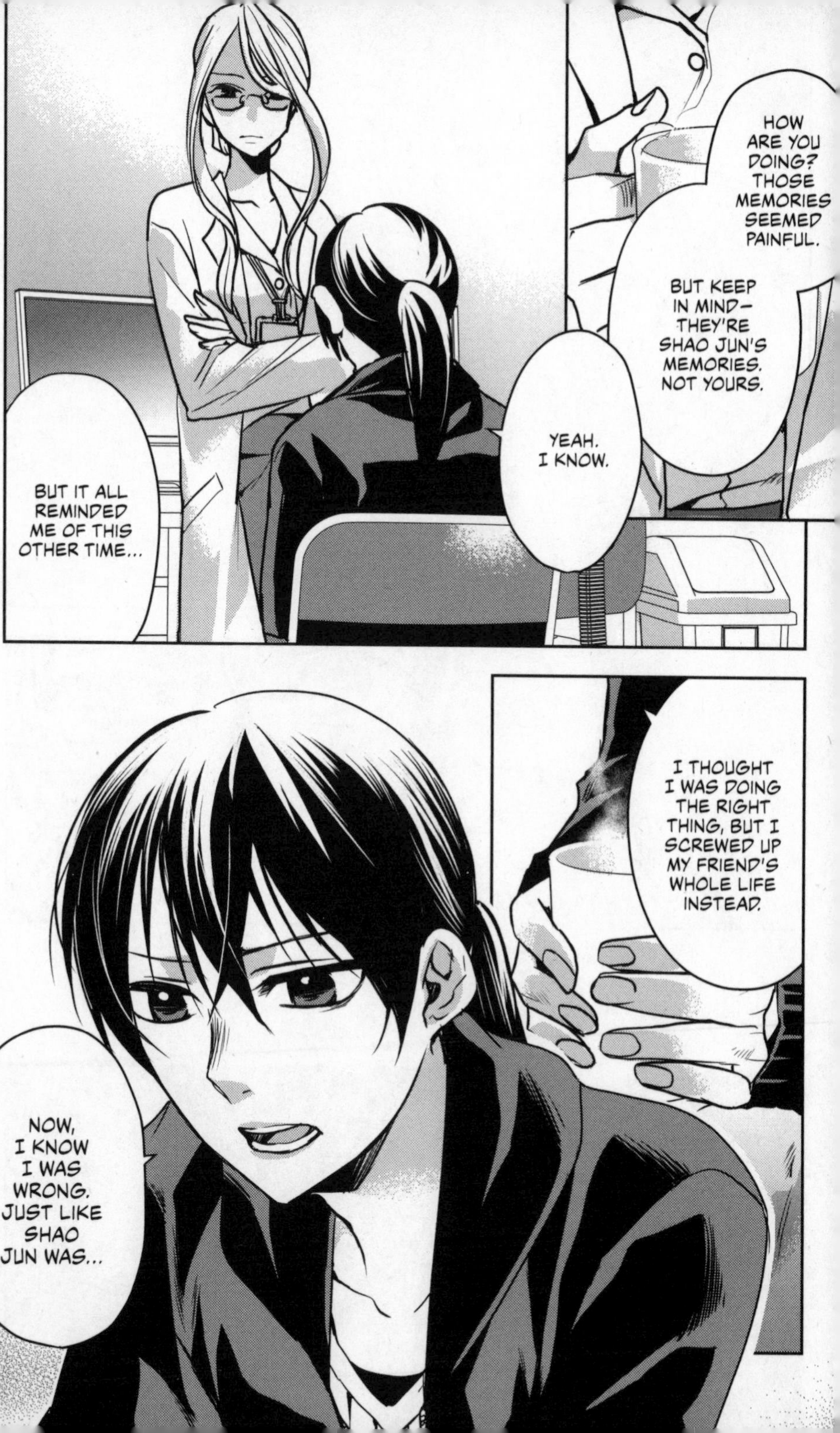
HOW ARE YOU DOING? THOSE MEMORIES SEEMED PAINFUL.
BUT KEEP IN MIND— THEY'RE SHAO JUN'S MEMORIES. NOT YOURS.
YEAH. I KNOW.
BUT IT ALL REMINDED ME OF THIS OTHER TIME...
I THOUGHT I WAS DOING THE RIGHT THING, BUT I SCREWED UP MY FRIEND'S WHOLE LIFE INSTEAD.
NOW, I KNOW I WAS WRONG. JUST LIKE SHAO JUN WAS...

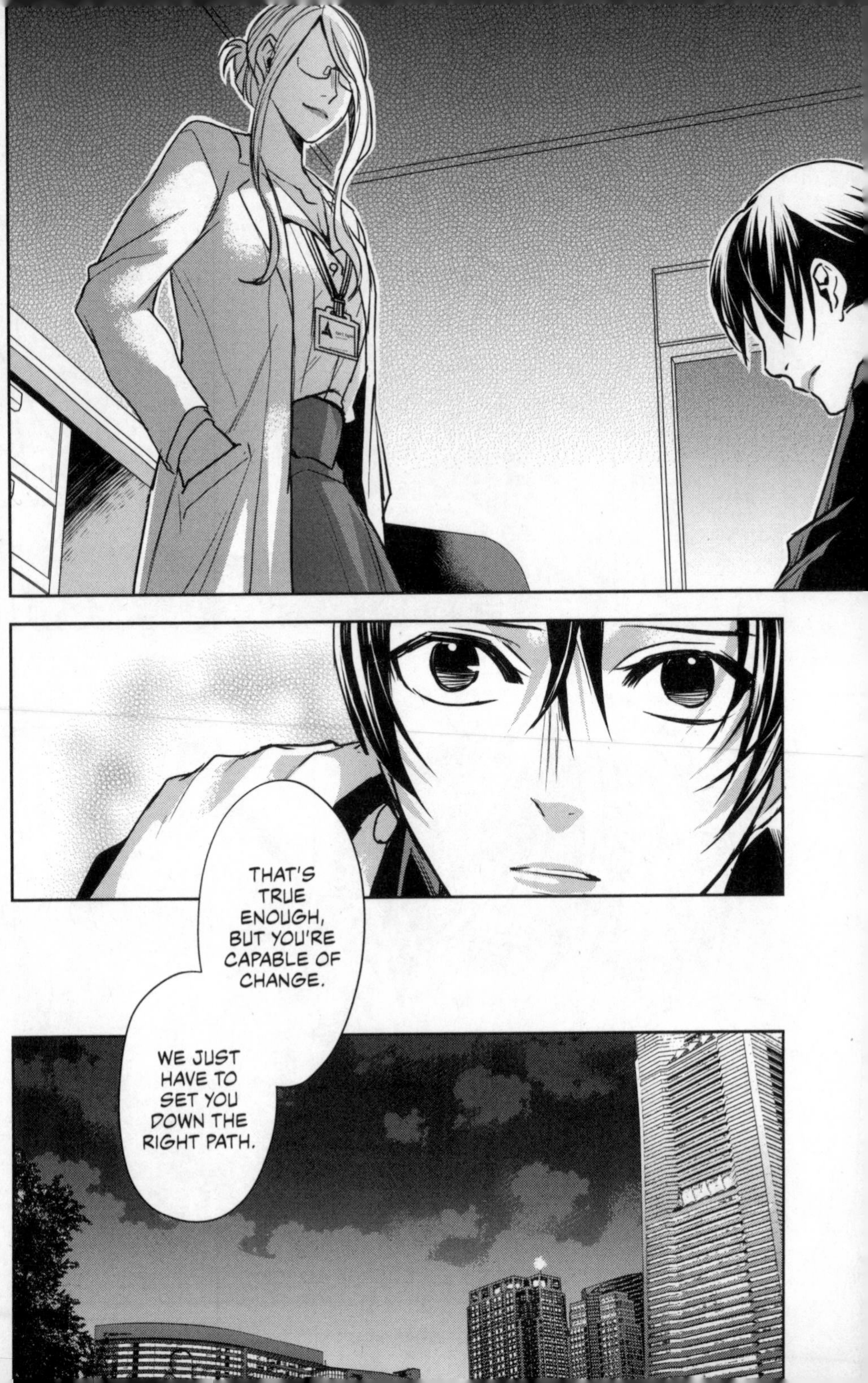
THAT'S TRUE ENOUGH, BUT YOU'RE CAPABLE OF CHANGE.
WE JUST HAVE TO SET YOU DOWN THE RIGHT PATH.

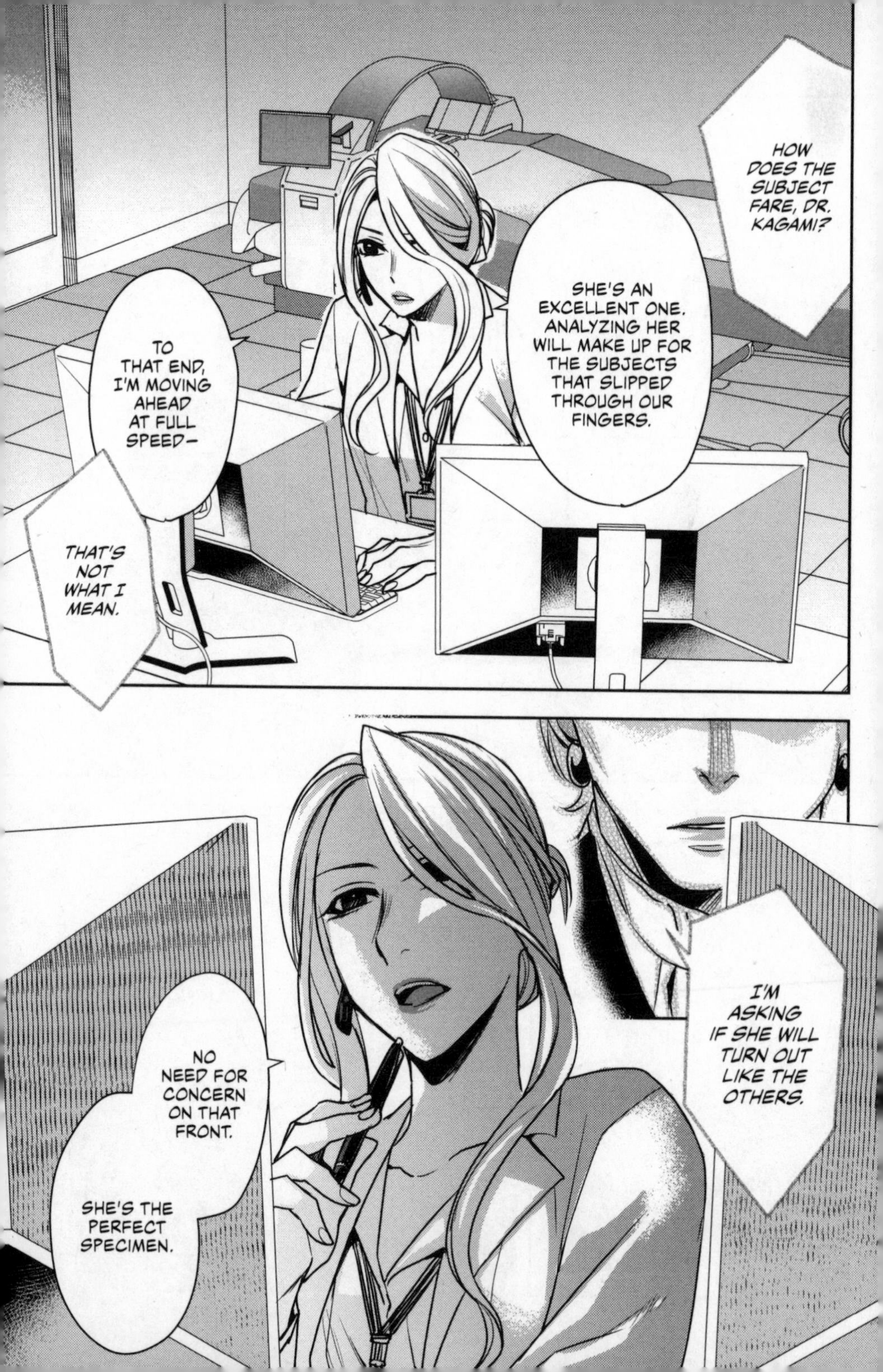
HOW DOES THE SUBJECT FARE, DR. KAGAMI?
SHE'S AN EXCELLENT ONE. ANALYZING HER WILL MAKE UP FOR THE SUBJECTS THAT SLIPPED THROUGH OUR FINGERS.
TO THAT END, I'M MOVING AHEAD AT FULL SPEED—
THAT'S NOT WHAT I MEAN.
I'M ASKING IF SHE WILL TURN OUT LIKE THE OTHERS.
NO NEED FOR CONCERN ON THAT FRONT.
SHE'S THE PERFECT SPECIMEN.

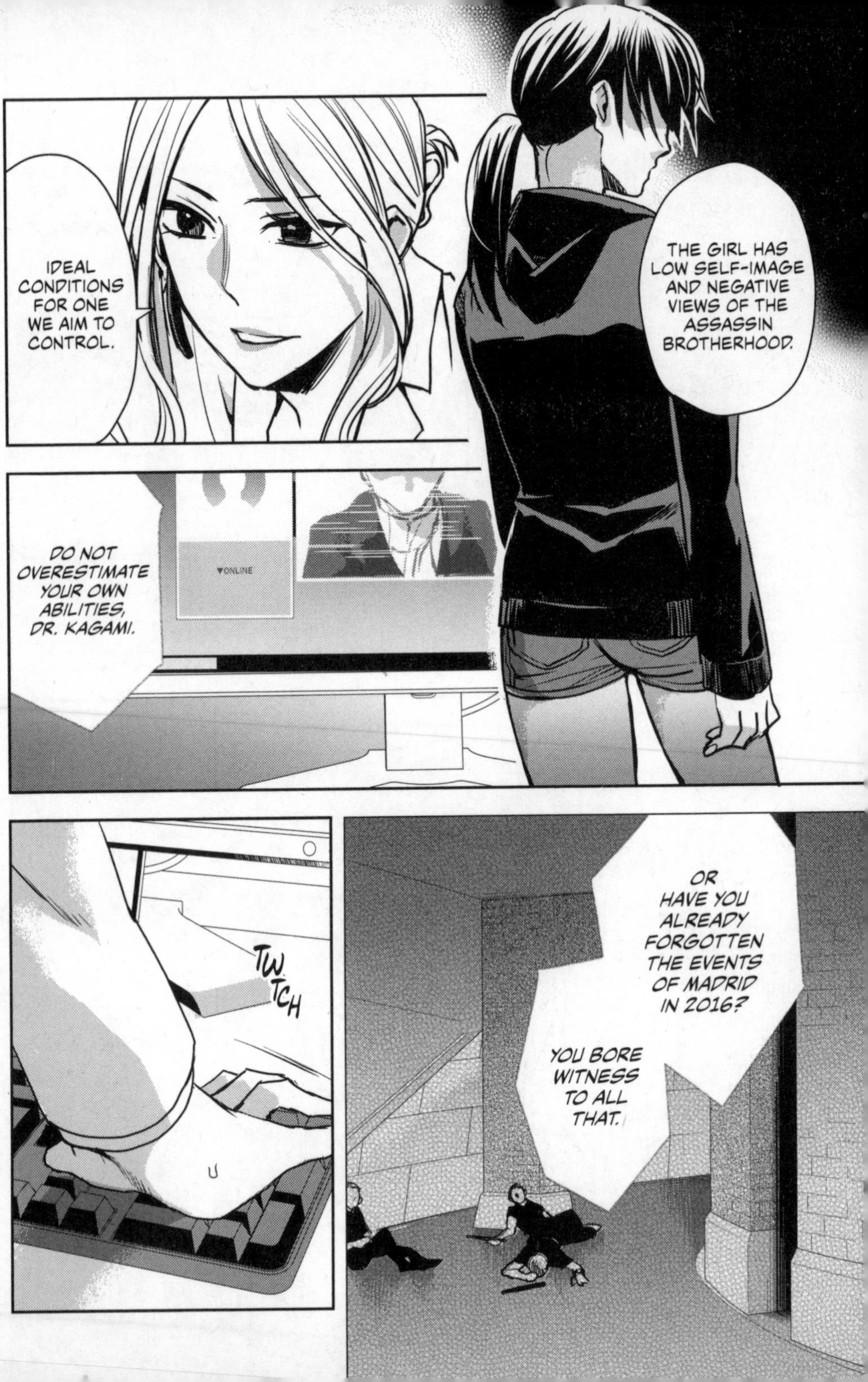
THE GIRL HAS LOW SELF-IMAGE AND NEGATIVE VIEWS OF THE ASSASSIN BROTHERHOOD.
IDEAL CONDITIONS FOR ONE WE AIM TO CONTROL.
▼ONLINE
DO NOT OVERESTIMATE YOUR OWN ABILITIES, DR. KAGAMI.
OR HAVE YOU ALREADY FORGOTTEN THE EVENTS OF MADRID IN 2016?
YOU BORE WITNESS TO ALL THAT.
TWITCH

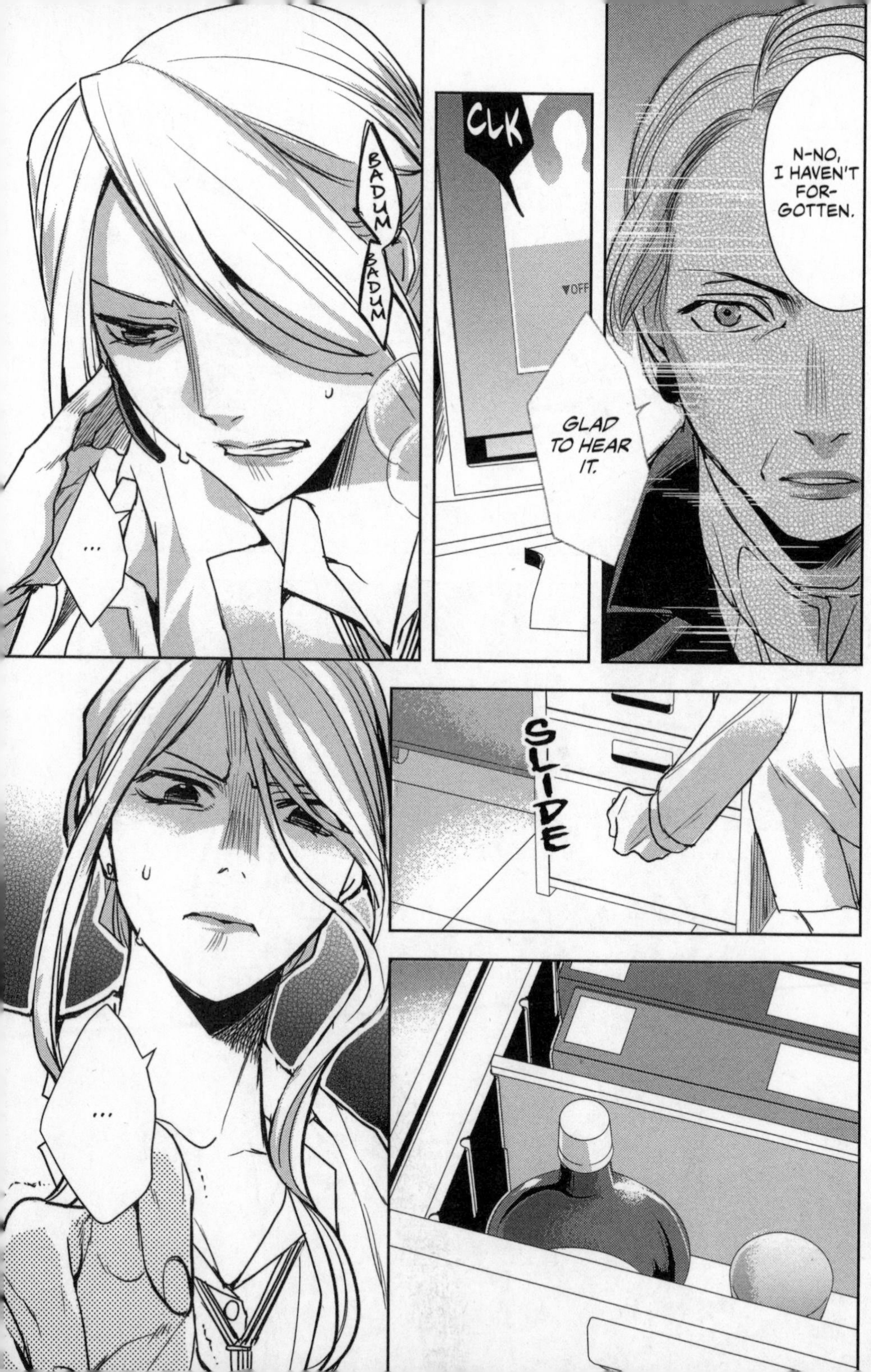

N-NO, I HAVEN'T FOR-GOTTEN.
GLAD TO HEAR IT.
CLK
OFF
BADUM BADUM
...
SLIDE
...

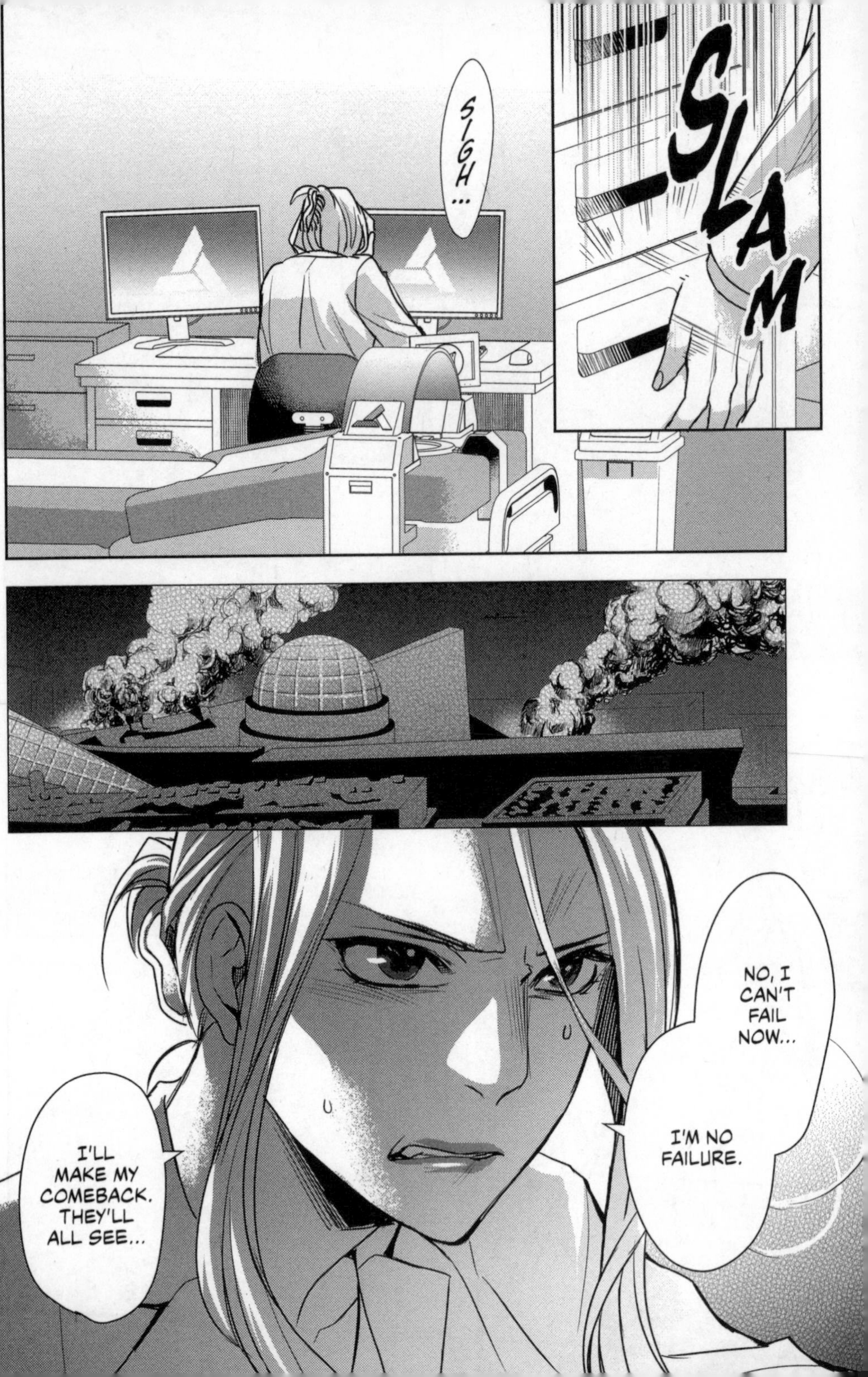
SLAM
SIGH...
NO, I CAN'T FAIL NOW...
I'M NO FAILURE.
I'LL MAKE MY COMEBACK. THEY'LL ALL SEE...

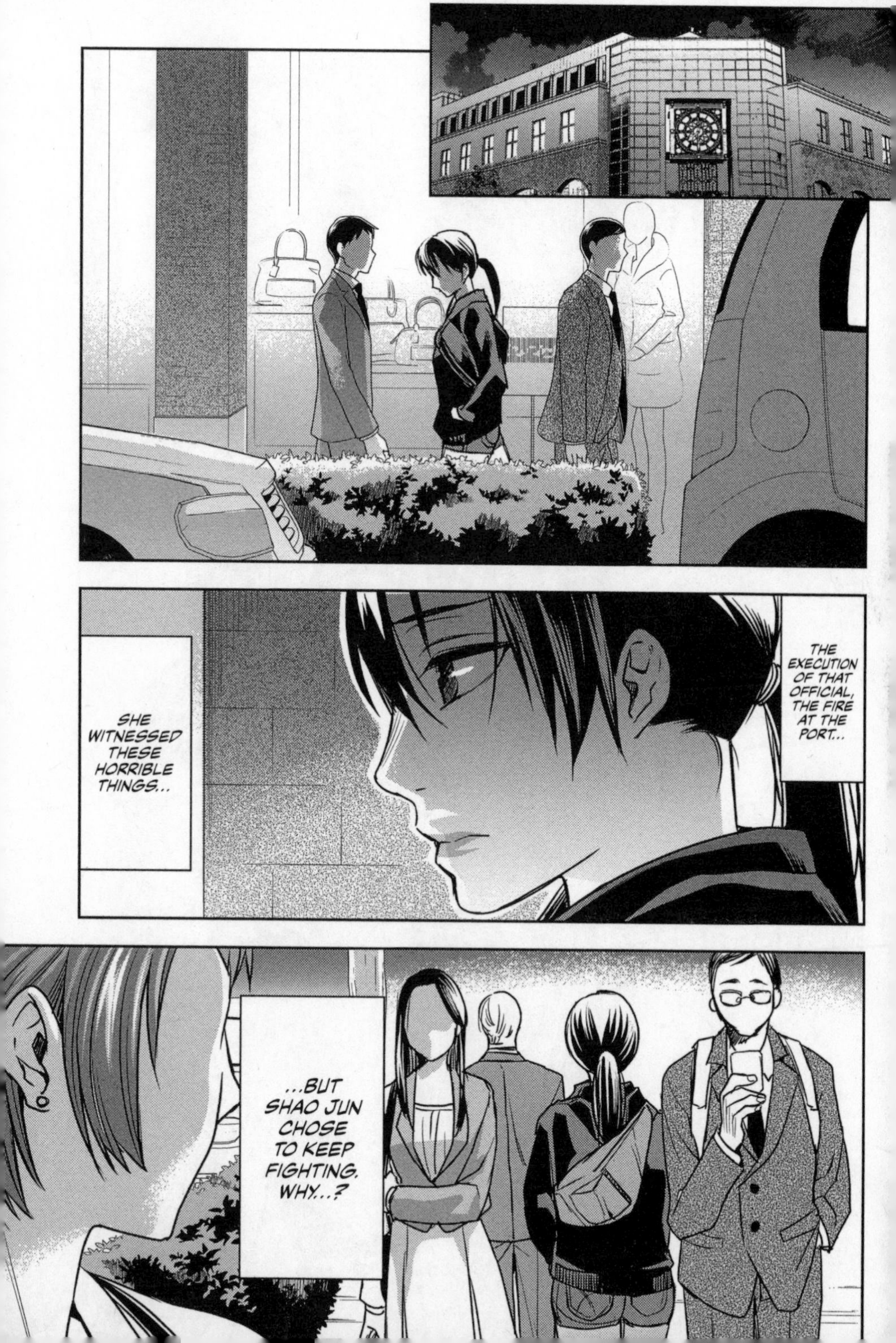
THE EXECUTION OF THAT OFFICIAL, THE FIRE AT THE PORT...
SHE WITNESSED THESE HORRIBLE THINGS...
...BUT SHAO JUN CHOSE TO KEEP FIGHTING. WHY...?

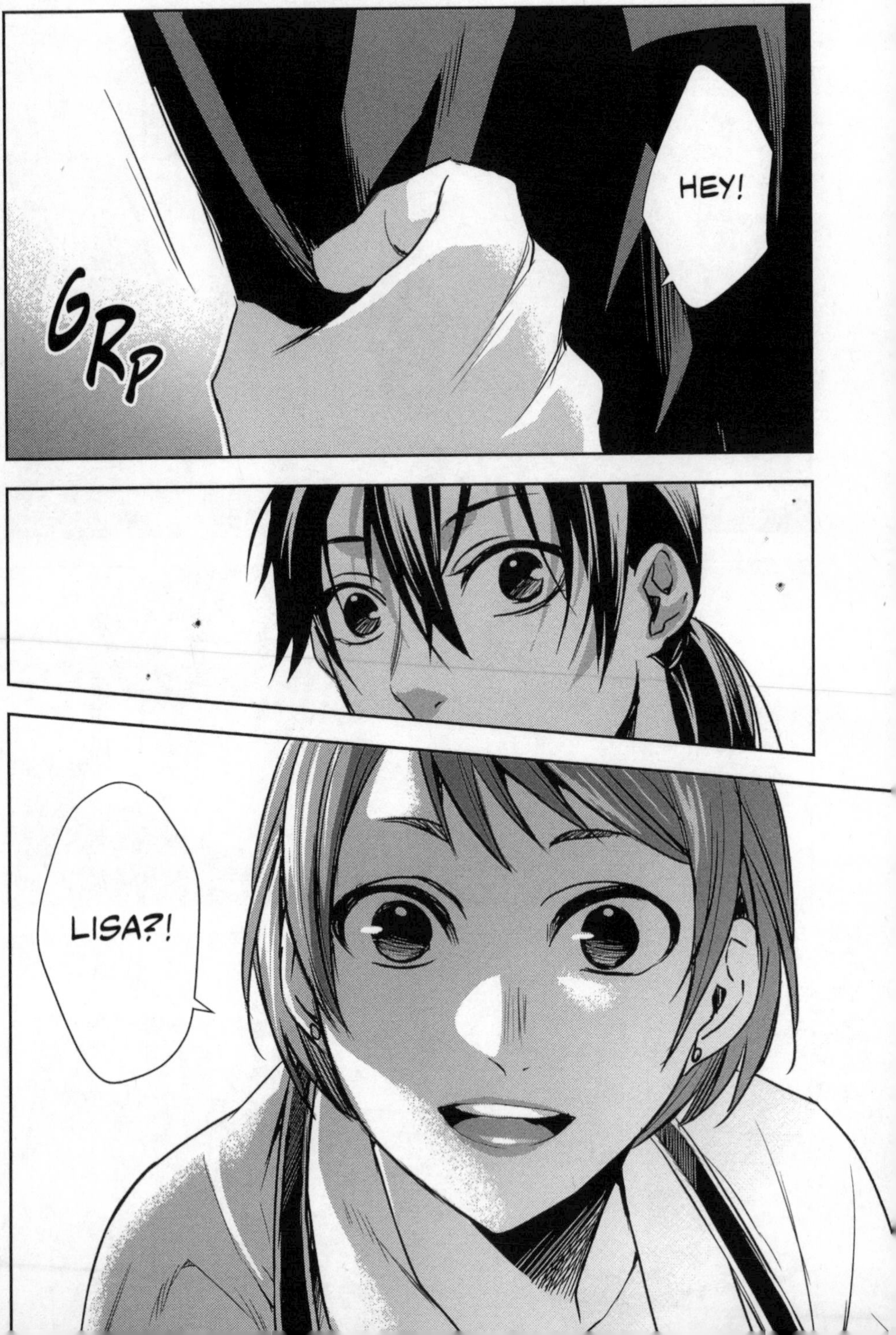
HEY!
GRP
LISA?!

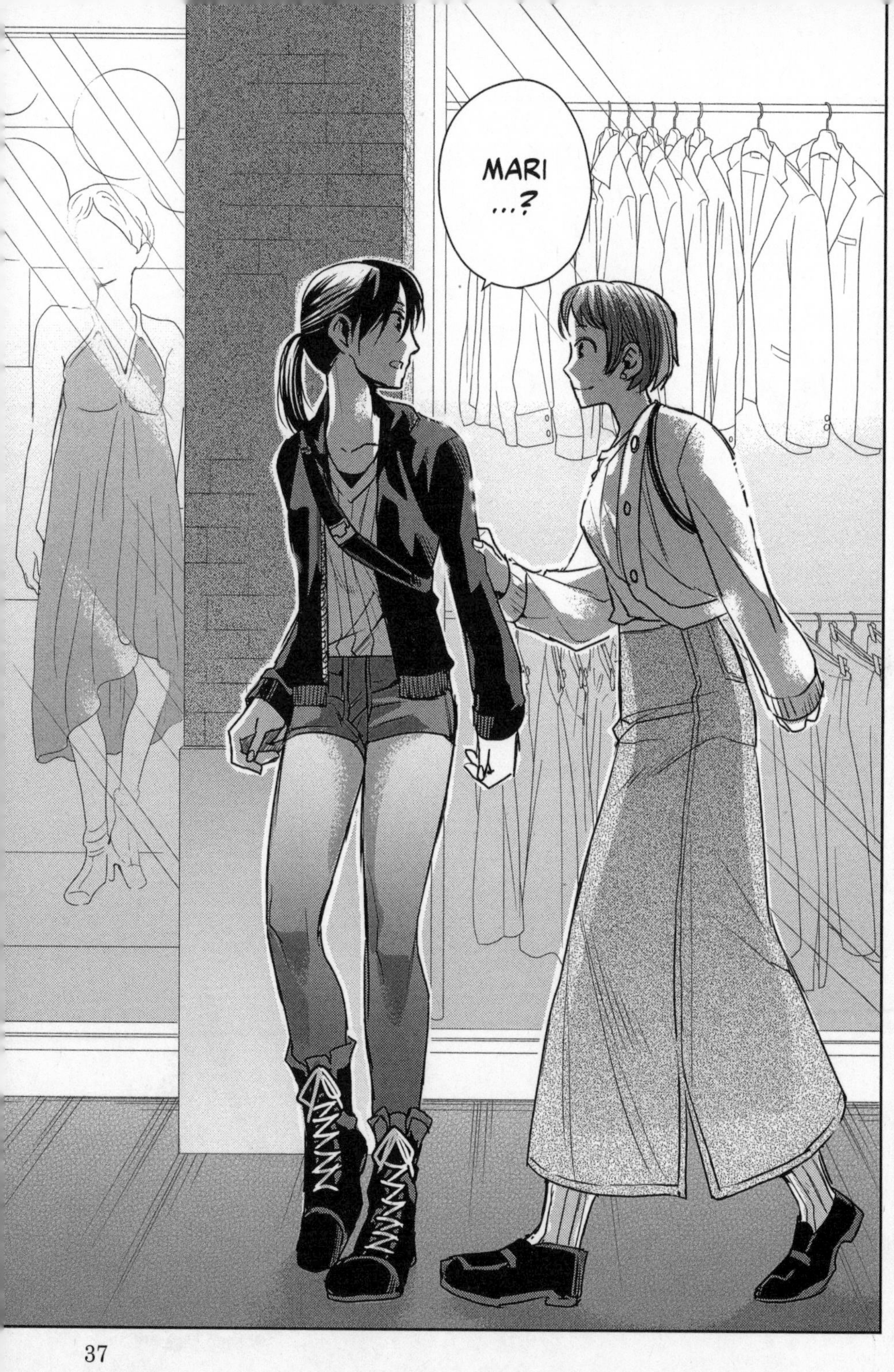
MARI ...?

## Chapter 6: The Bleeding Effect

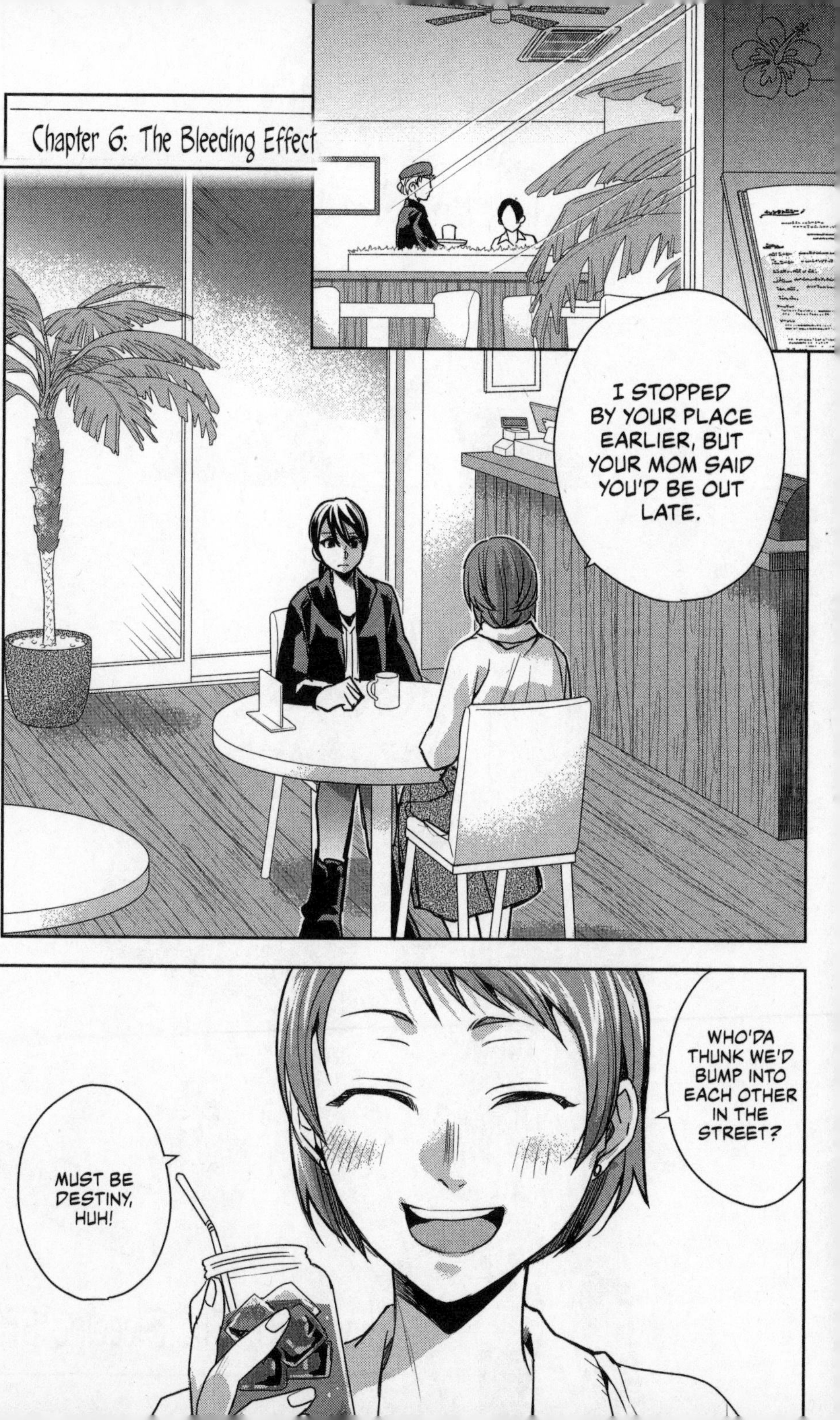
I STOPPED BY YOUR PLACE EARLIER, BUT YOUR MOM SAID YOU'D BE OUT LATE.
WHO'DA THUNK WE'D BUMP INTO EACH OTHER IN THE STREET?
MUST BE DESTINY, HUH!

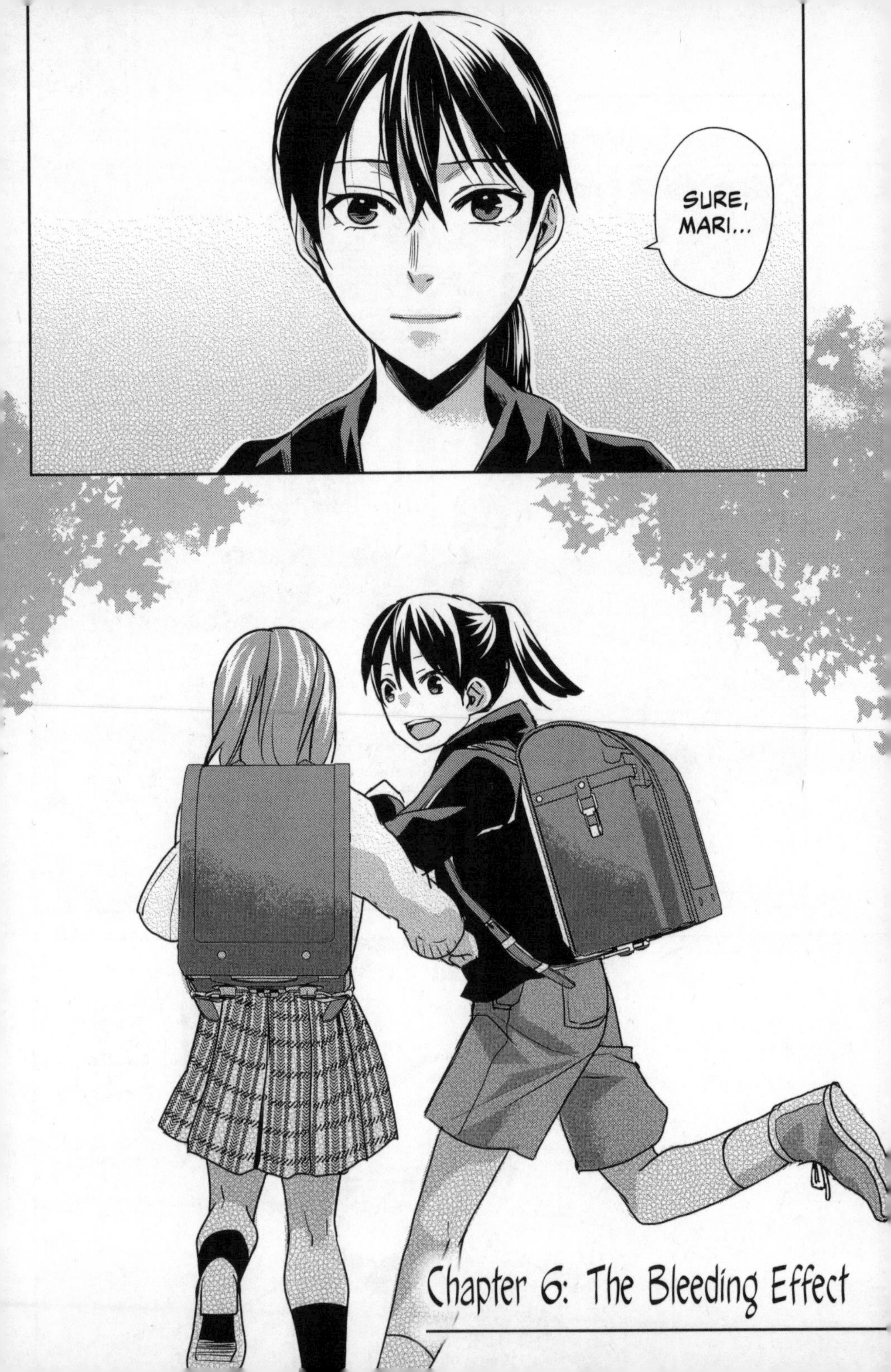
SURE, MARI...
Chapter 6: The Bleeding Effect

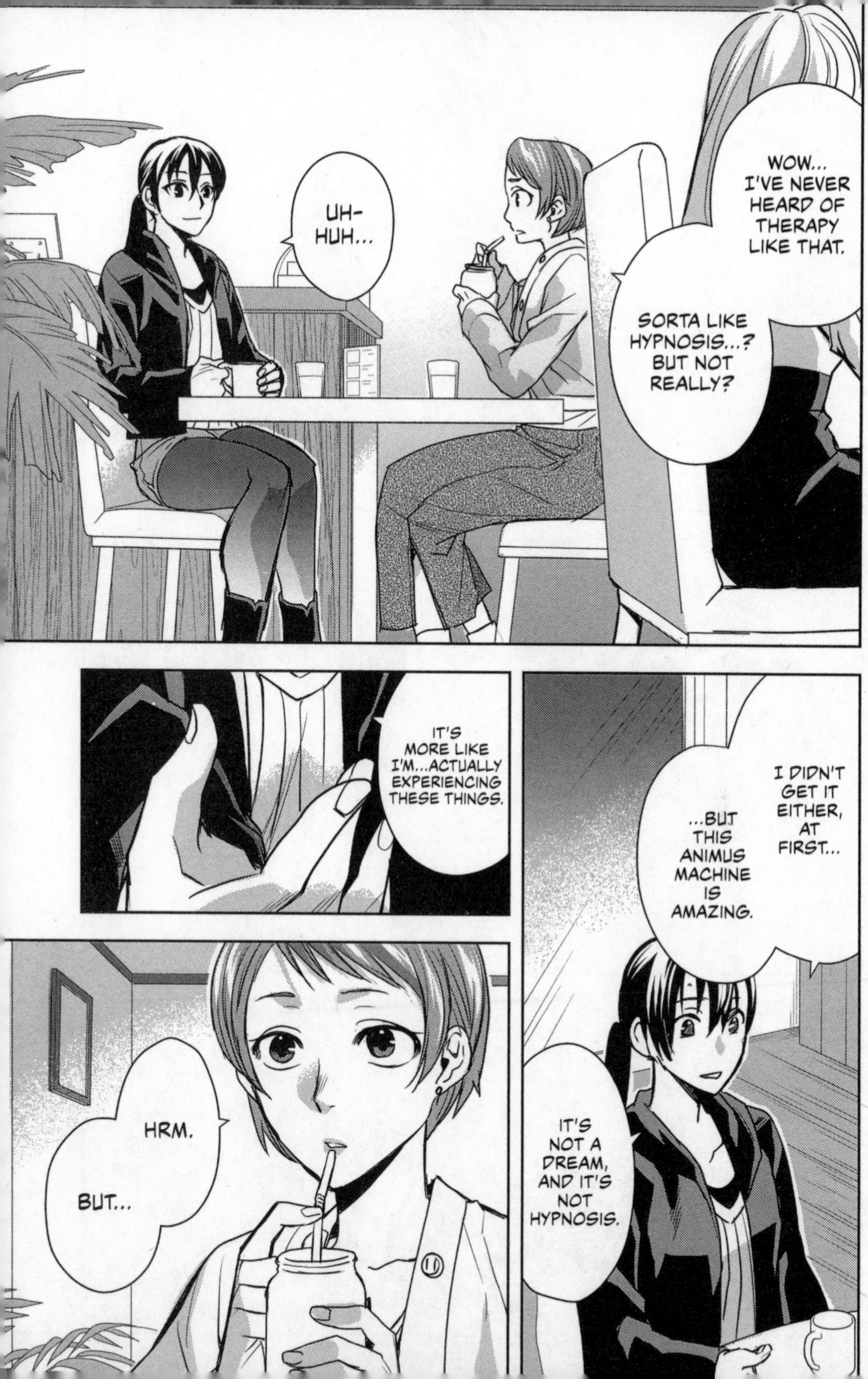
WOW... I'VE NEVER HEARD OF THERAPY LIKE THAT.
SORTA LIKE HYPNOSIS...? BUT NOT REALLY?
UH-HUH...
I DIDN'T GET IT EITHER, AT FIRST...
...BUT THIS ANIMUS MACHINE IS AMAZING.
IT'S MORE LIKE I'M...ACTUALLY EXPERIENCING THESE THINGS.
IT'S NOT A DREAM, AND IT'S NOT HYPNOSIS.
HRM.
BUT...

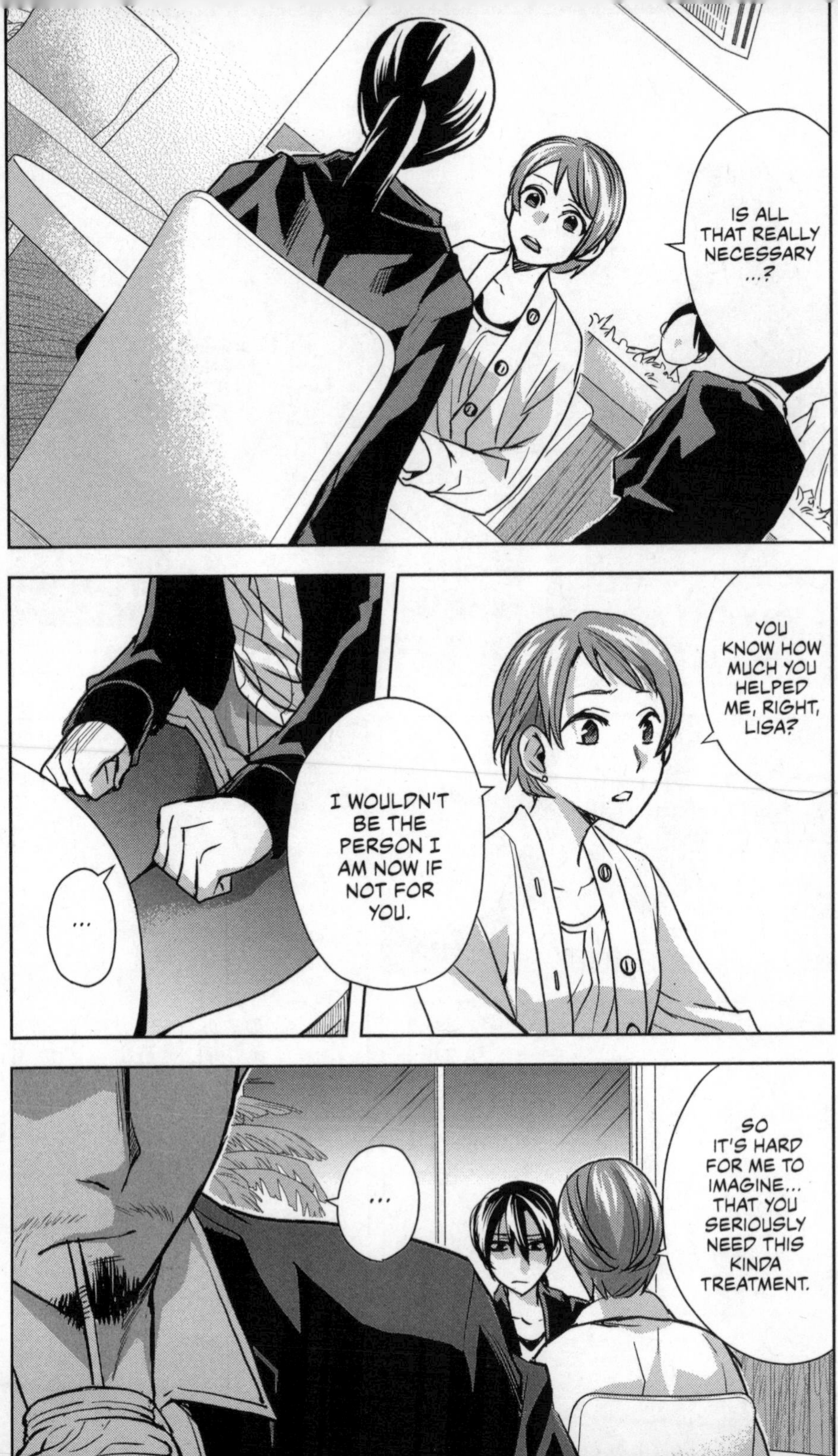
IS ALL THAT REALLY NECESSARY ...?
YOU KNOW HOW MUCH YOU HELPED ME, RIGHT, LISA?
I WOULDN'T BE THE PERSON I AM NOW IF NOT FOR YOU.
...
SO IT'S HARD FOR ME TO IMAGINE... THAT YOU SERIOUSLY NEED THIS KINDA TREATMENT.
...

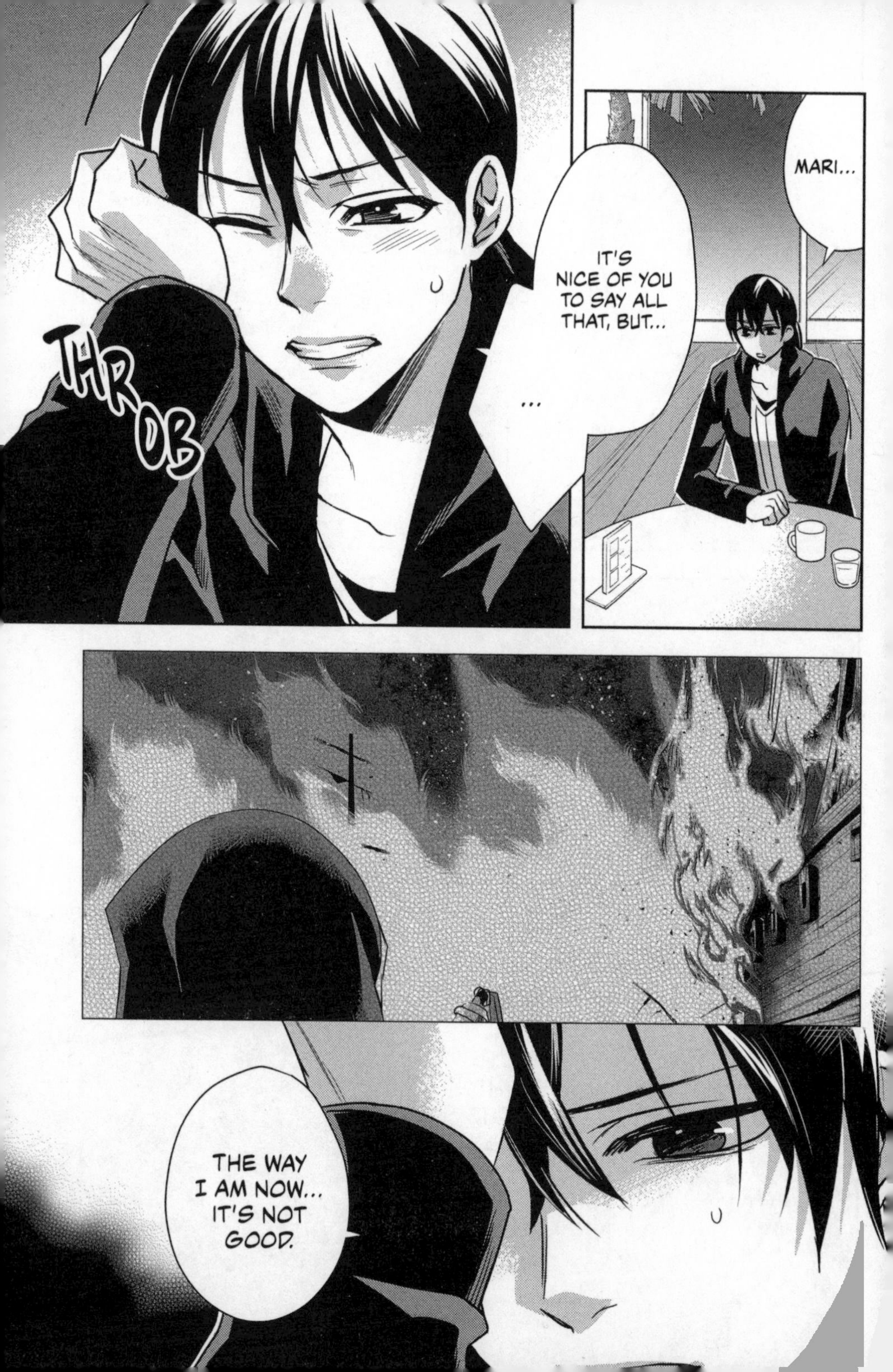
MARI...
IT'S NICE OF YOU TO SAY ALL THAT, BUT...
...
THROB
THE WAY I AM NOW... IT'S NOT GOOD.

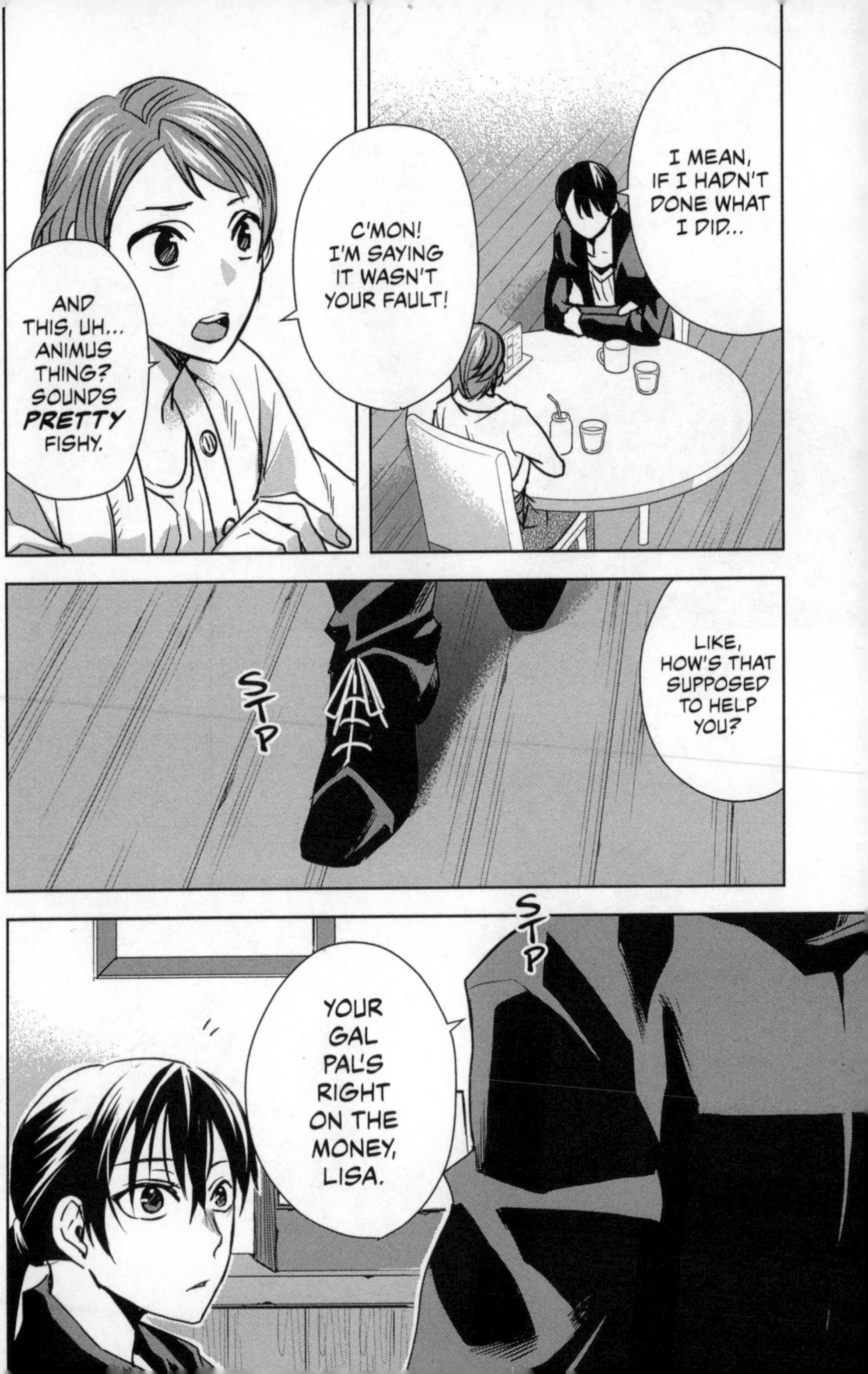
I MEAN, IF I HADN'T DONE WHAT I DID...
C'MON! I'M SAYING IT WASN'T YOUR FAULT!
AND THIS, UH... ANIMUS THING? SOUNDS PRETTY FISHY.
LIKE, HOW'S THAT SUPPOSED TO HELP YOU?
STP
STP
YOUR GAL PAL'S RIGHT ON THE MONEY, LISA.

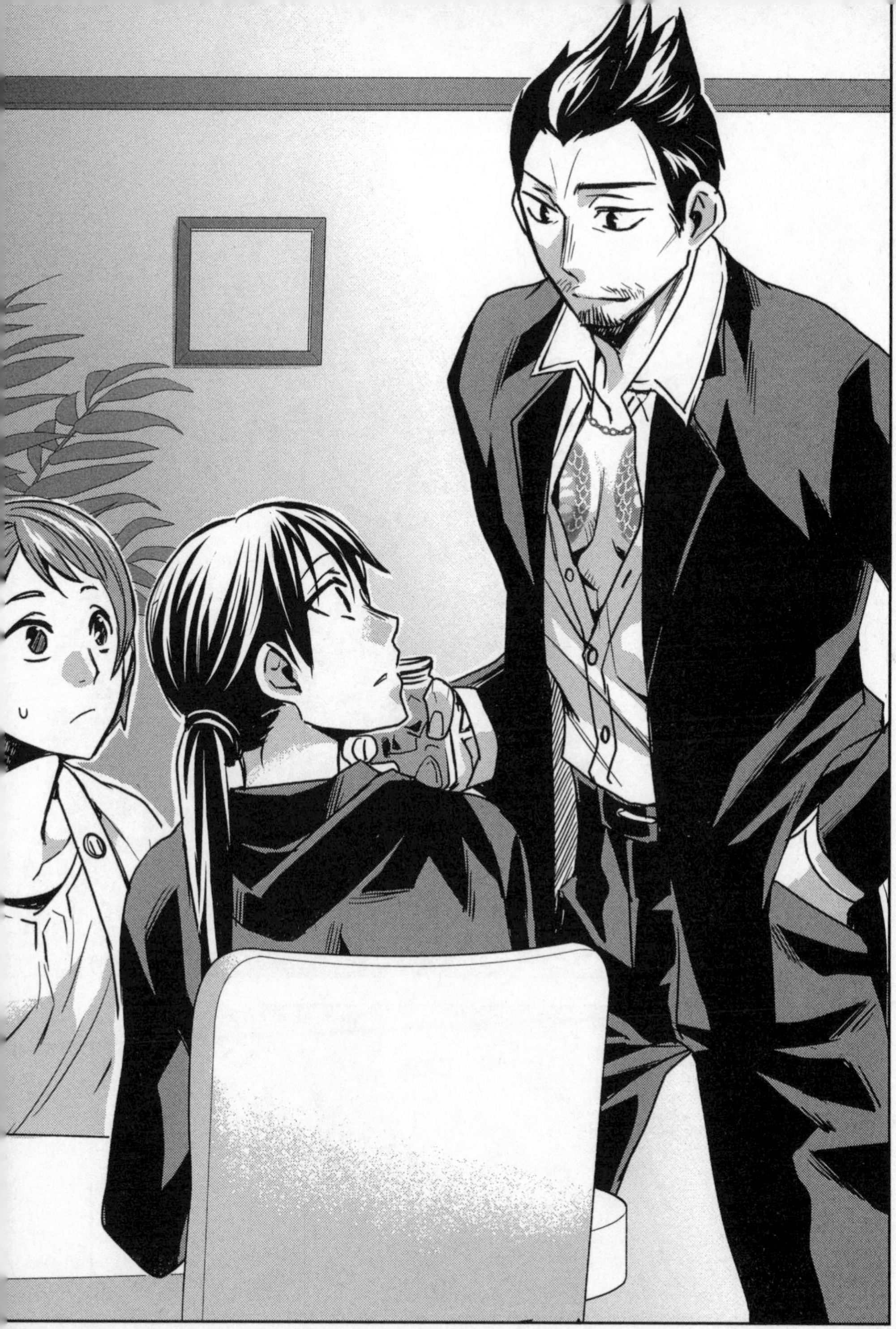

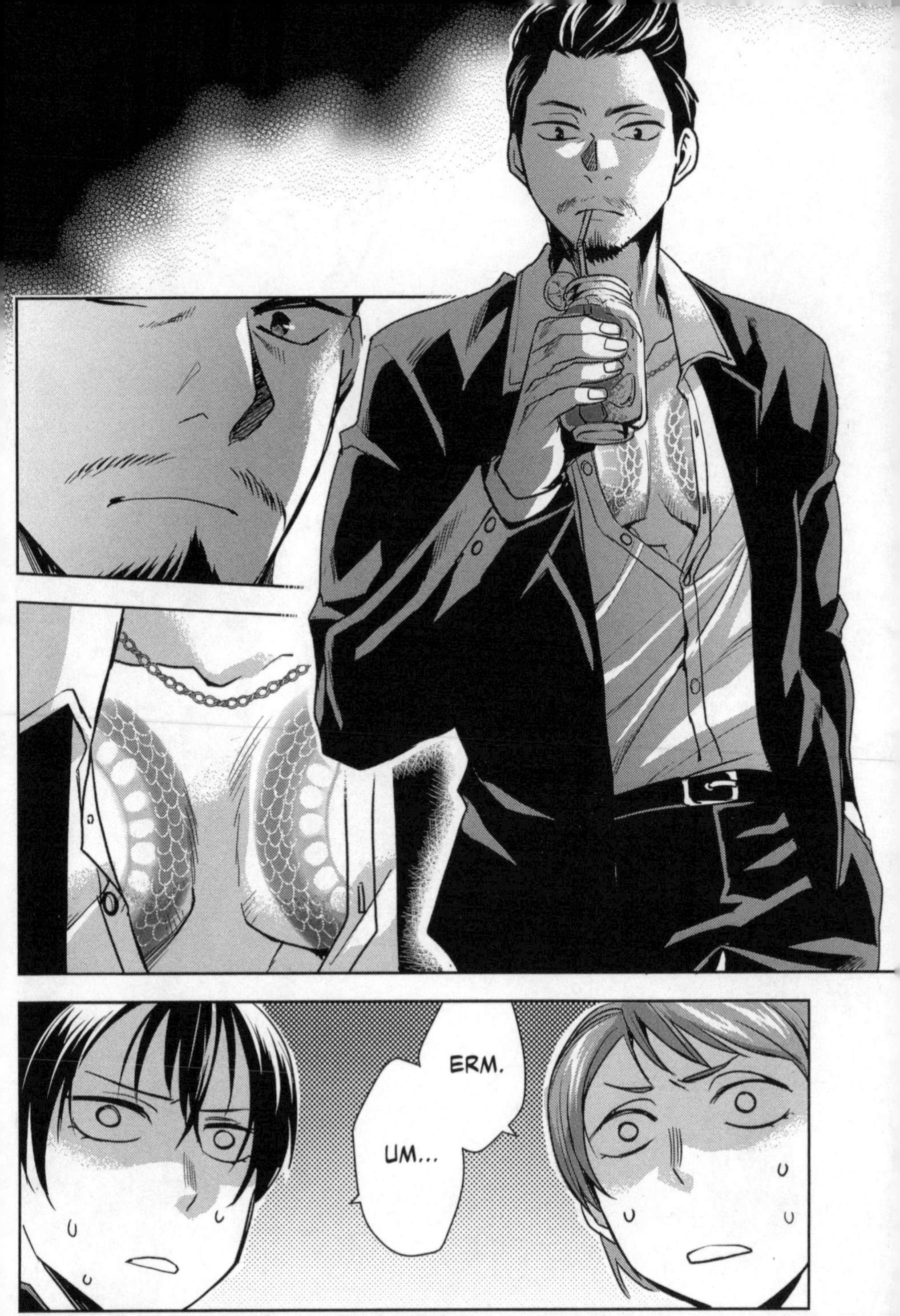
ERM.
UM...

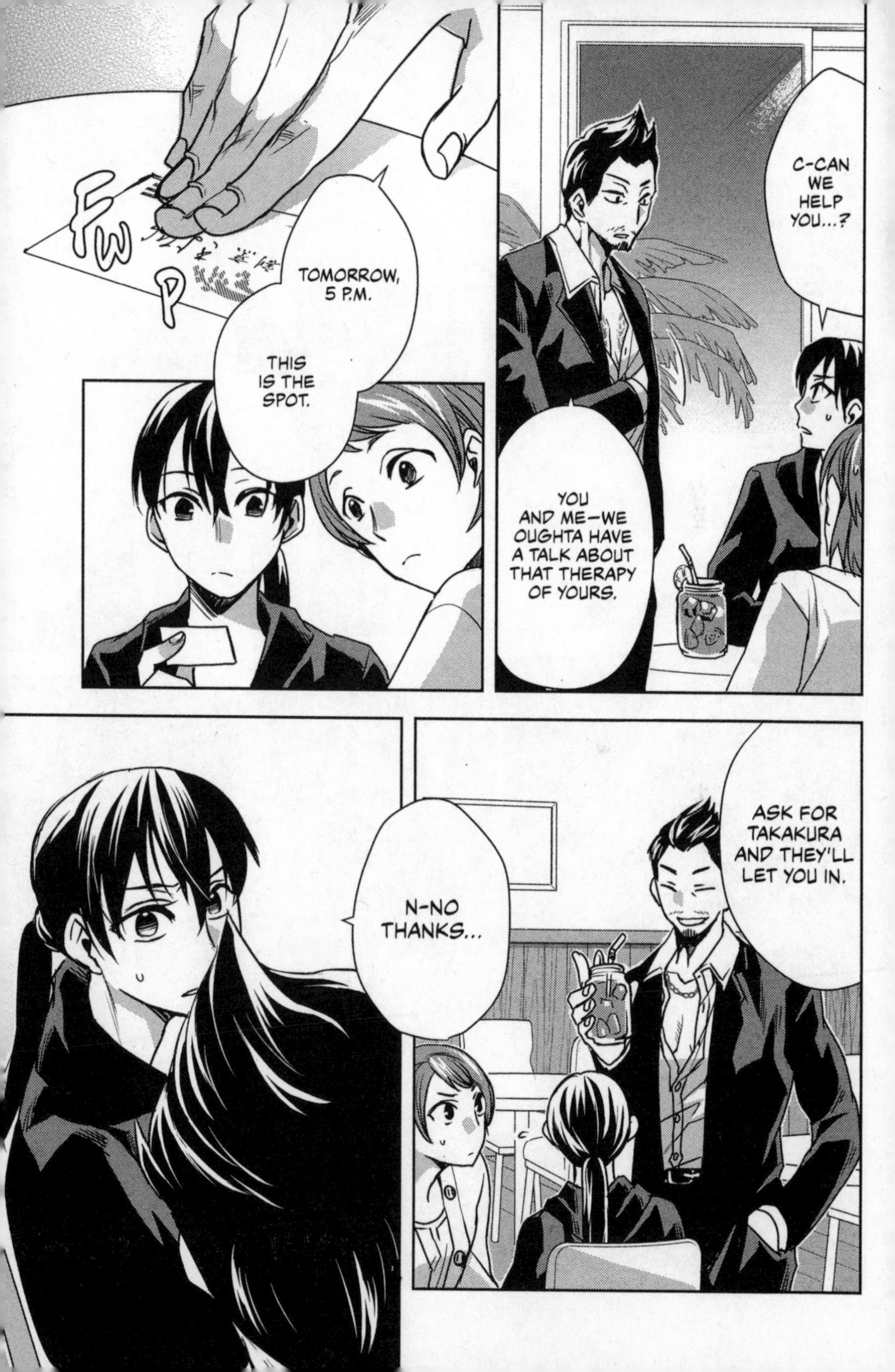
C-CAN WE HELP YOU...?
YOU AND ME—WE OUGHTA HAVE A TALK ABOUT THAT THERAPY OF YOURS.
FWP
TOMORROW, 5 P.M.
THIS IS THE SPOT.
ASK FOR TAKAKURA AND THEY'LL LET YOU IN.
N-NO THANKS...

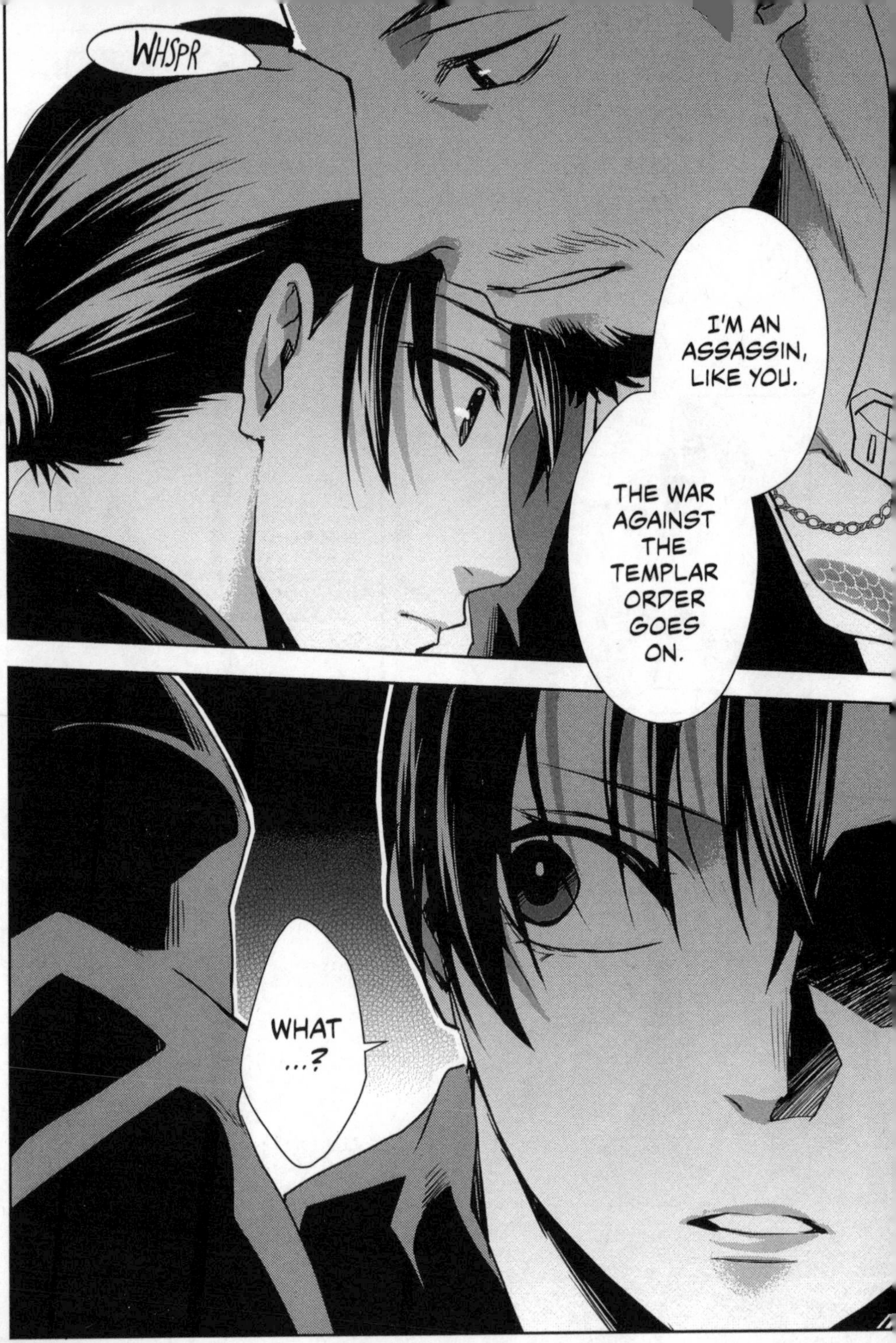
WHSPR
I'M AN ASSASSIN, LIKE YOU.
THE WAR AGAINST THE TEMPLAR ORDER GOES ON.
WHAT ...?

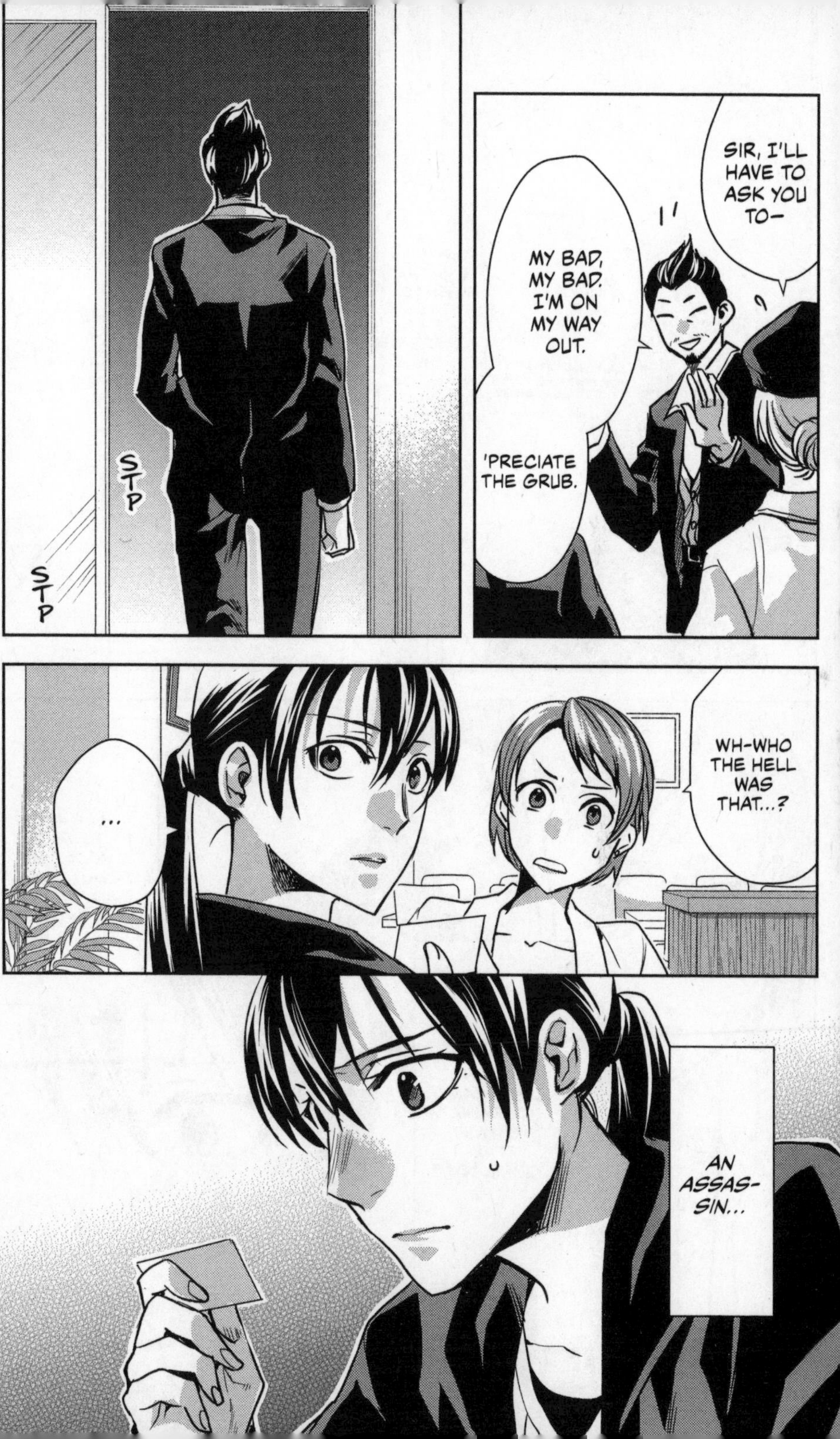
SIR, I'LL HAVE TO ASK YOU TO—
MY BAD, MY BAD. I'M ON MY WAY OUT.
'PRECIATE THE GRUB.
STP
STP
WH-WHO THE HELL WAS THAT...?
...
AN ASSAS-SIN...

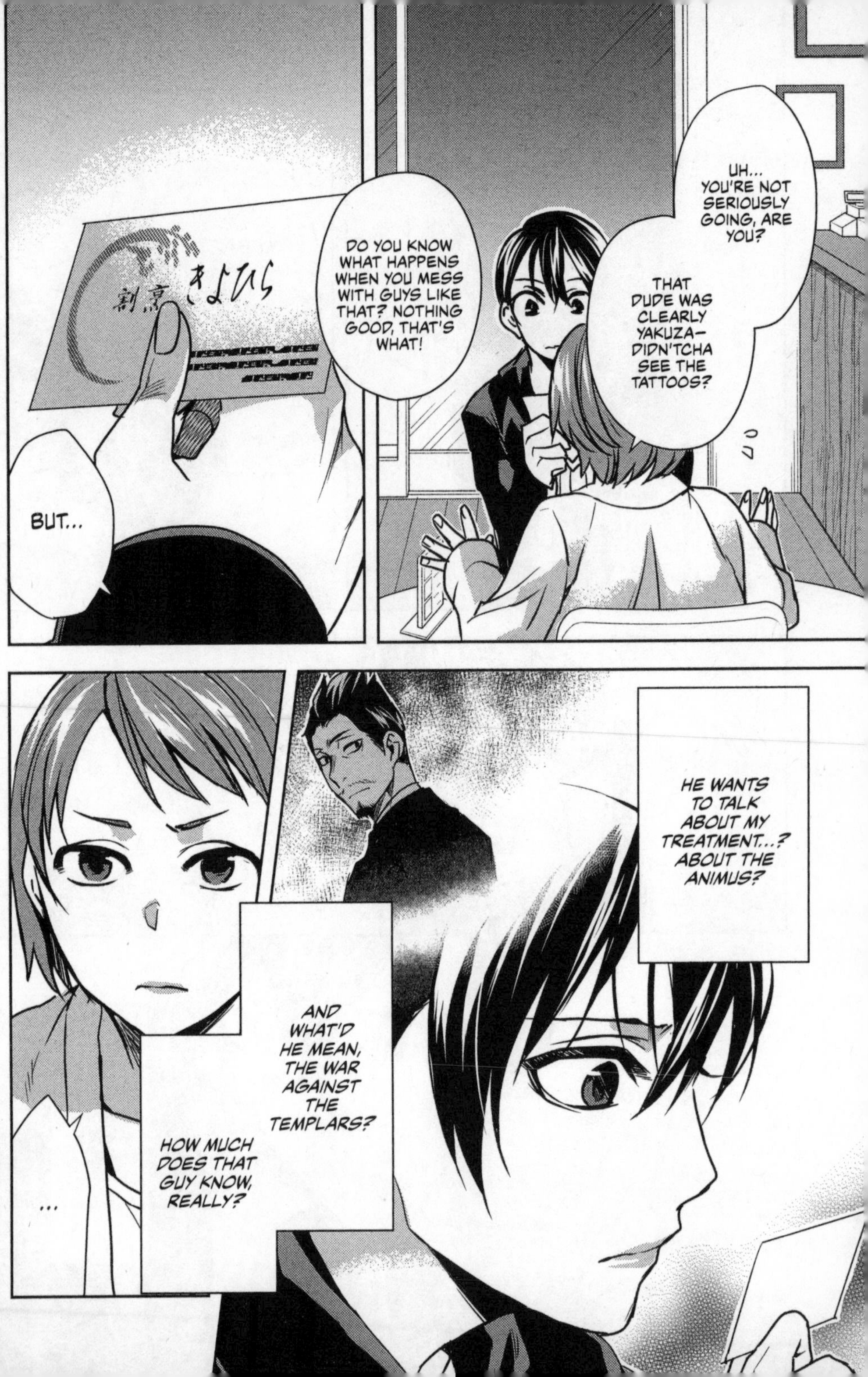
UH... YOU'RE NOT SERIOUSLY GOING, ARE YOU?
THAT DUDE WAS CLEARLY YAKUZA-DIDN'TCHA SEE THE TATTOOS?
DO YOU KNOW WHAT HAPPENS WHEN YOU MESS WITH GUYS LIKE THAT? NOTHING GOOD, THAT'S WHAT!
割烹 きよひら
BUT...
HE WANTS TO TALK ABOUT MY TREATMENT...? ABOUT THE ANIMUS?
AND WHAT'D HE MEAN, THE WAR AGAINST THE TEMPLARS?
HOW MUCH DOES THAT GUY KNOW, REALLY?
...

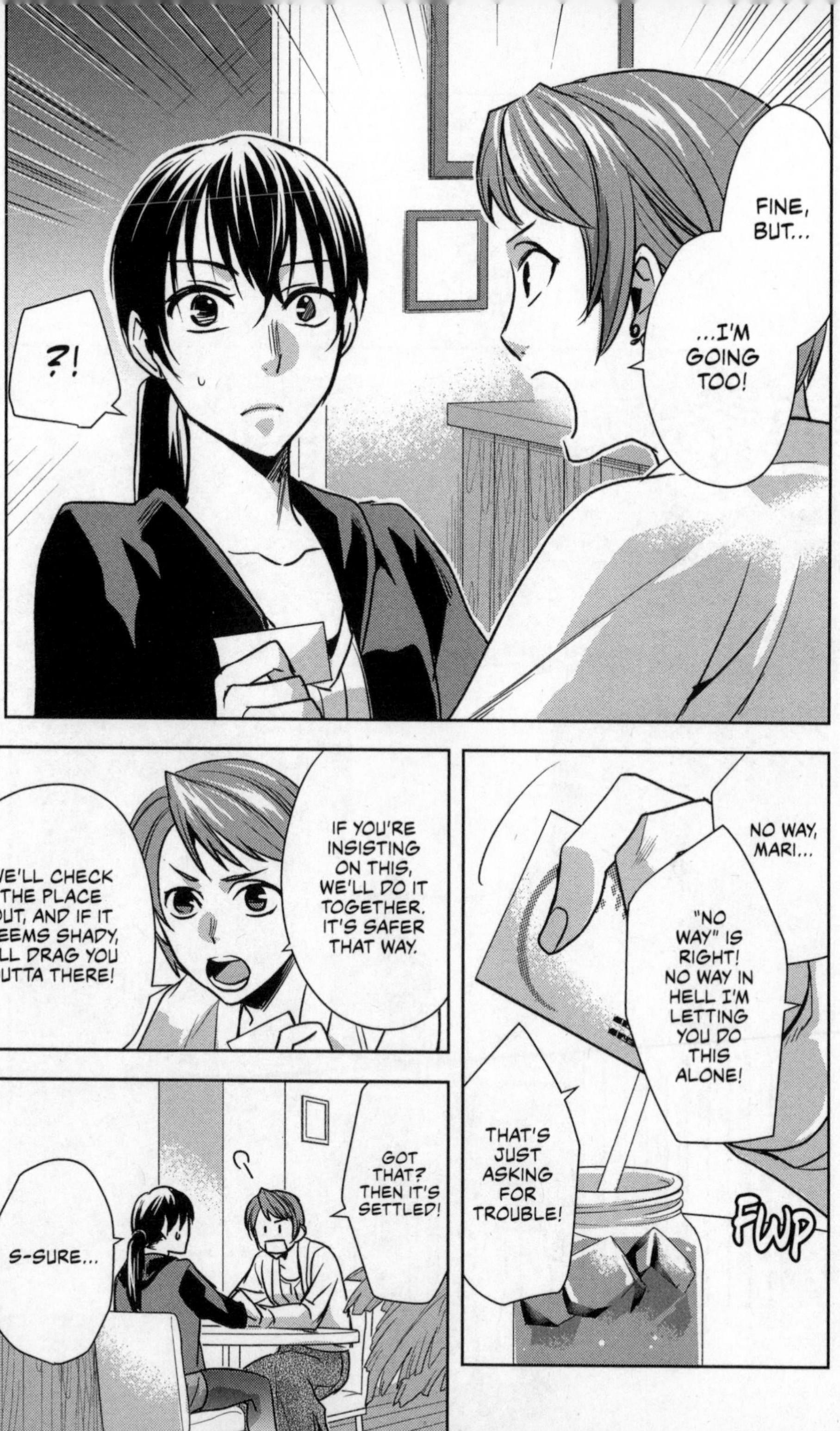
FINE, BUT...
...I'M GOING TOO!
?!
NO WAY, MARI...
"NO WAY" IS RIGHT! NO WAY IN HELL I'M LETTING YOU DO THIS ALONE!
THAT'S JUST ASKING FOR TROUBLE!
FWP
IF YOU'RE INSISTING ON THIS, WE'LL DO IT TOGETHER. IT'S SAFER THAT WAY.
WE'LL CHECK THE PLACE OUT, AND IF IT SEEMS SHADY, I'LL DRAG YOU OUTTA THERE!
GOT THAT? THEN IT'S SETTLED!
S-SURE...

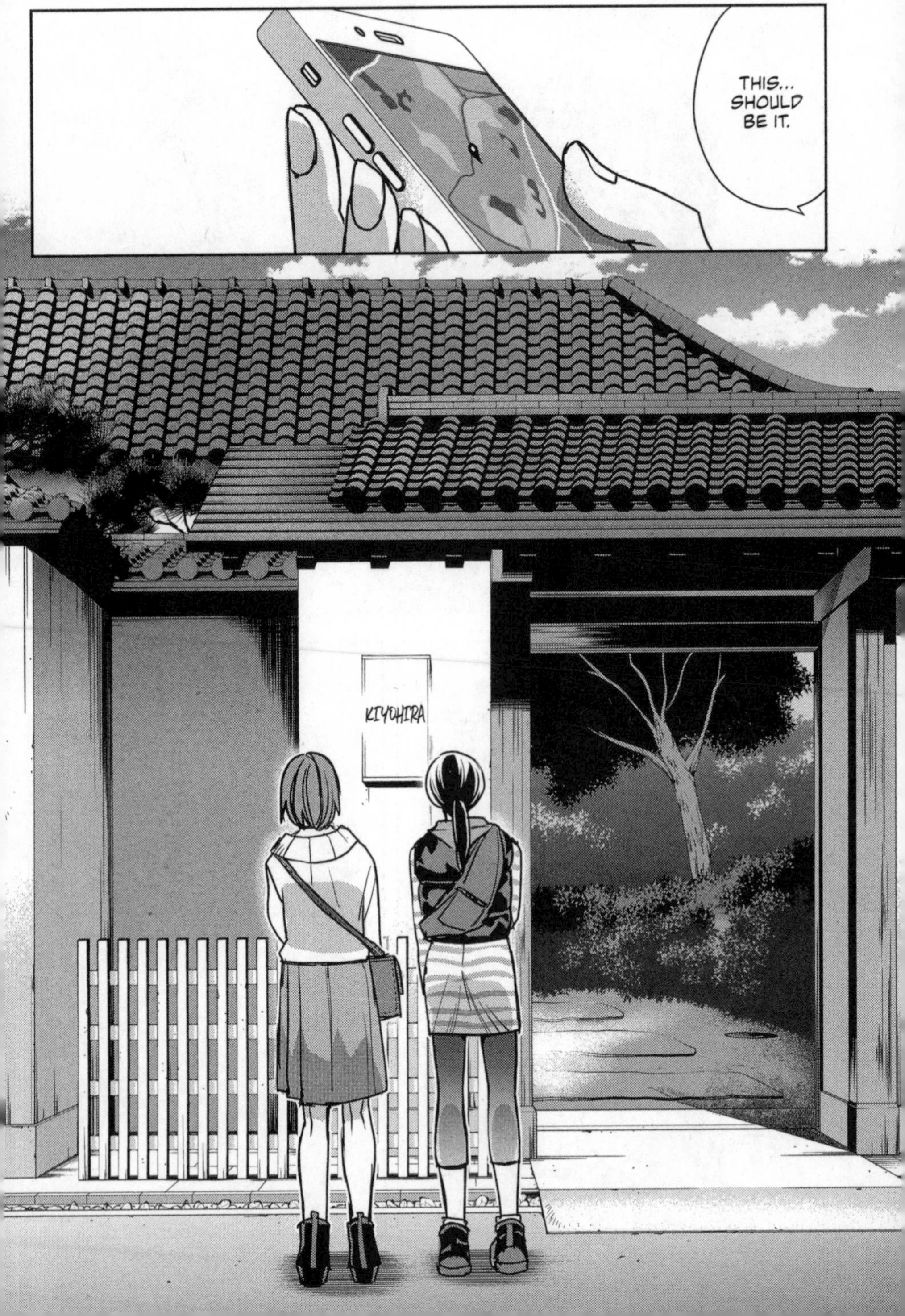
THIS... SHOULD BE IT.
KIYOHIRA

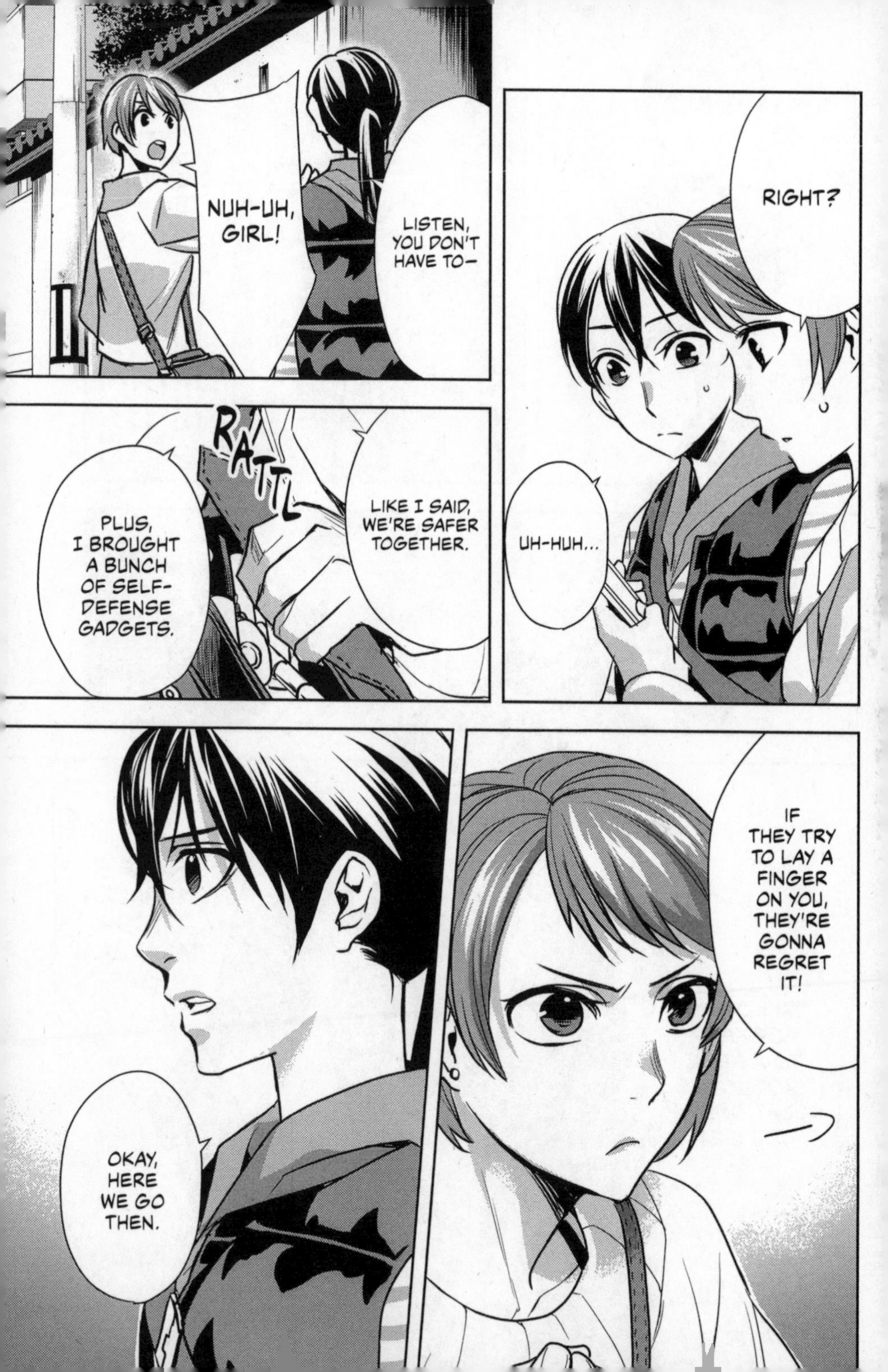
LISTEN, YOU DON'T HAVE TO—
NUH-UH, GIRL!
LIKE I SAID, WE'RE SAFER TOGETHER.
RATTL
PLUS, I BROUGHT A BUNCH OF SELF-DEFENSE GADGETS.
RIGHT?
UH-HUH...
IF THEY TRY TO LAY A FINGER ON YOU, THEY'RE GONNA REGRET IT!
OKAY, HERE WE GO THEN.

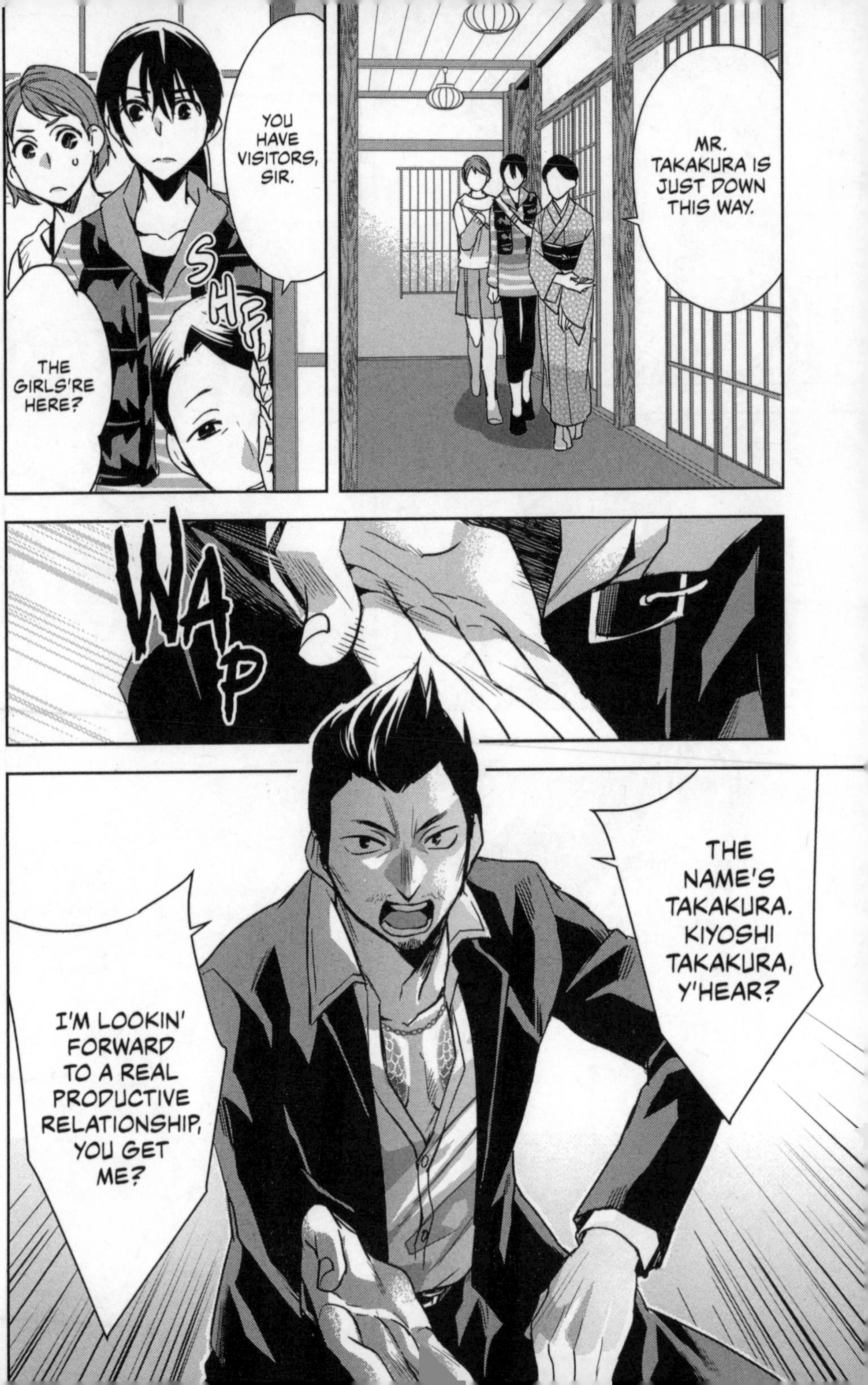
MR. TAKAKURA IS JUST DOWN THIS WAY.
YOU HAVE VISITORS, SIR.
SHF
THE GIRLS'RE HERE?
WAP
THE NAME'S TAKAKURA. KIYOSHI TAKAKURA, Y'HEAR?
I'M LOOKIN' FORWARD TO A REAL PRODUCTIVE RELATIONSHIP, YOU GET ME?

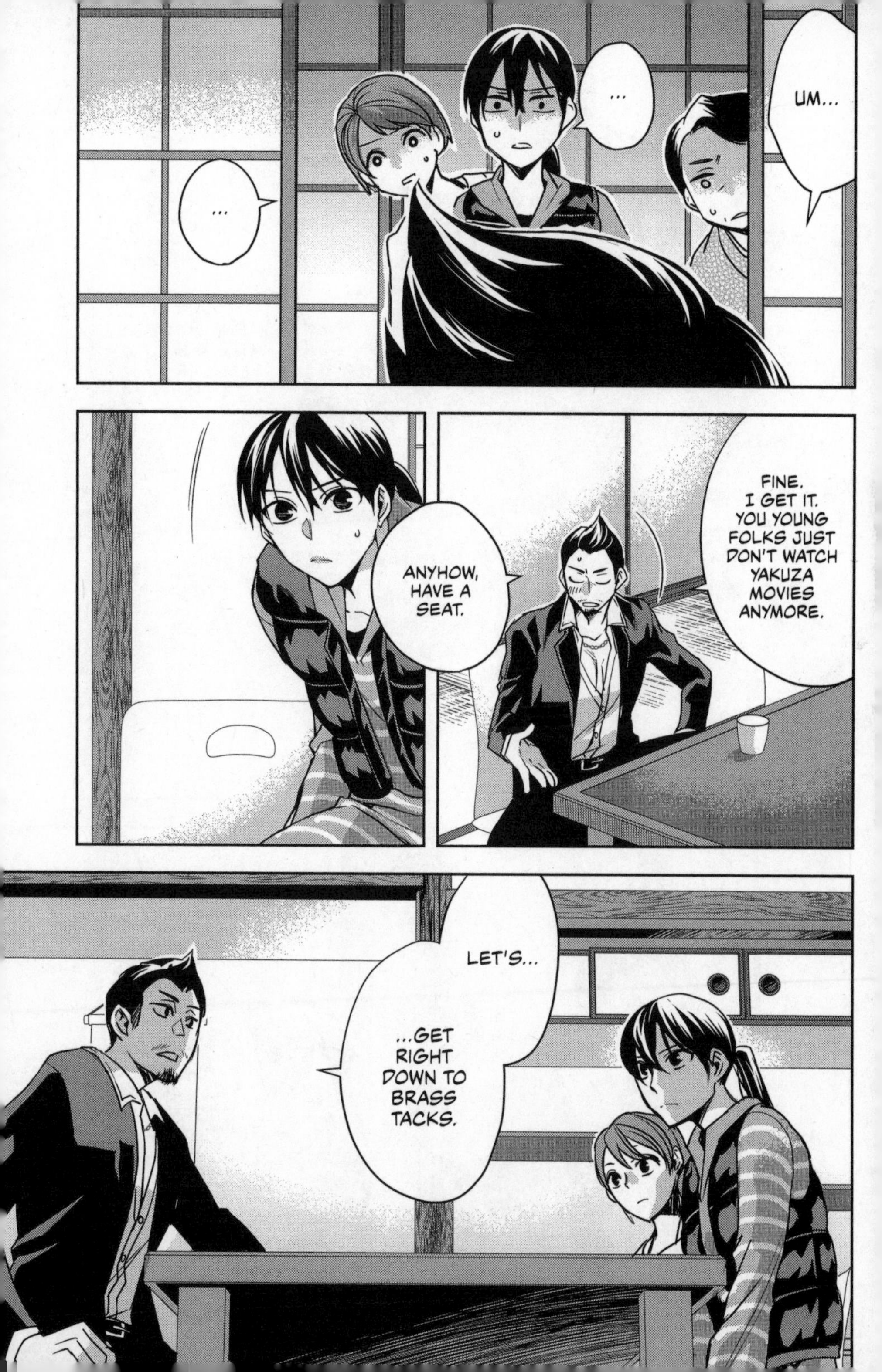
UM...
...
...
FINE. I GET IT. YOU YOUNG FOLKS JUST DON'T WATCH YAKUZA MOVIES ANYMORE.
ANYHOW, HAVE A SEAT.
LET'S...
...GET RIGHT DOWN TO BRASS TACKS.

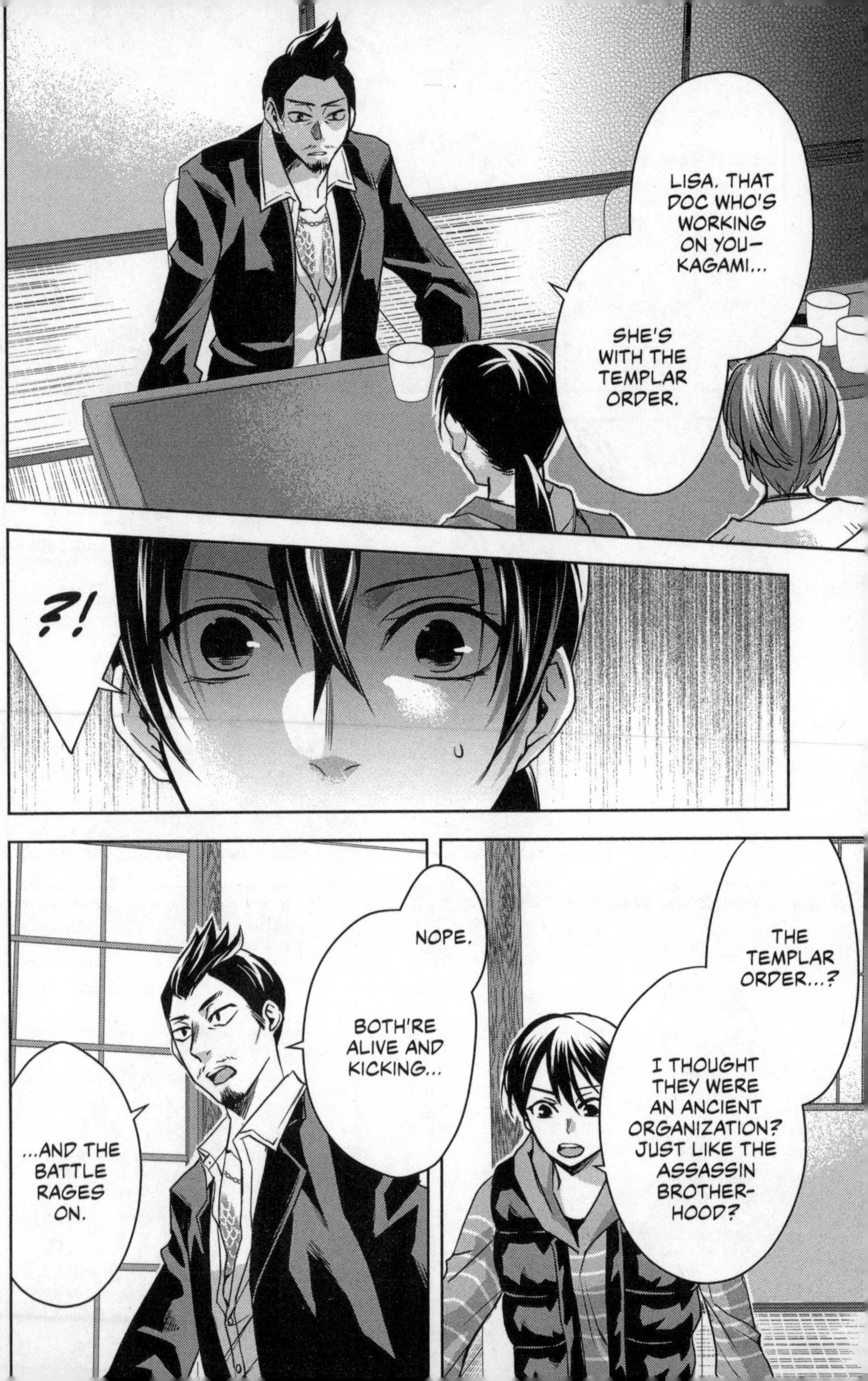
LISA. THAT DOC WHO'S WORKING ON YOU— KAGAMI...
SHE'S WITH THE TEMPLAR ORDER.
?!
THE TEMPLAR ORDER...?
I THOUGHT THEY WERE AN ANCIENT ORGANIZATION? JUST LIKE THE ASSASSIN BROTHER-HOOD?
NOPE.
BOTH'RE ALIVE AND KICKING...
...AND THE BATTLE RAGES ON.

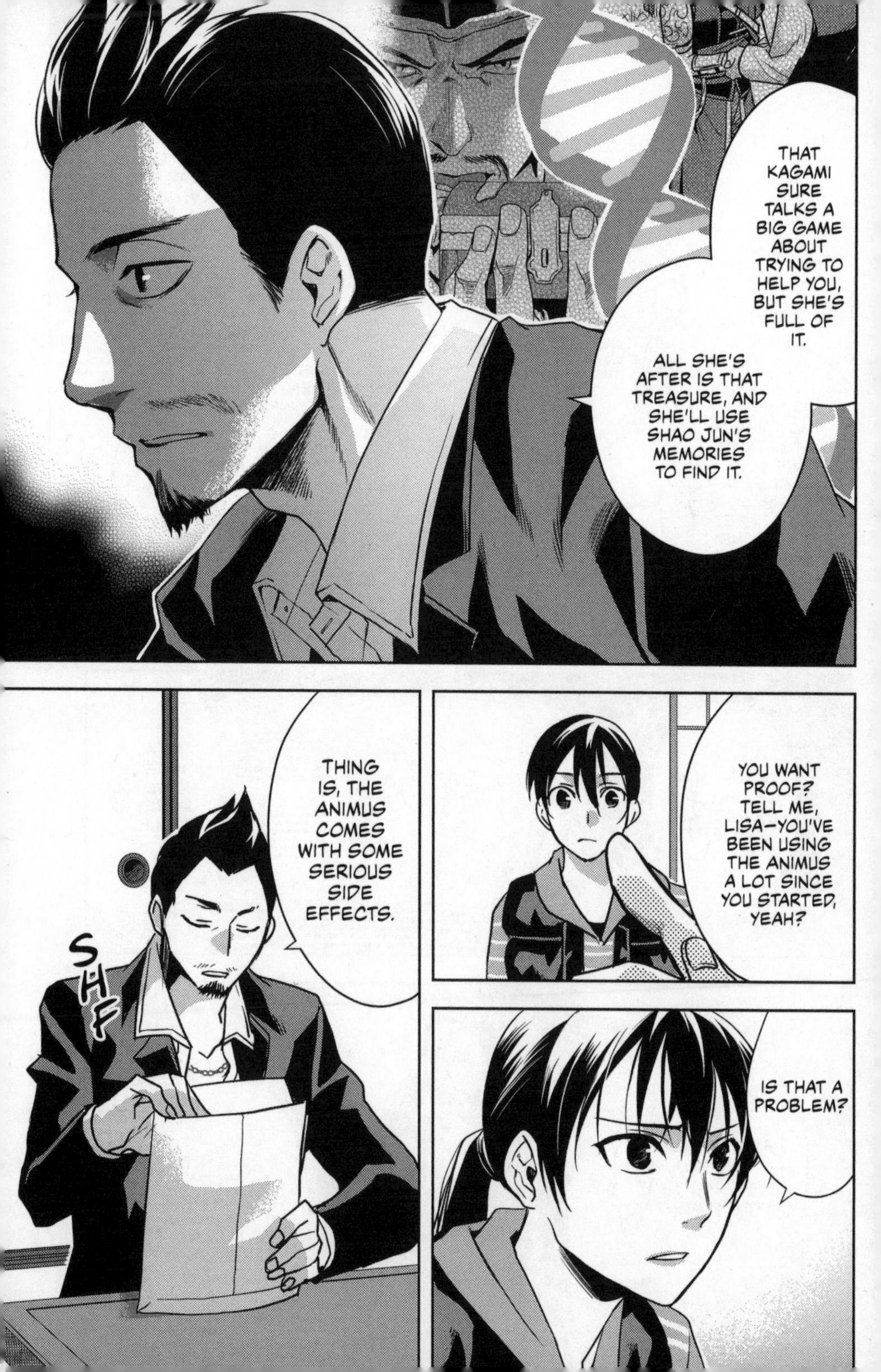
THAT KAGAMI SURE TALKS A BIG GAME ABOUT TRYING TO HELP YOU, BUT SHE'S FULL OF IT.
ALL SHE'S AFTER IS THAT TREASURE, AND SHE'LL USE SHAO JUN'S MEMORIES TO FIND IT.
YOU WANT PROOF? TELL ME, LISA—YOU'VE BEEN USING THE ANIMUS A LOT SINCE YOU STARTED, YEAH?
IS THAT A PROBLEM?
THING IS, THE ANIMUS COMES WITH SOME SERIOUS SIDE EFFECTS.
SHF

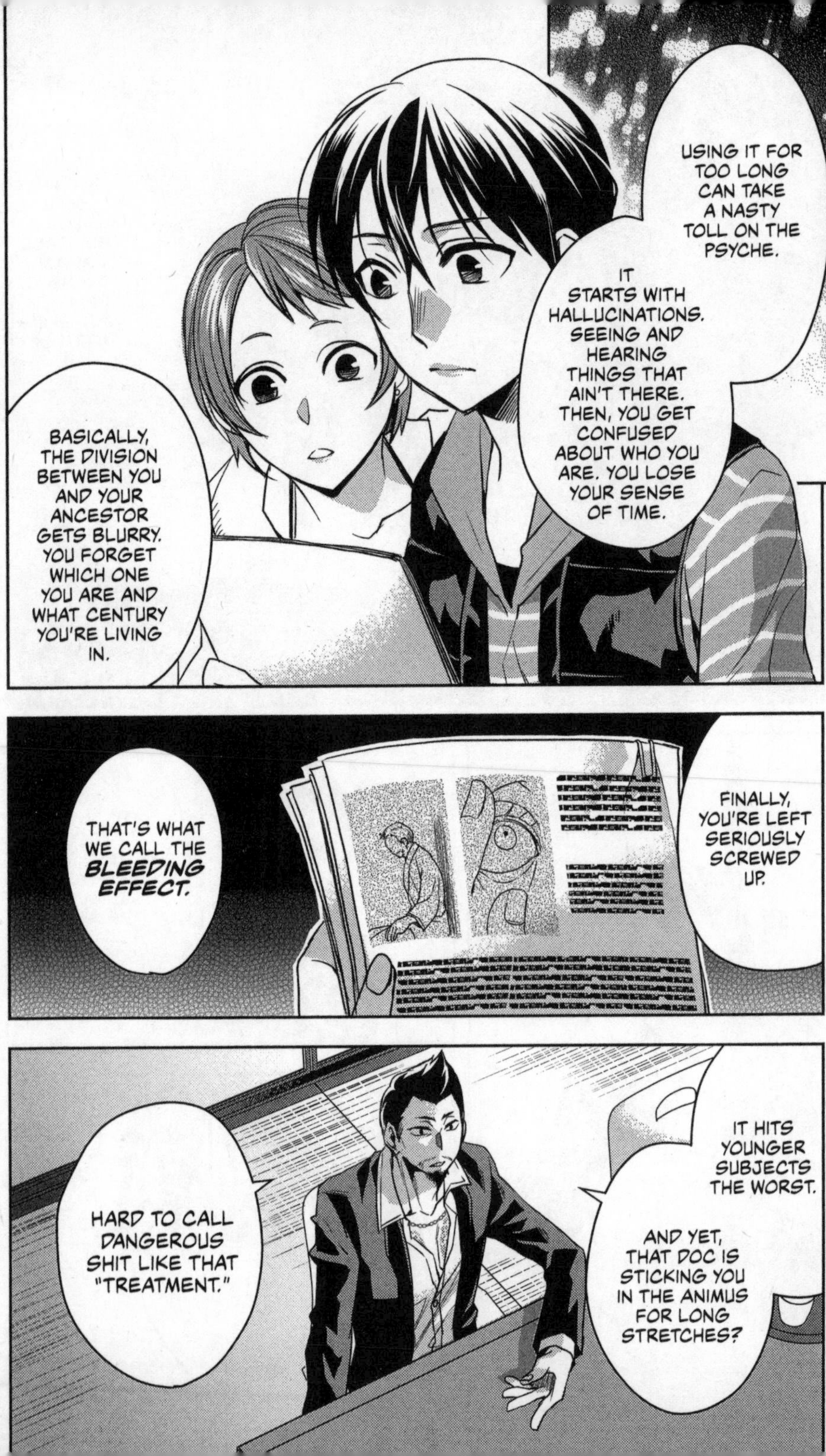
USING IT FOR TOO LONG CAN TAKE A NASTY TOLL ON THE PSYCHE.
IT STARTS WITH HALLUCINATIONS. SEEING AND HEARING THINGS THAT AIN'T THERE. THEN, YOU GET CONFUSED ABOUT WHO YOU ARE. YOU LOSE YOUR SENSE OF TIME.
BASICALLY, THE DIVISION BETWEEN YOU AND YOUR ANCESTOR GETS BLURRY. YOU FORGET WHICH ONE YOU ARE AND WHAT CENTURY YOU'RE LIVING IN.
FINALLY, YOU'RE LEFT SERIOUSLY SCREWED UP.
THAT'S WHAT WE CALL THE *BLEEDING EFFECT.*
IT HITS YOUNGER SUBJECTS THE WORST.
AND YET, THAT DOC IS STICKING YOU IN THE ANIMUS FOR LONG STRETCHES?
HARD TO CALL DANGEROUS SHIT LIKE THAT "TREATMENT."

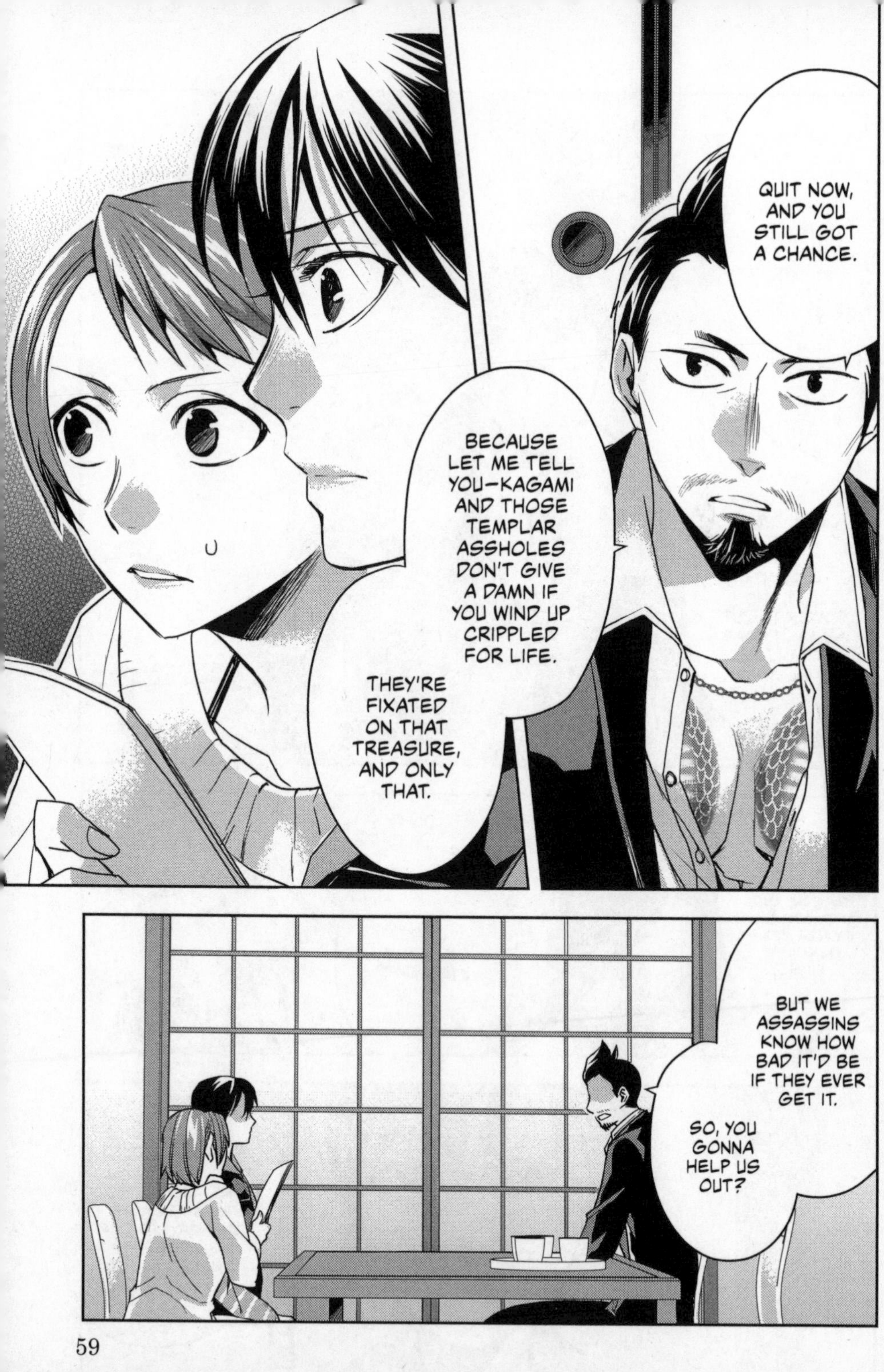
QUIT NOW, AND YOU STILL GOT A CHANCE.
BECAUSE LET ME TELL YOU—KAGAMI AND THOSE TEMPLAR ASSHOLES DON'T GIVE A DAMN IF YOU WIND UP CRIPPLED FOR LIFE.
THEY'RE FIXATED ON THAT TREASURE, AND ONLY THAT.
BUT WE ASSASSINS KNOW HOW BAD IT'D BE IF THEY EVER GET IT.
SO, YOU GONNA HELP US OUT?

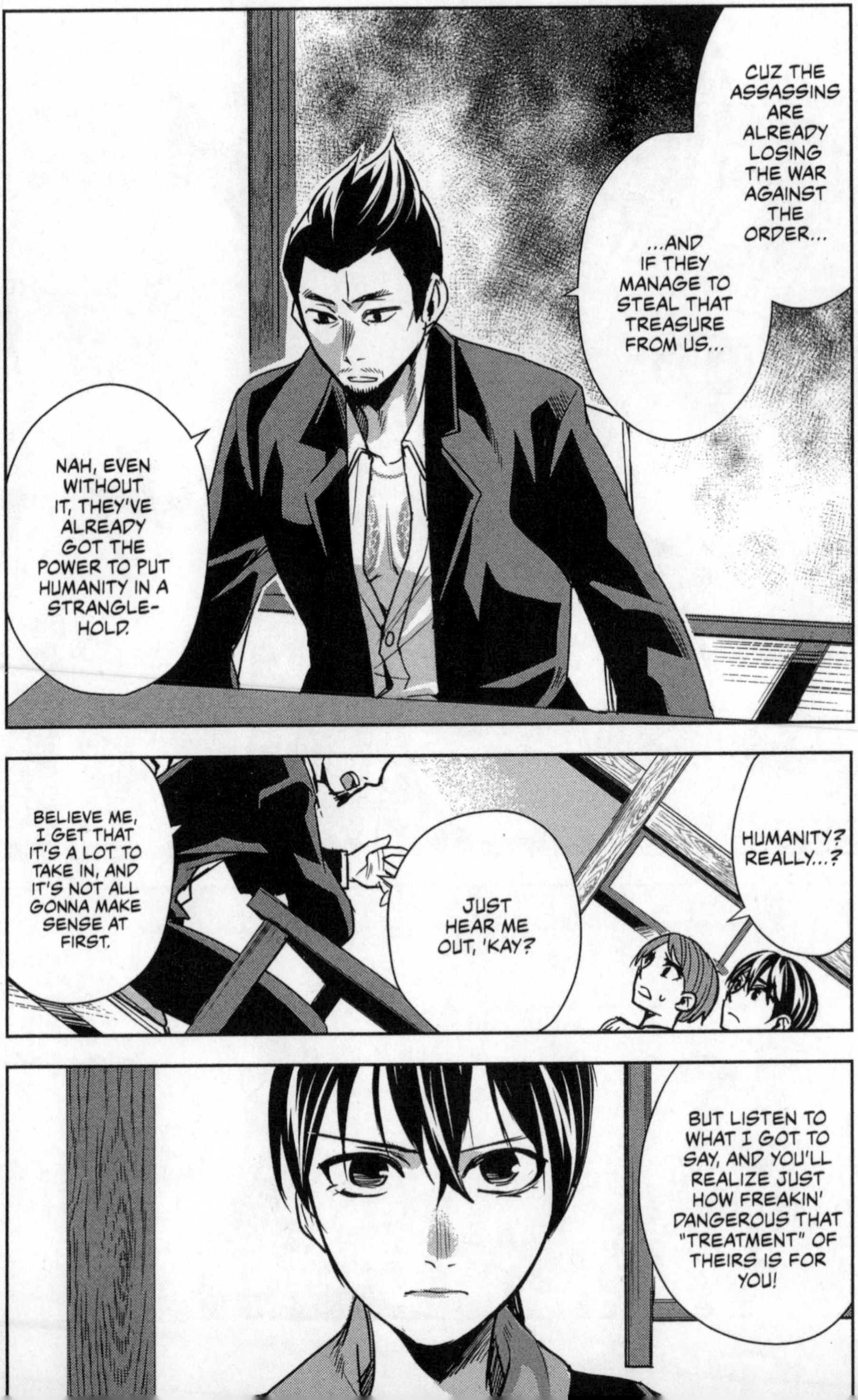
CUZ THE ASSASSINS ARE ALREADY LOSING THE WAR AGAINST THE ORDER...
...AND IF THEY MANAGE TO STEAL THAT TREASURE FROM US...
NAH, EVEN WITHOUT IT, THEY'VE ALREADY GOT THE POWER TO PUT HUMANITY IN A STRANGLE-HOLD.
HUMANITY? REALLY...?
BELIEVE ME, I GET THAT IT'S A LOT TO TAKE IN, AND IT'S NOT ALL GONNA MAKE SENSE AT FIRST.
JUST HEAR ME OUT, 'KAY?
BUT LISTEN TO WHAT I GOT TO SAY, AND YOU'LL REALIZE JUST HOW FREAKIN' DANGEROUS THAT "TREATMENT" OF THEIRS IS FOR YOU!

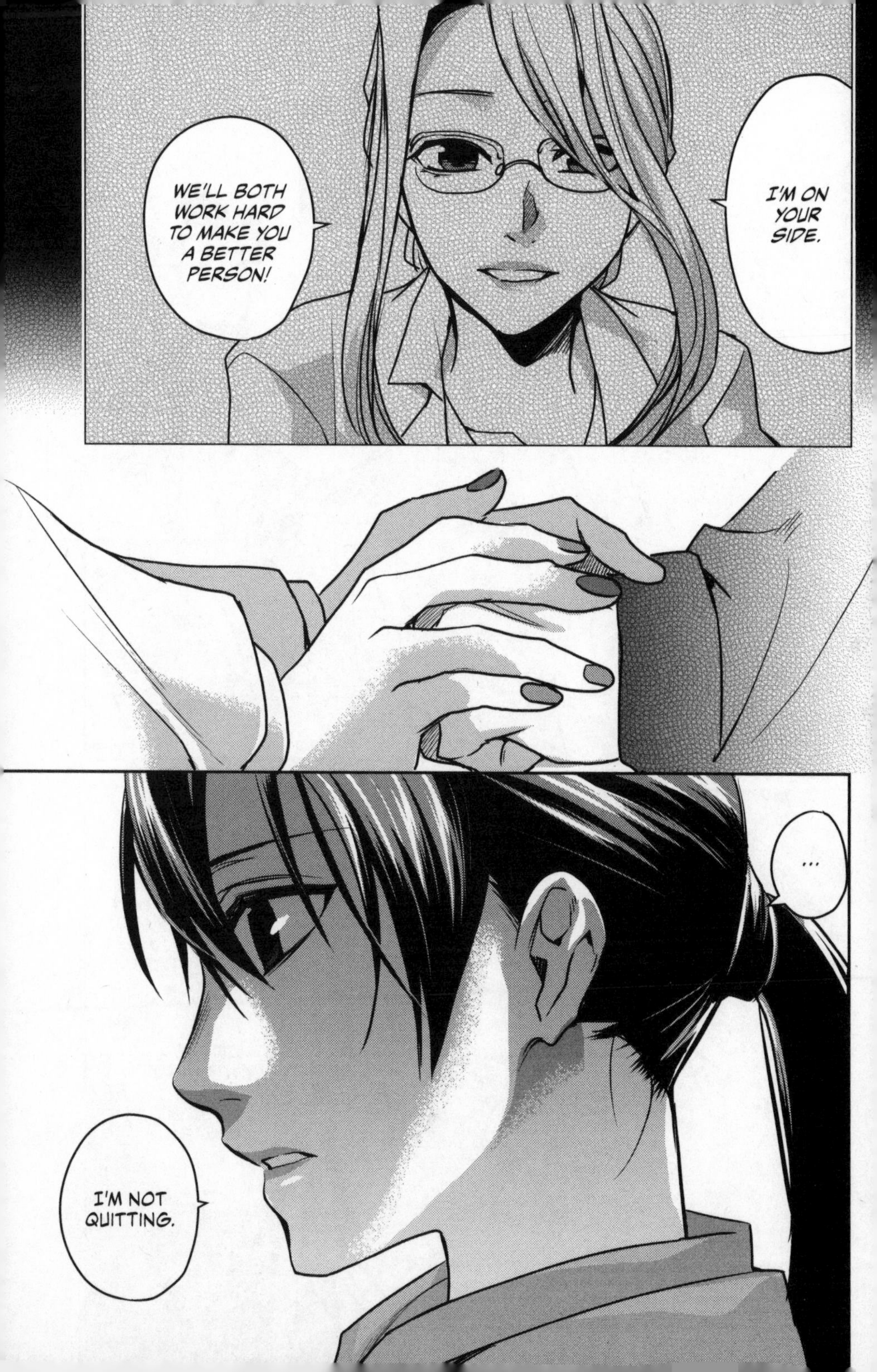
I'M ON YOUR SIDE.
WE'LL BOTH WORK HARD TO MAKE YOU A BETTER PERSON!
...
I'M NOT QUITTING.

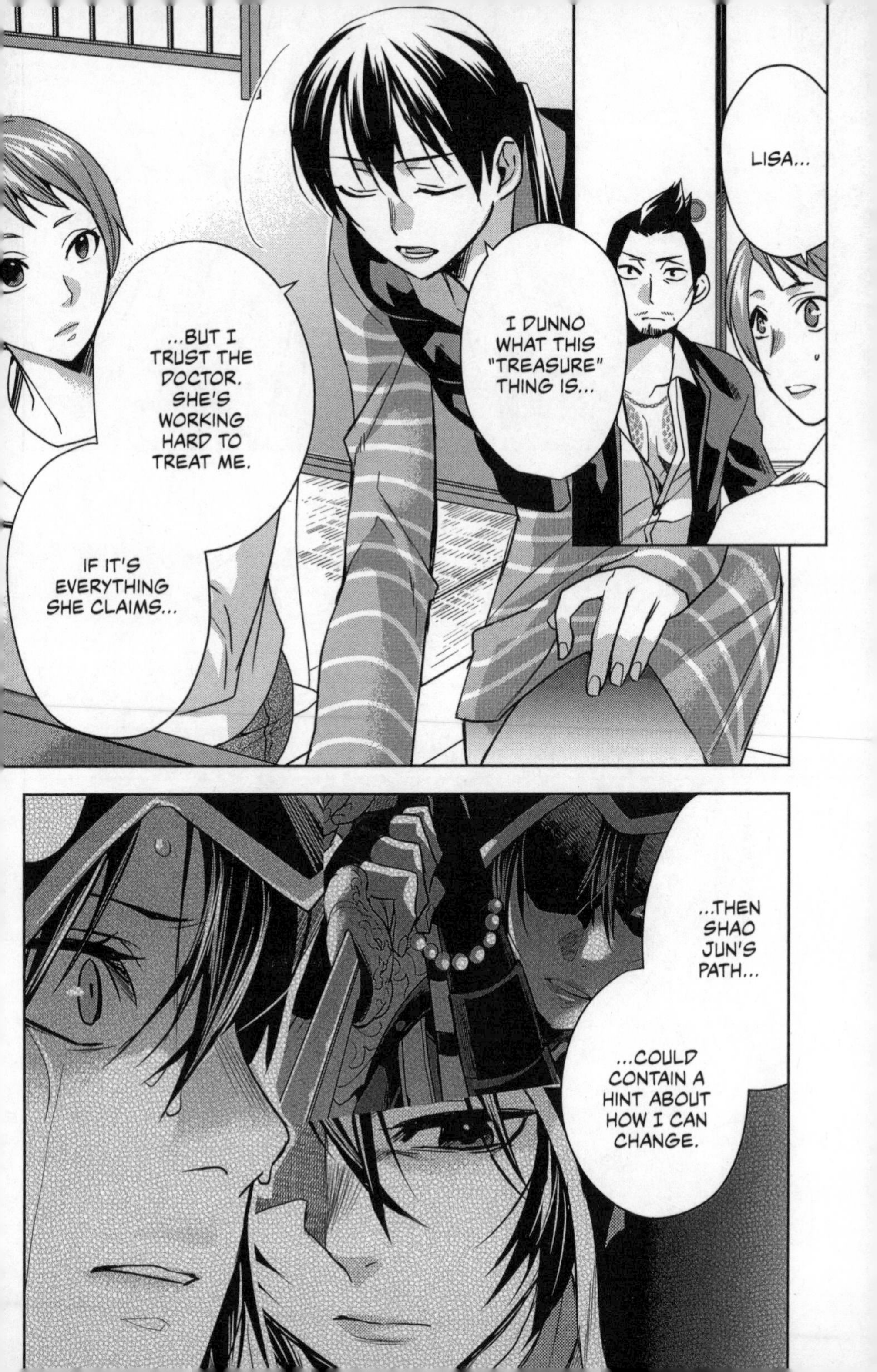
LISA...
I DUNNO WHAT THIS "TREASURE" THING IS...
...BUT I TRUST THE DOCTOR. SHE'S WORKING HARD TO TREAT ME.
IF IT'S EVERYTHING SHE CLAIMS...
...THEN SHAO JUN'S PATH...
...COULD CONTAIN A HINT ABOUT HOW I CAN CHANGE.

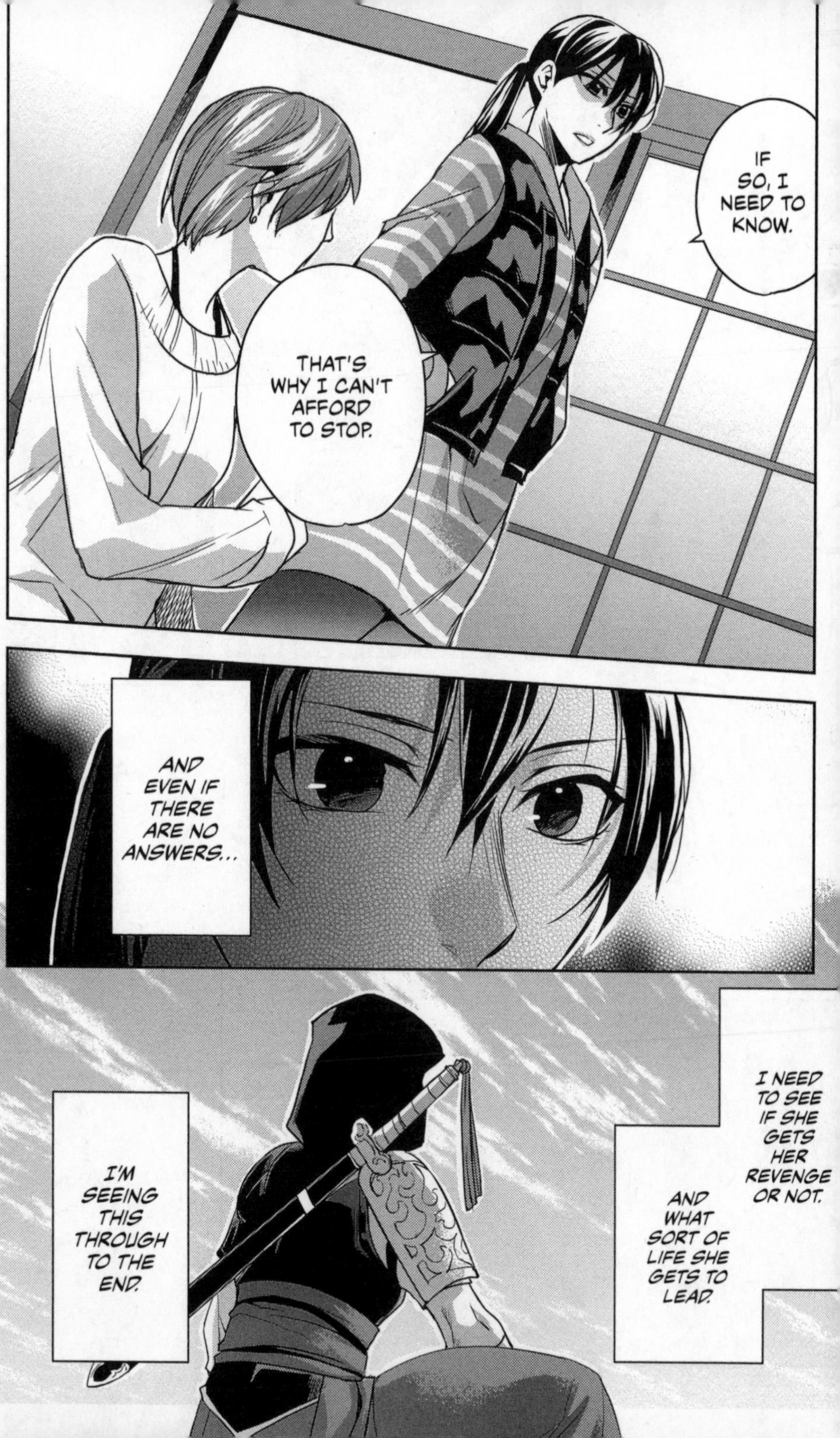
IF SO, I NEED TO KNOW.
THAT'S WHY I CAN'T AFFORD TO STOP.
AND EVEN IF THERE ARE NO ANSWERS...
I NEED TO SEE IF SHE GETS HER REVENGE OR NOT.
AND WHAT SORT OF LIFE SHE GETS TO LEAD.
I'M SEEING THIS THROUGH TO THE END.

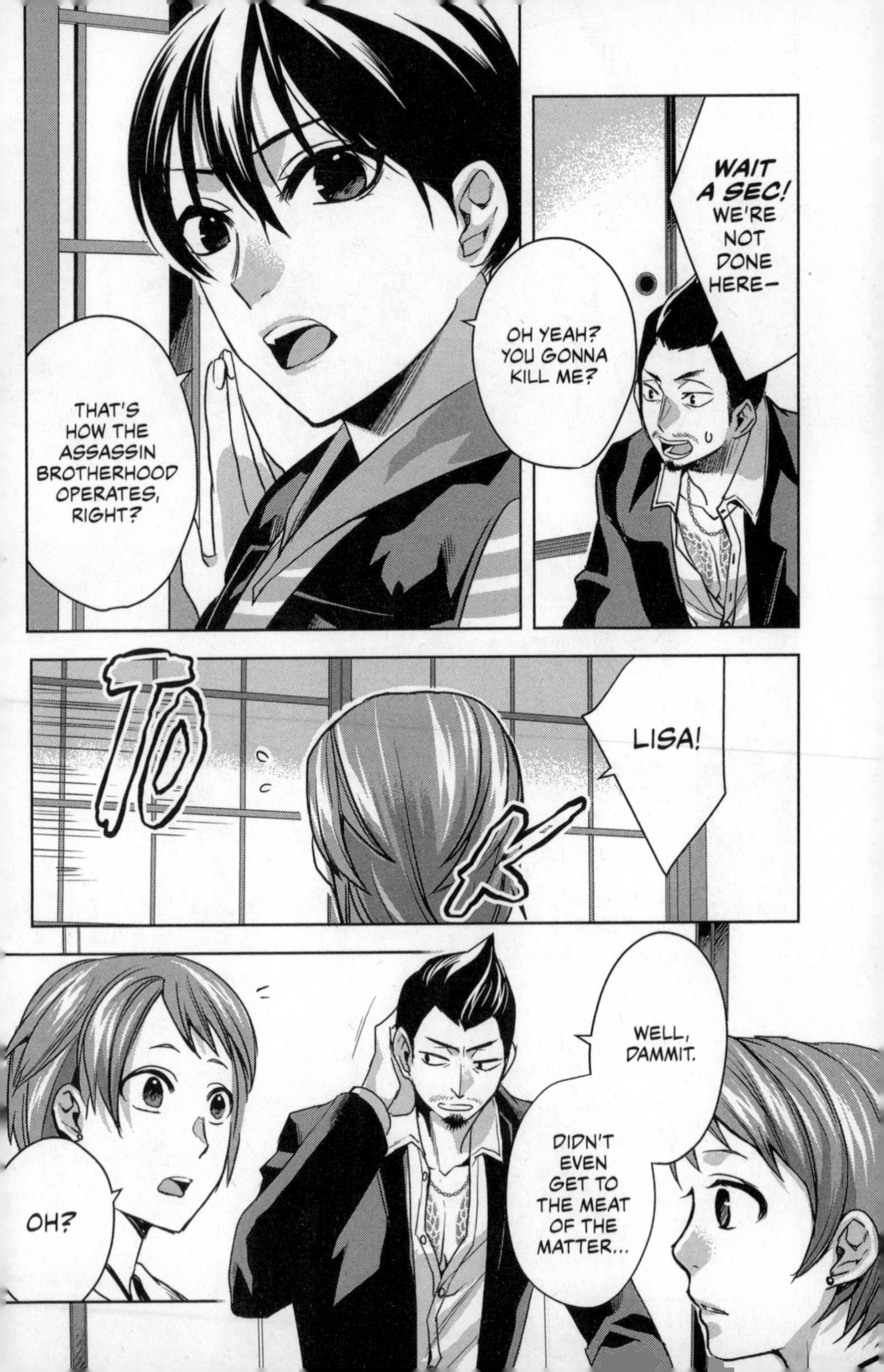
WAIT A SEC! WE'RE NOT DONE HERE—
OH YEAH? YOU GONNA KILL ME?
THAT'S HOW THE ASSASSIN BROTHERHOOD OPERATES, RIGHT?
LISA!
TOK
WELL, DAMMIT.
DIDN'T EVEN GET TO THE MEAT OF THE MATTER...
OH?

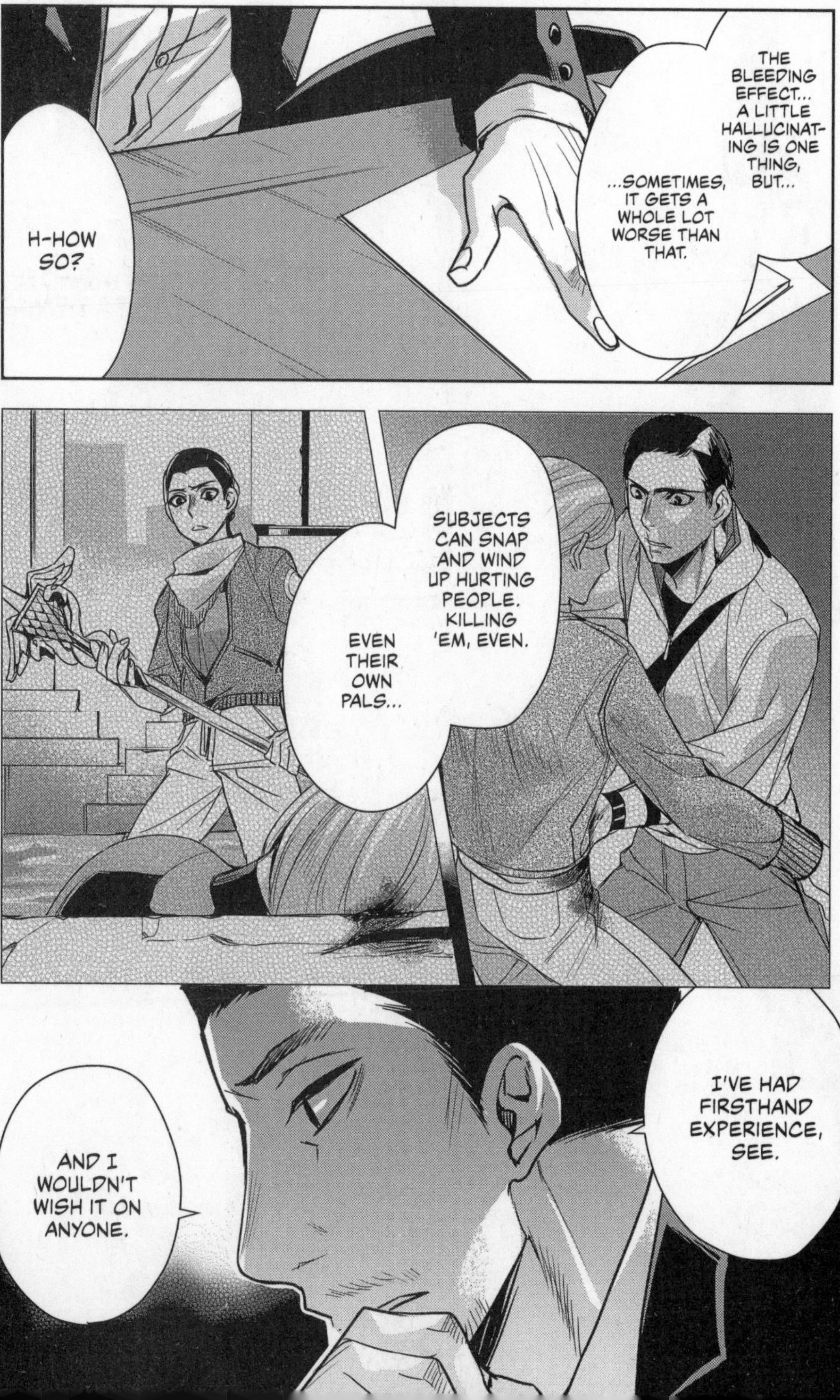
THE BLEEDING EFFECT... A LITTLE HALLUCINATING IS ONE THING, BUT...
...SOMETIMES, IT GETS A WHOLE LOT WORSE THAN THAT.
H-HOW SO?
SUBJECTS CAN SNAP AND WIND UP HURTING PEOPLE. KILLING 'EM, EVEN.
EVEN THEIR OWN PALS...
I'VE HAD FIRSTHAND EXPERIENCE, SEE.
AND I WOULDN'T WISH IT ON ANYONE.

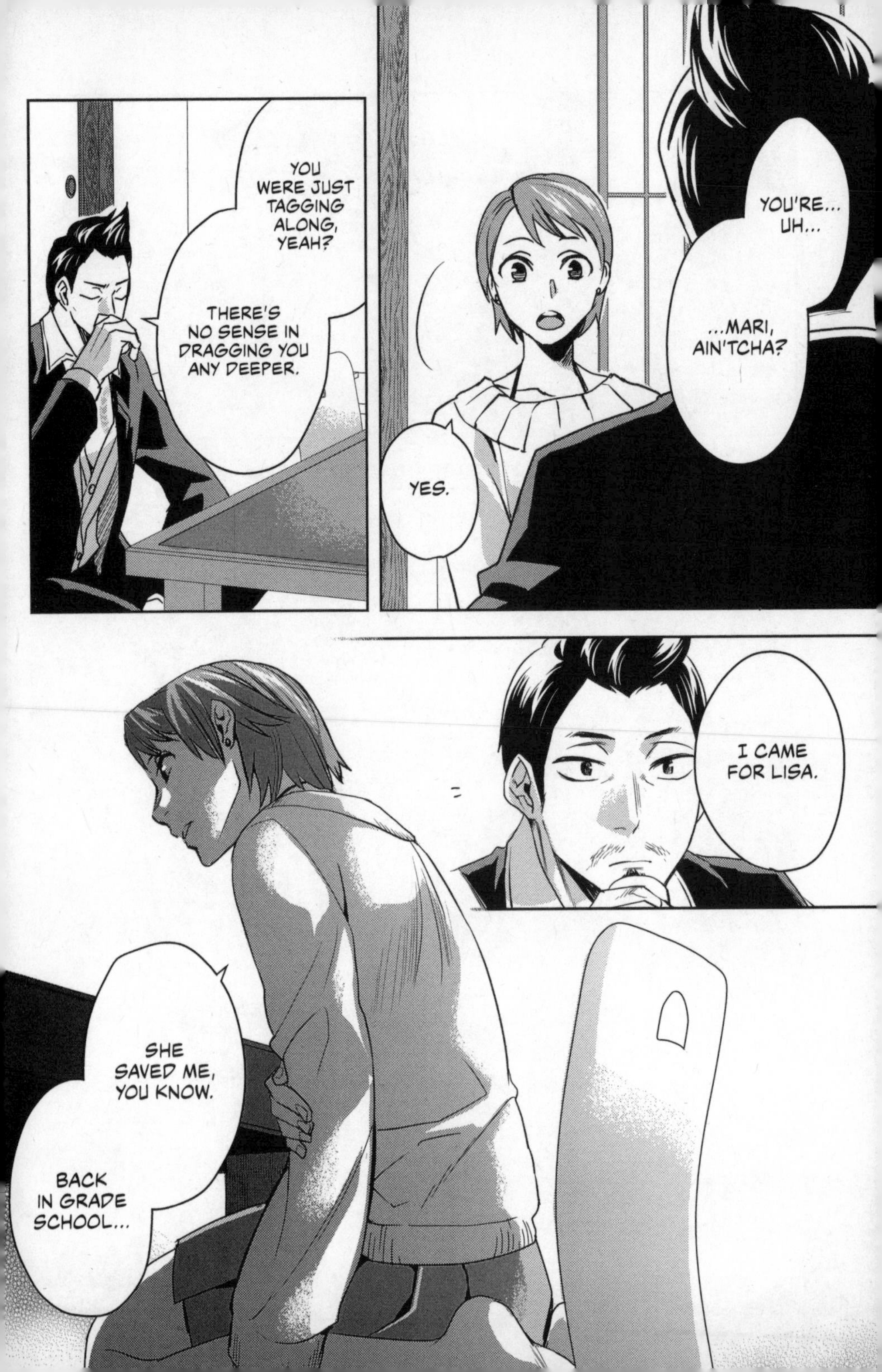
YOU'RE... UH...
...MARI, AIN'TCHA?
YES.
YOU WERE JUST TAGGING ALONG, YEAH?
THERE'S NO SENSE IN DRAGGING YOU ANY DEEPER.
I CAME FOR LISA.
SHE SAVED ME, YOU KNOW.
BACK IN GRADE SCHOOL...

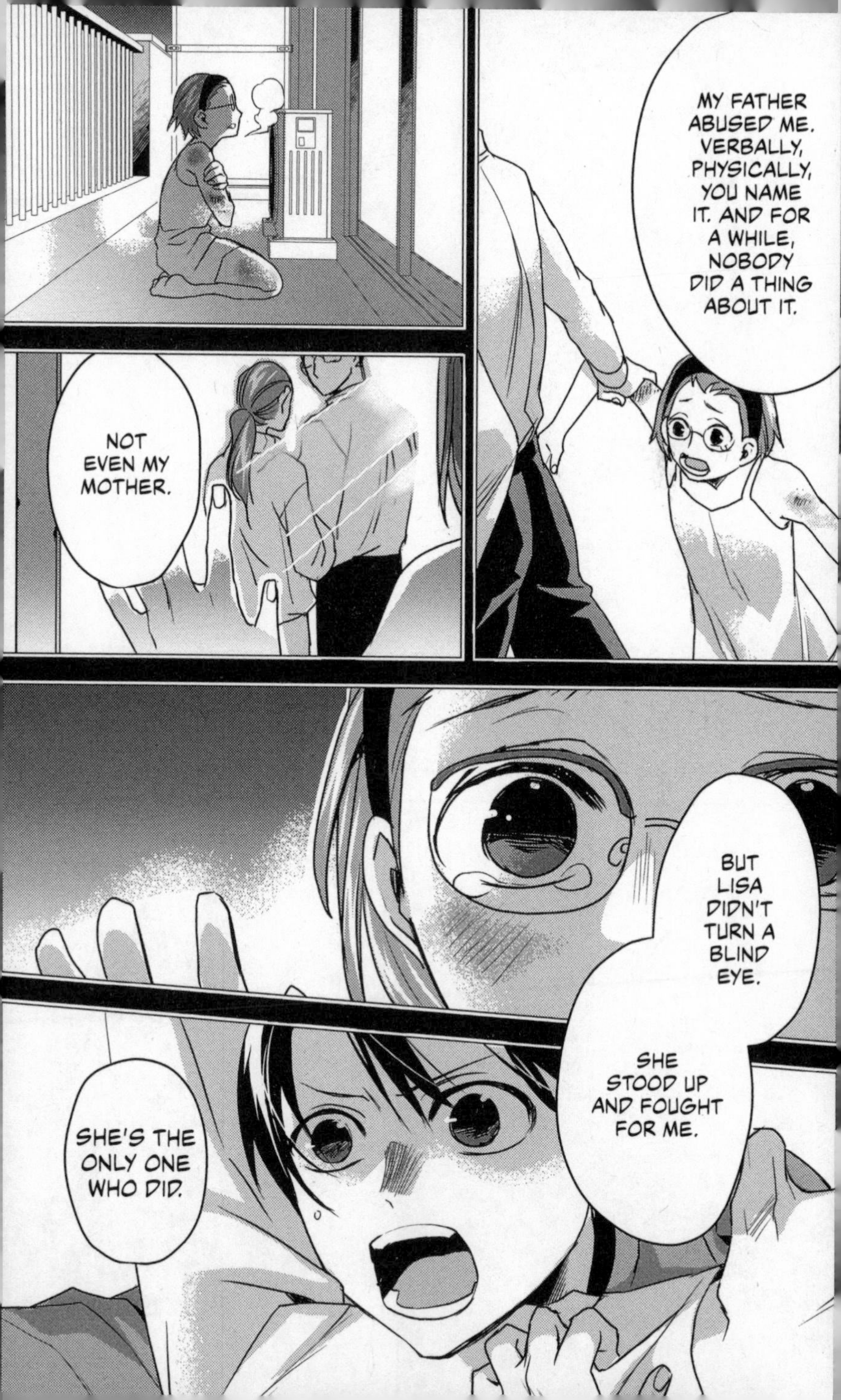
MY FATHER ABUSED ME. VERBALLY, PHYSICALLY, YOU NAME IT. AND FOR A WHILE, NOBODY DID A THING ABOUT IT.
NOT EVEN MY MOTHER.
BUT LISA DIDN'T TURN A BLIND EYE.
SHE STOOD UP AND FOUGHT FOR ME.
SHE'S THE ONLY ONE WHO DID.

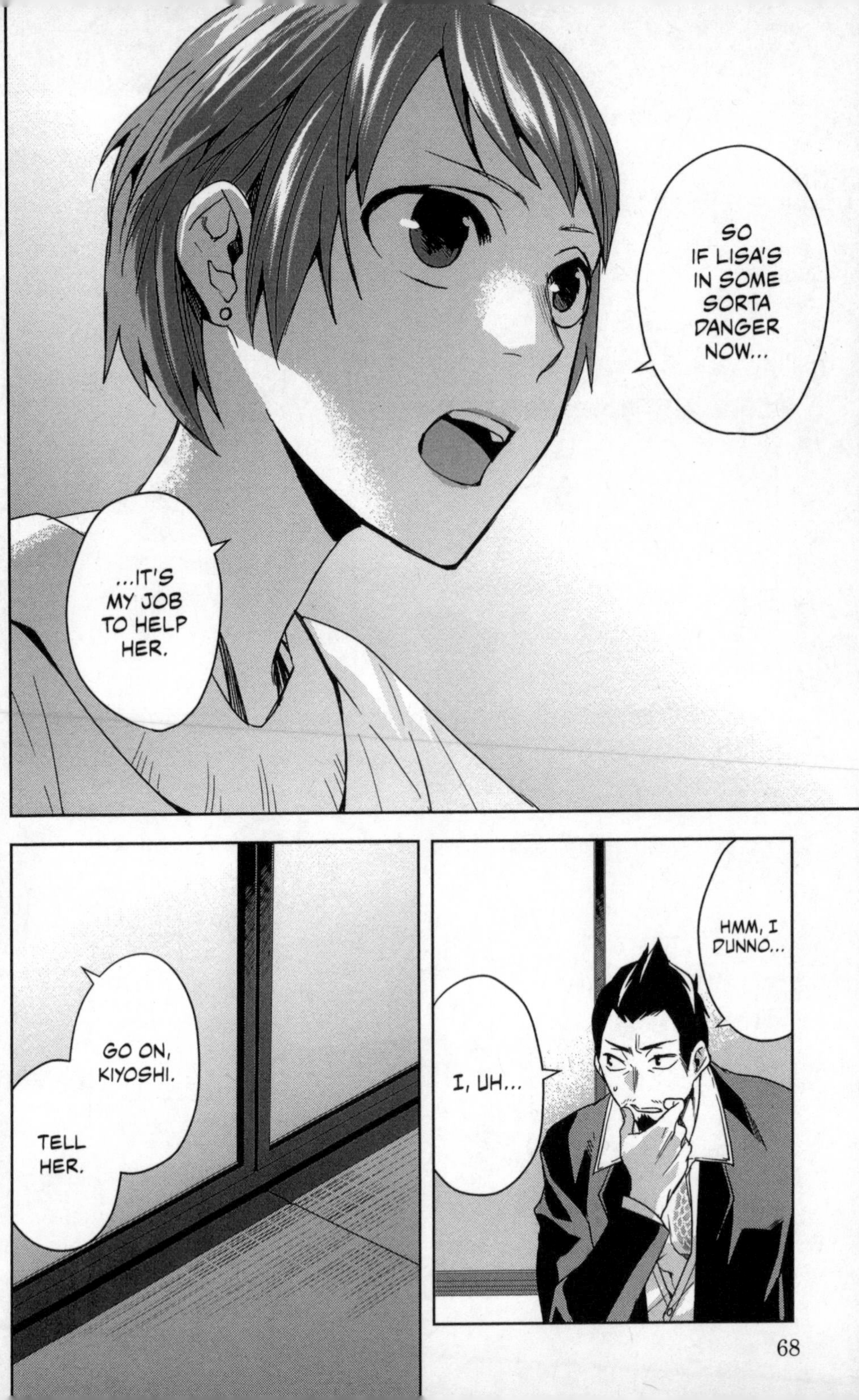
SO IF LISA'S IN SOME SORTA DANGER NOW...
...IT'S MY JOB TO HELP HER.
HMM, I DUNNO...
I, UH...
GO ON, KIYOSHI.
TELL HER.

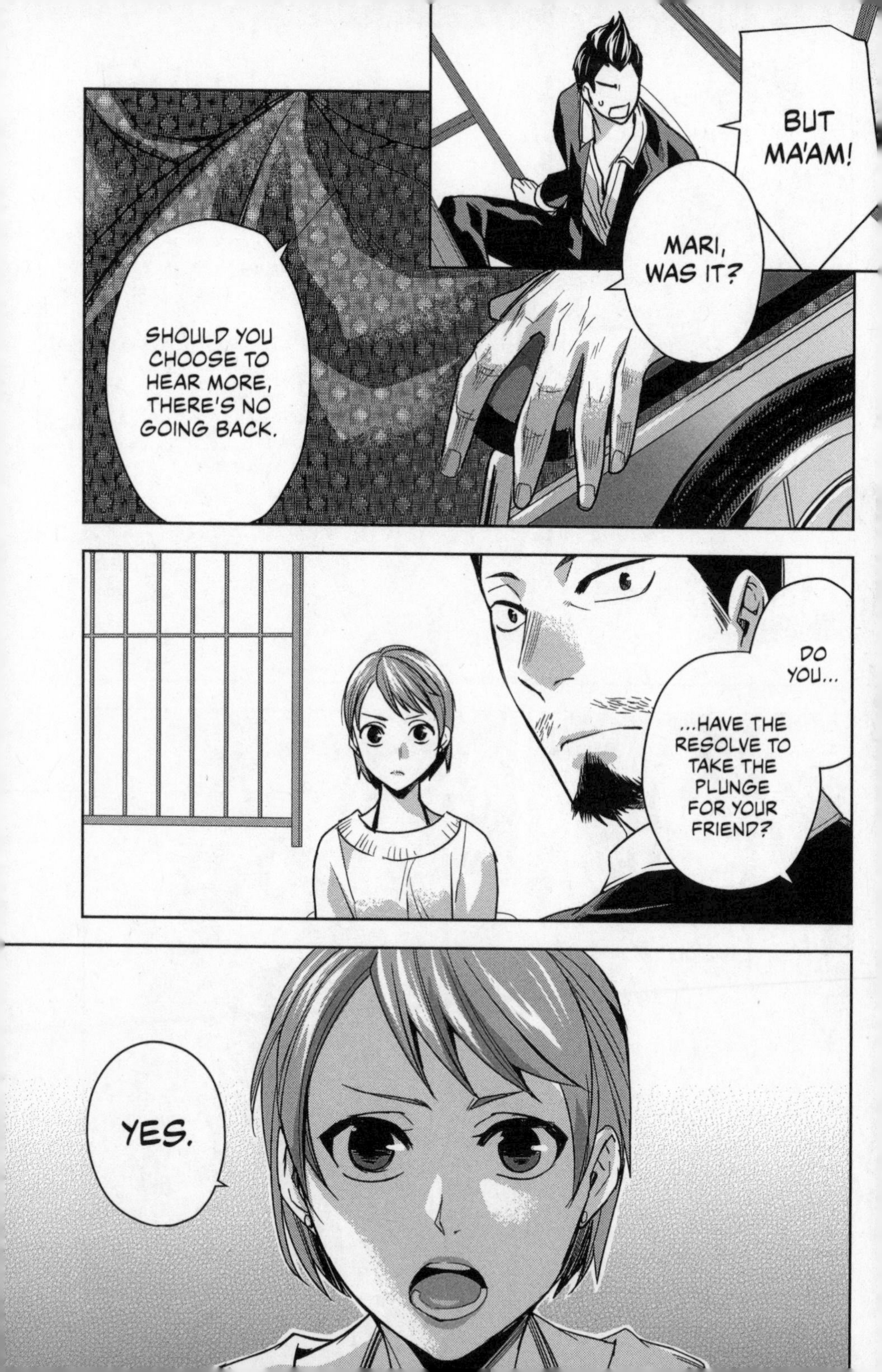
BUT MA'AM!
MARI, WAS IT?
SHOULD YOU CHOOSE TO HEAR MORE, THERE'S NO GOING BACK.
DO YOU...
...HAVE THE RESOLVE TO TAKE THE PLUNGE FOR YOUR FRIEND?
YES.

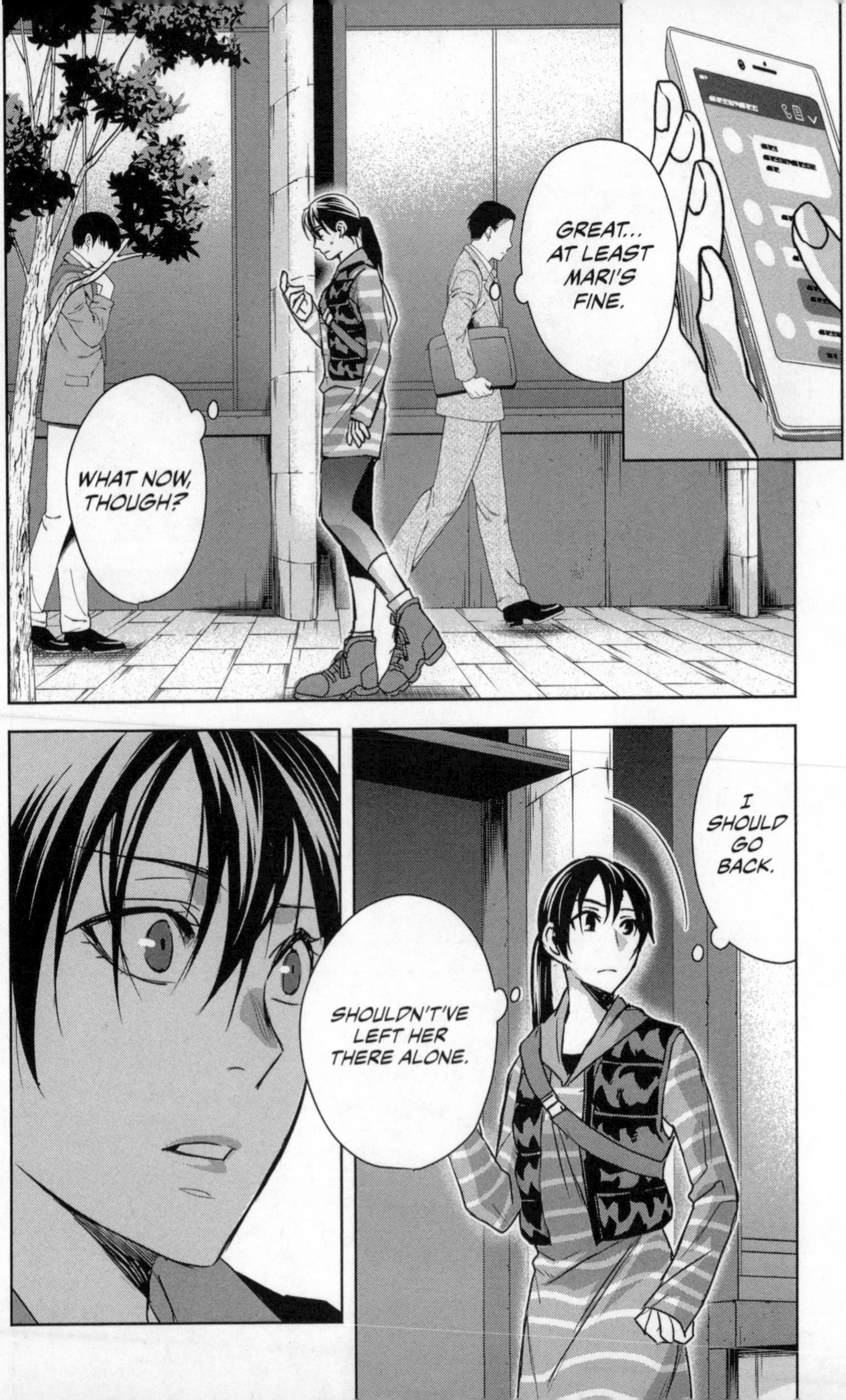
GREAT... AT LEAST MARI'S FINE.
WHAT NOW, THOUGH?
I SHOULD GO BACK.
SHOULDN'T'VE LEFT HER THERE ALONE.

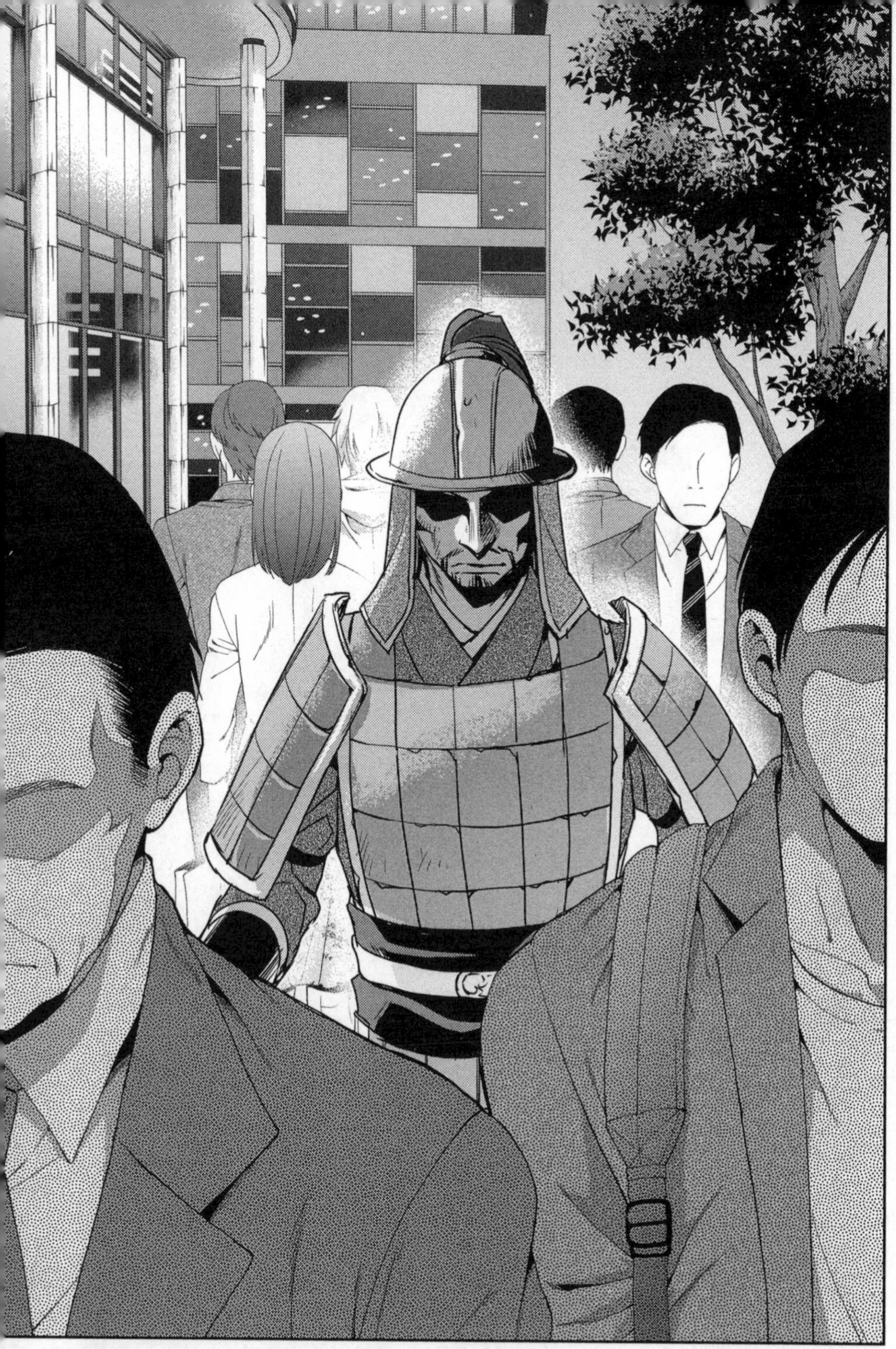

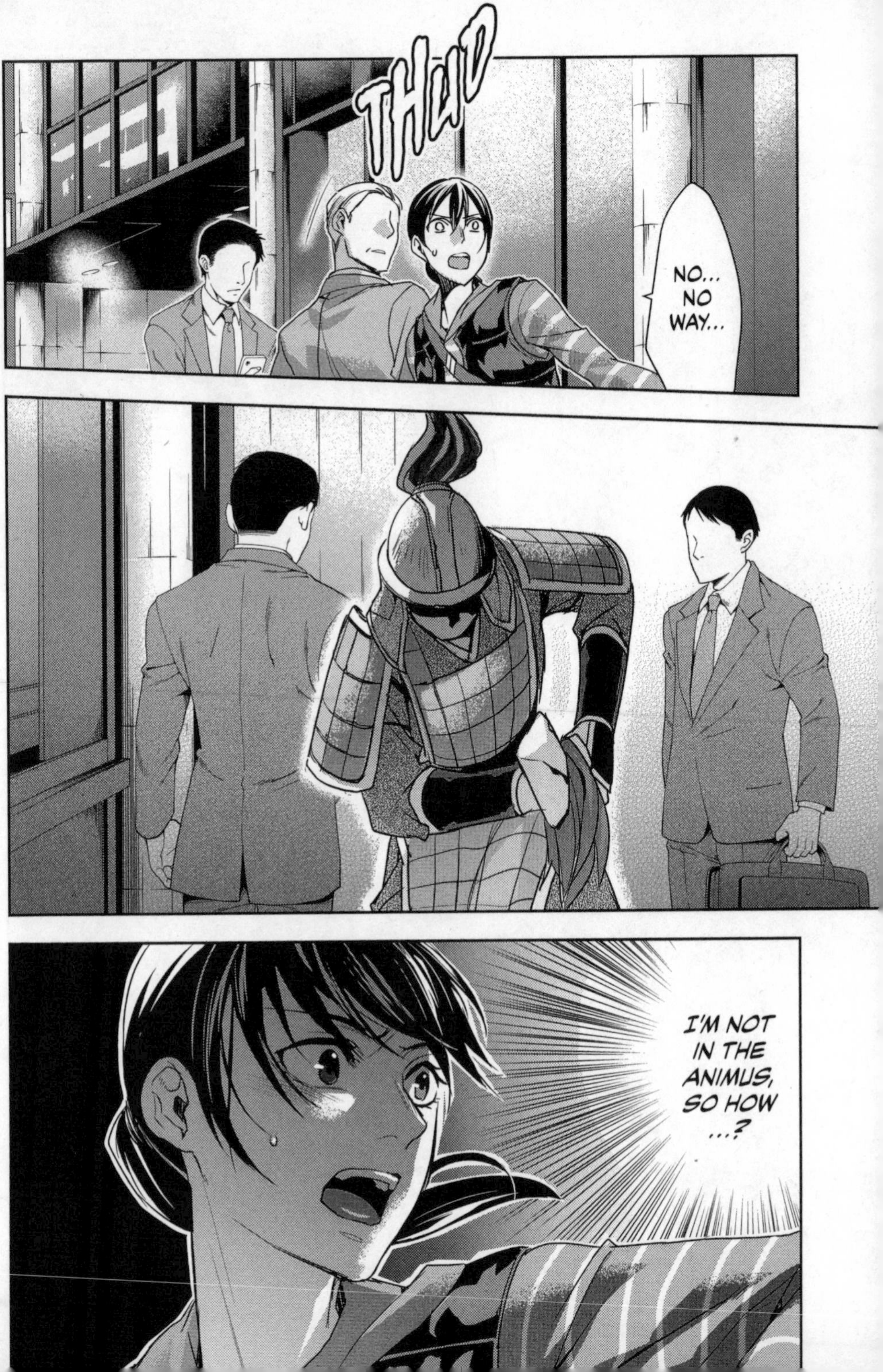
NO... NO WAY...
THUD
I'M NOT IN THE ANIMUS, SO HOW ...?

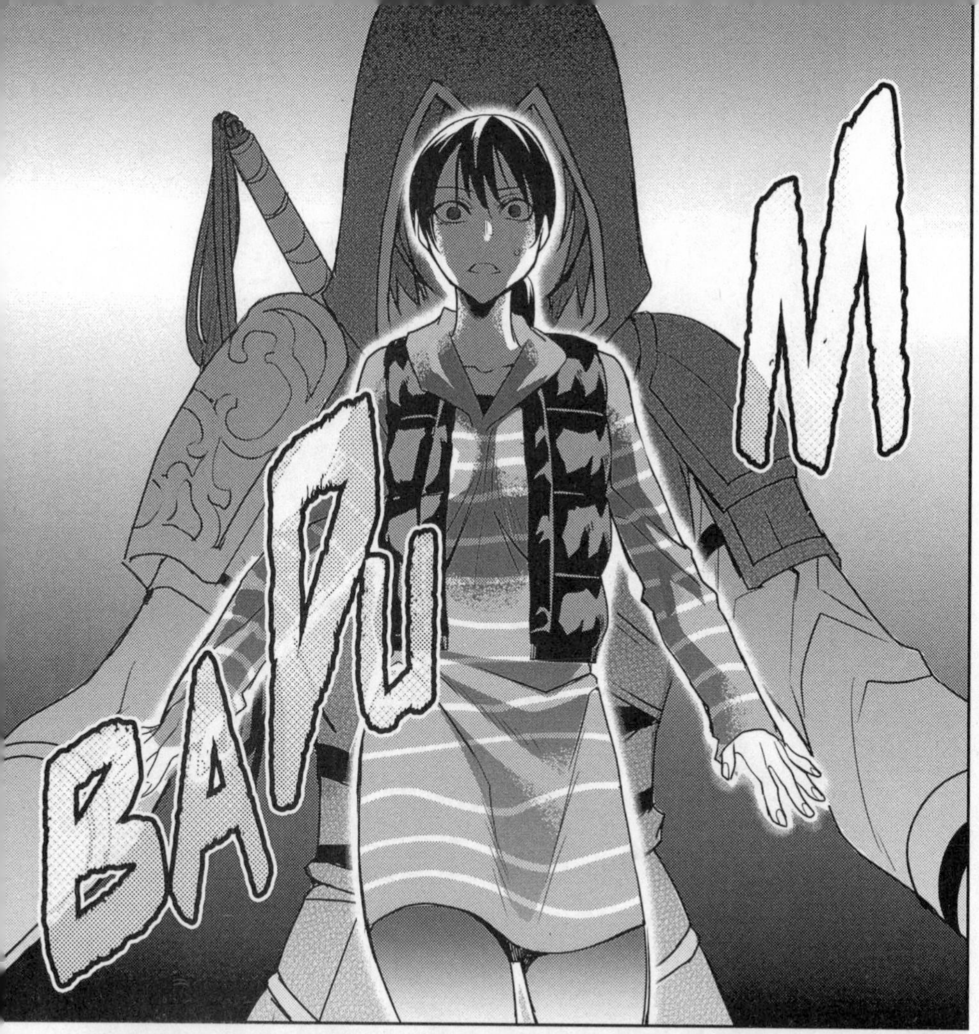
BADUMM
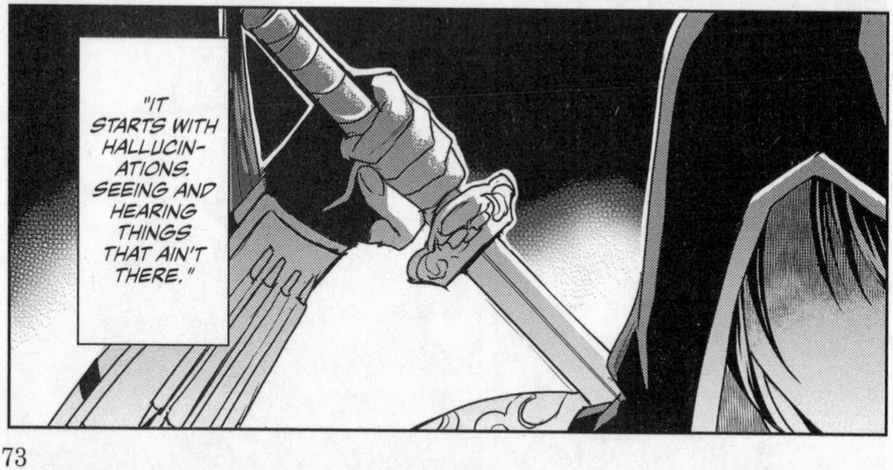
"IT STARTS WITH HALLUCIN-ATIONS. SEEING AND HEARING THINGS THAT AIN'T THERE."

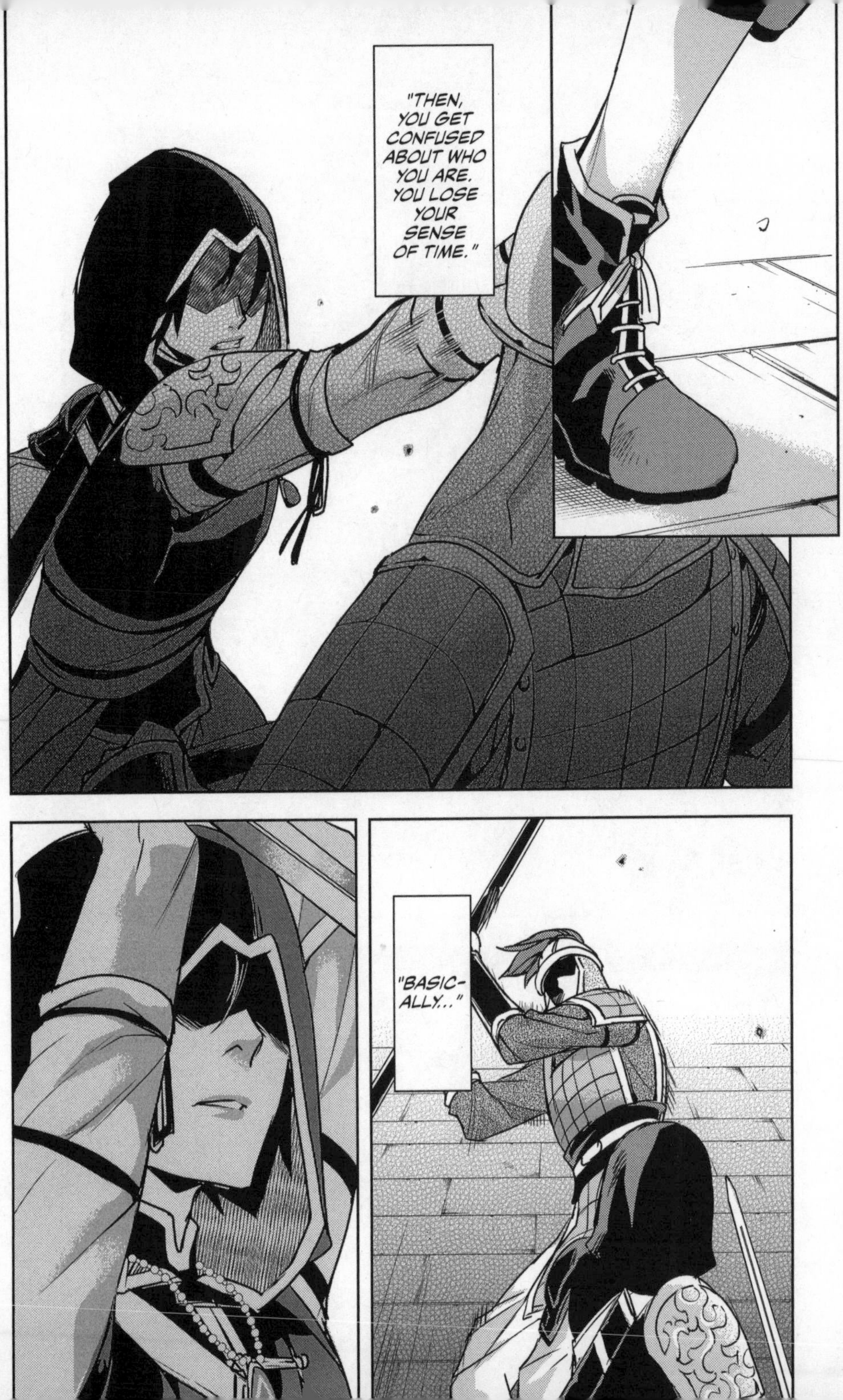
"THEN, YOU GET CONFUSED ABOUT WHO YOU ARE. YOU LOSE YOUR SENSE OF TIME."
"BASIC-ALLY..."

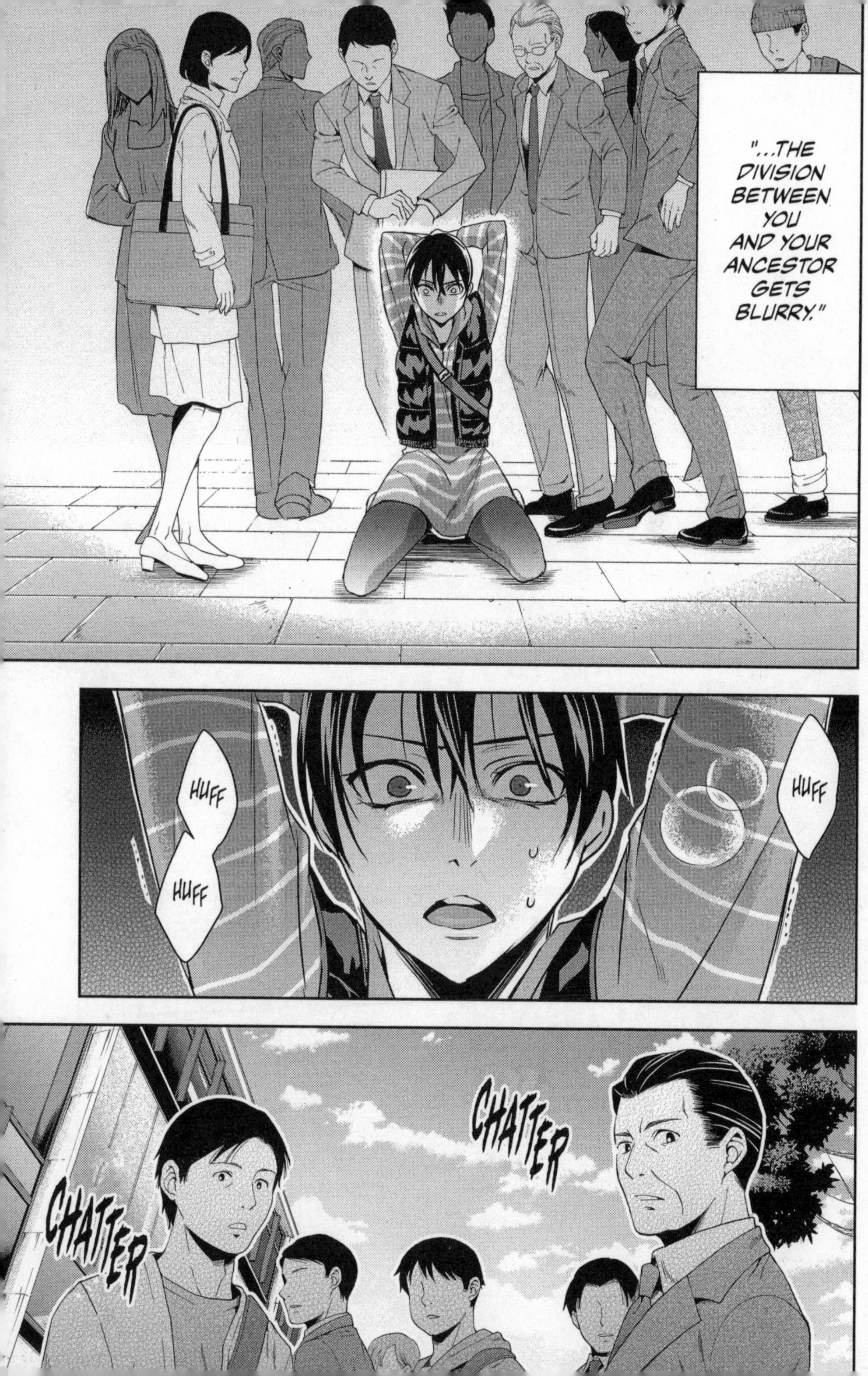
"...THE DIVISION BETWEEN YOU AND YOUR ANCESTOR GETS BLURRY."
HUFF
HUFF
HUFF
CHATTER
CHATTER

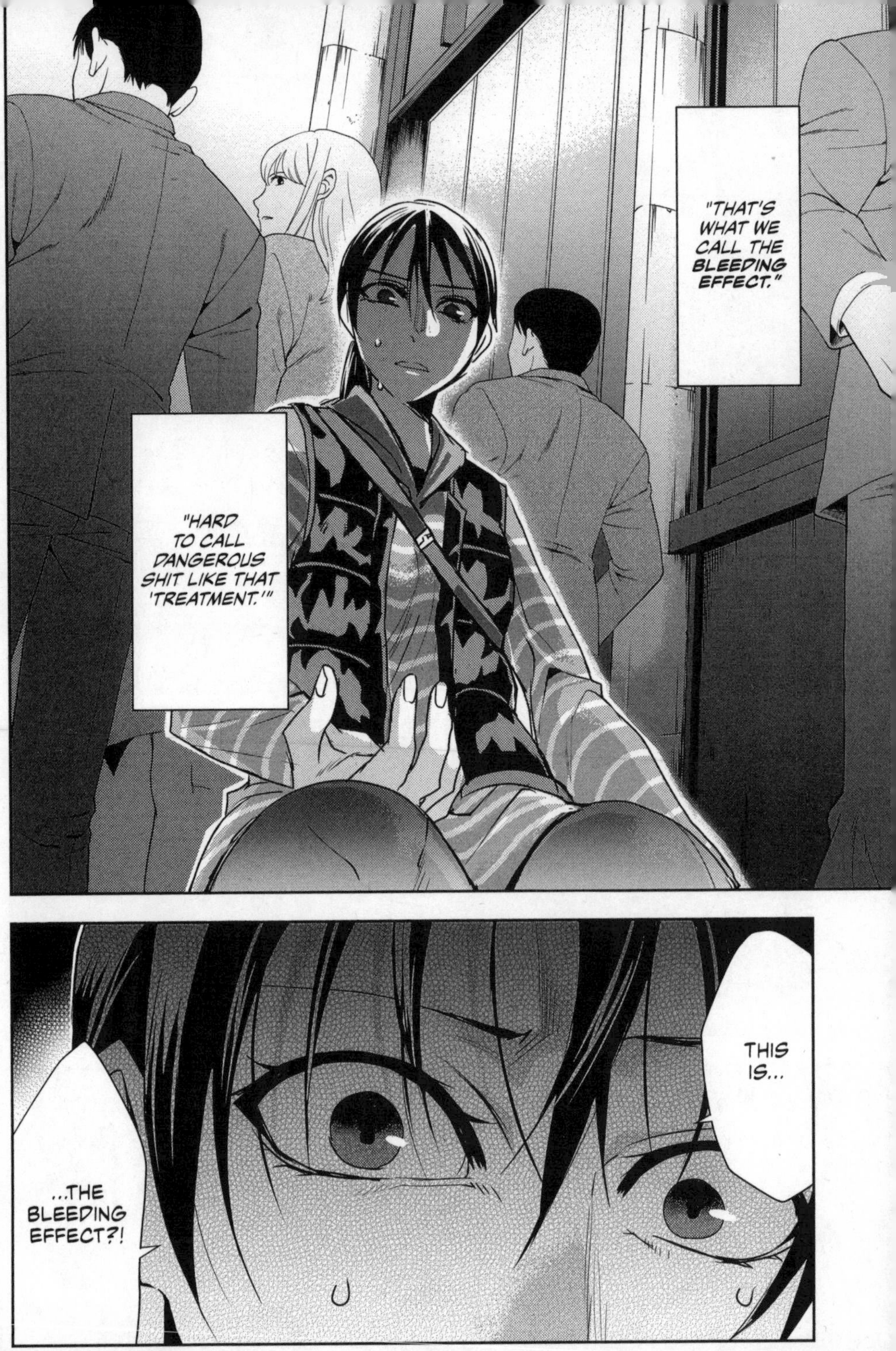
"THAT'S WHAT WE CALL THE BLEEDING EFFECT."
"HARD TO CALL DANGEROUS SHIT LIKE THAT 'TREATMENT.'"
THIS IS...
...THE BLEEDING EFFECT?!

# Chapter 7: Shao Jun and Qixie

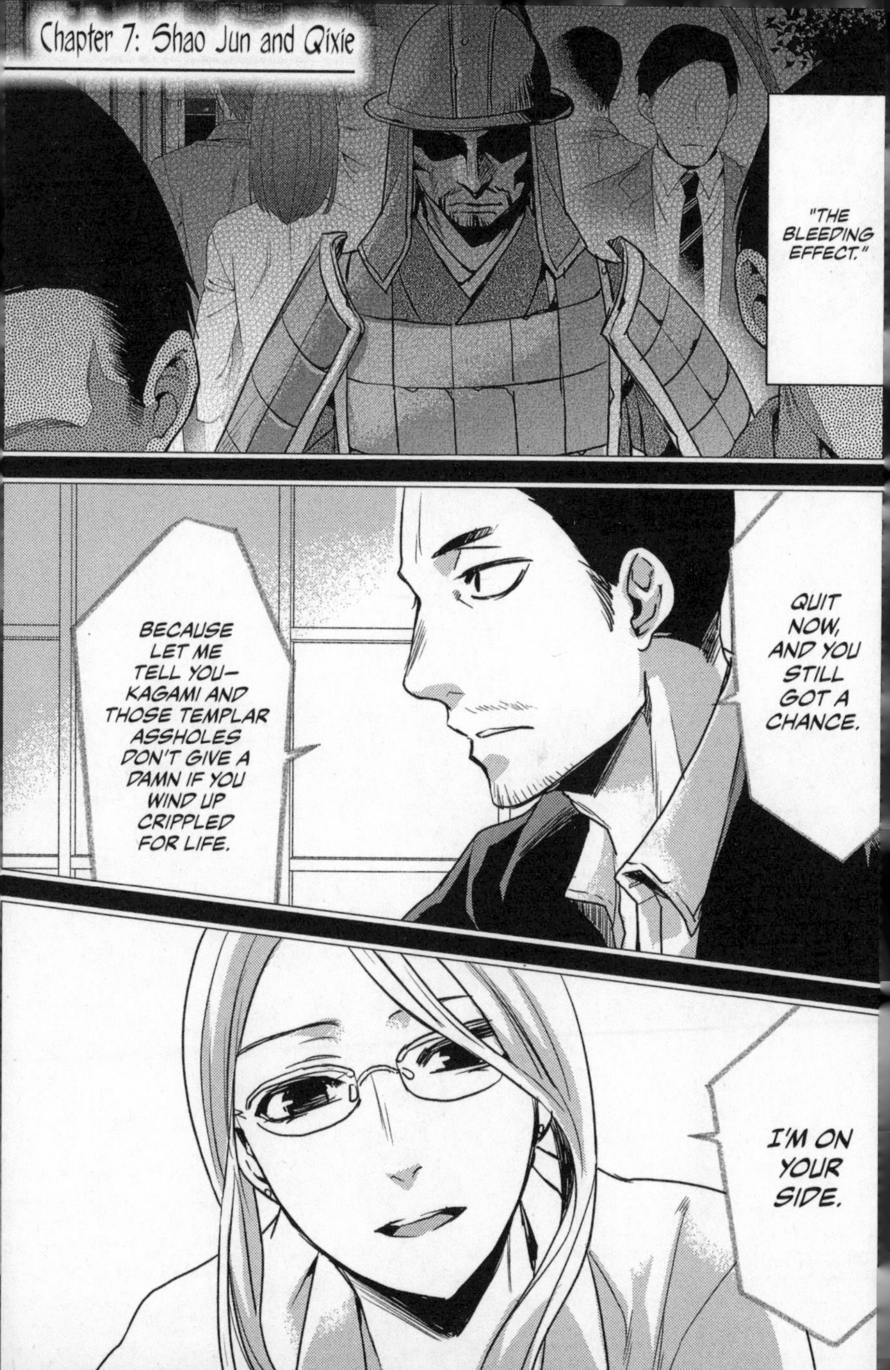

"THE BLEEDING EFFECT."
QUIT NOW, AND YOU STILL GOT A CHANCE.
BECAUSE LET ME TELL YOU— KAGAMI AND THOSE TEMPLAR ASSHOLES DON'T GIVE A DAMN IF YOU WIND UP CRIPPLED FOR LIFE.
I'M ON YOUR SIDE.

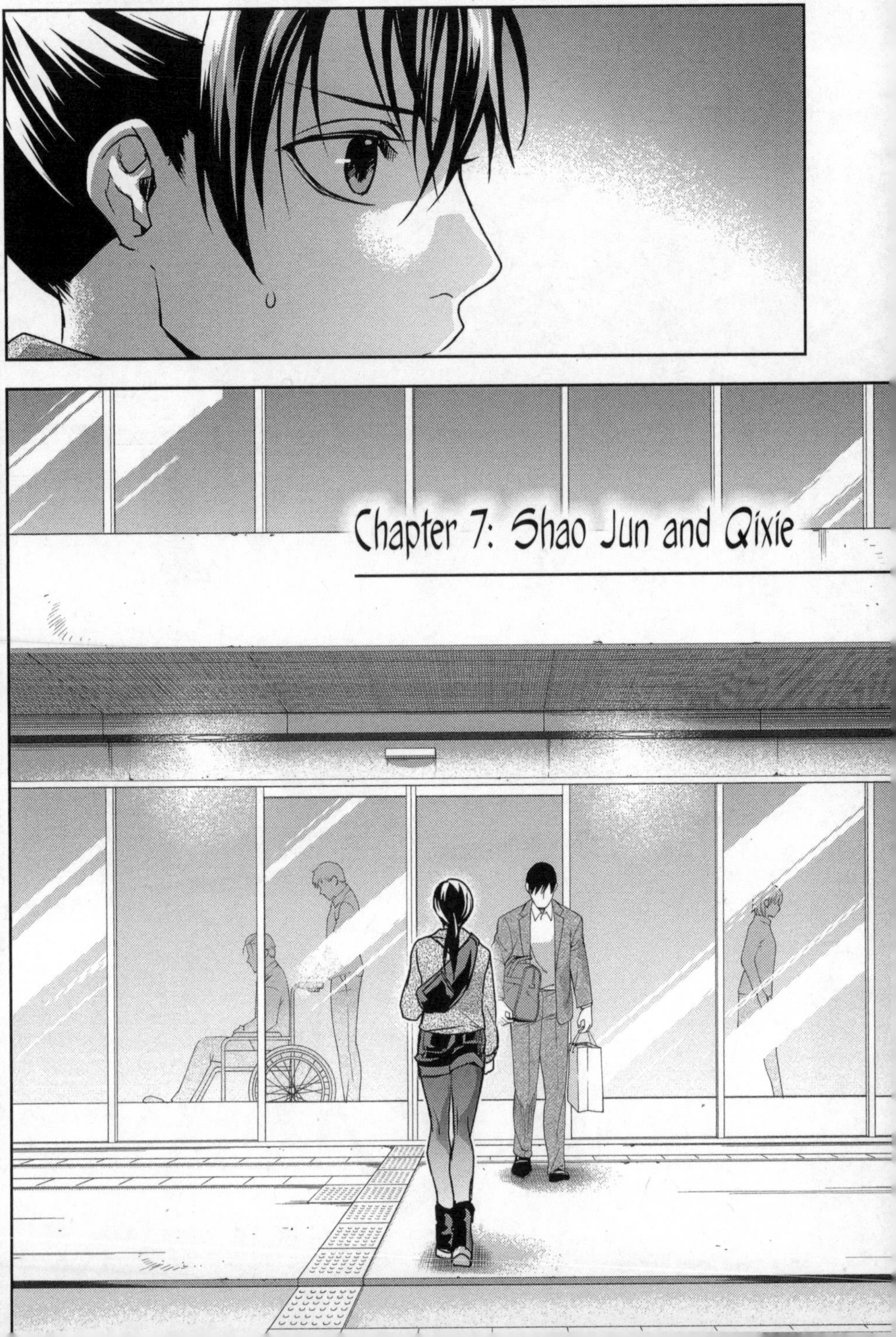
Chapter 7: Shao Jun and Qixie

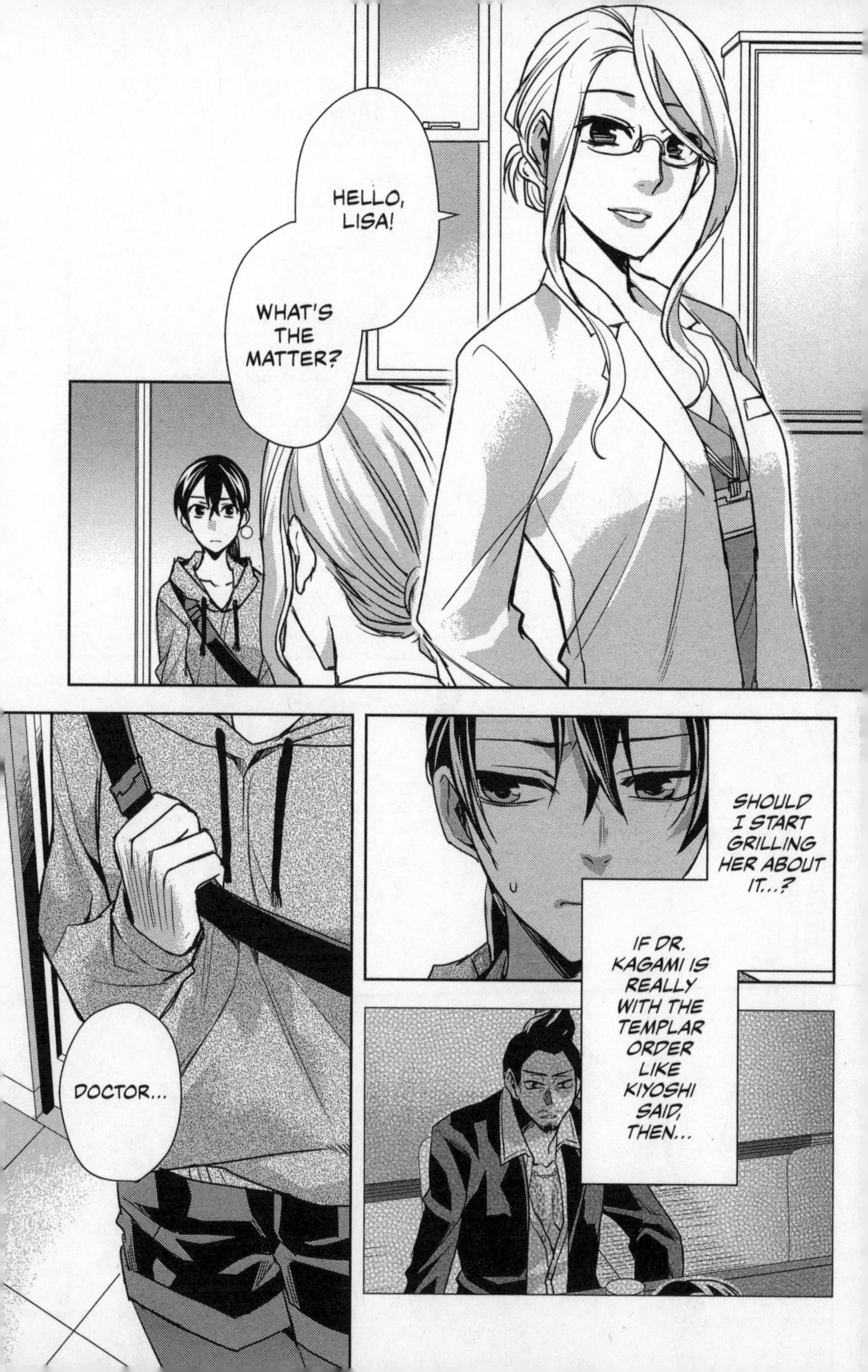
HELLO, LISA!
WHAT'S THE MATTER?
SHOULD I START GRILLING HER ABOUT IT...?
IF DR. KAGAMI IS REALLY WITH THE TEMPLAR ORDER LIKE KIYOSHI SAID, THEN...
DOCTOR...

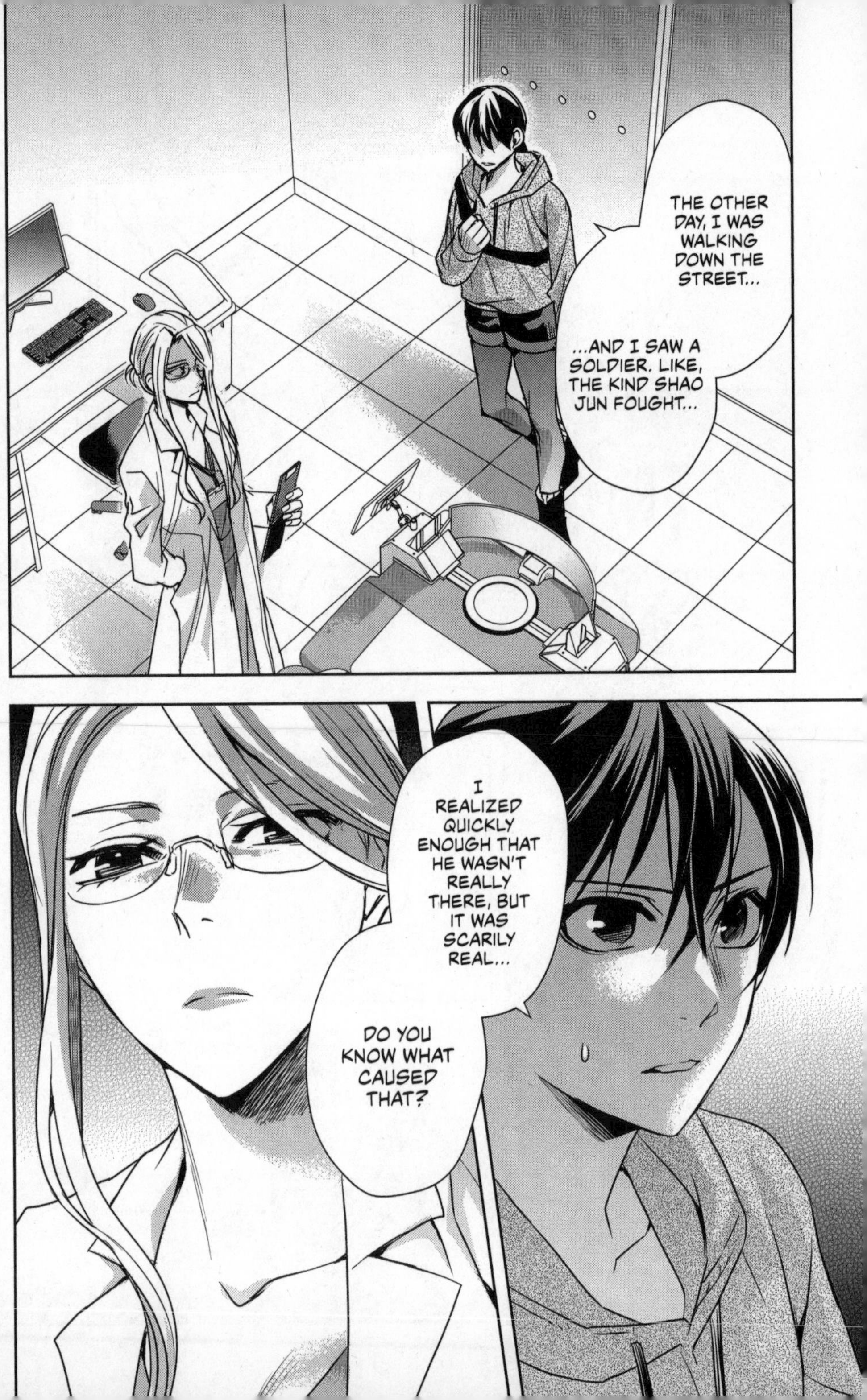
THE OTHER DAY, I WAS WALKING DOWN THE STREET...
...AND I SAW A SOLDIER. LIKE, THE KIND SHAO JUN FOUGHT...
I REALIZED QUICKLY ENOUGH THAT HE WASN'T REALLY THERE, BUT IT WAS SCARILY REAL...
DO YOU KNOW WHAT CAUSED THAT?

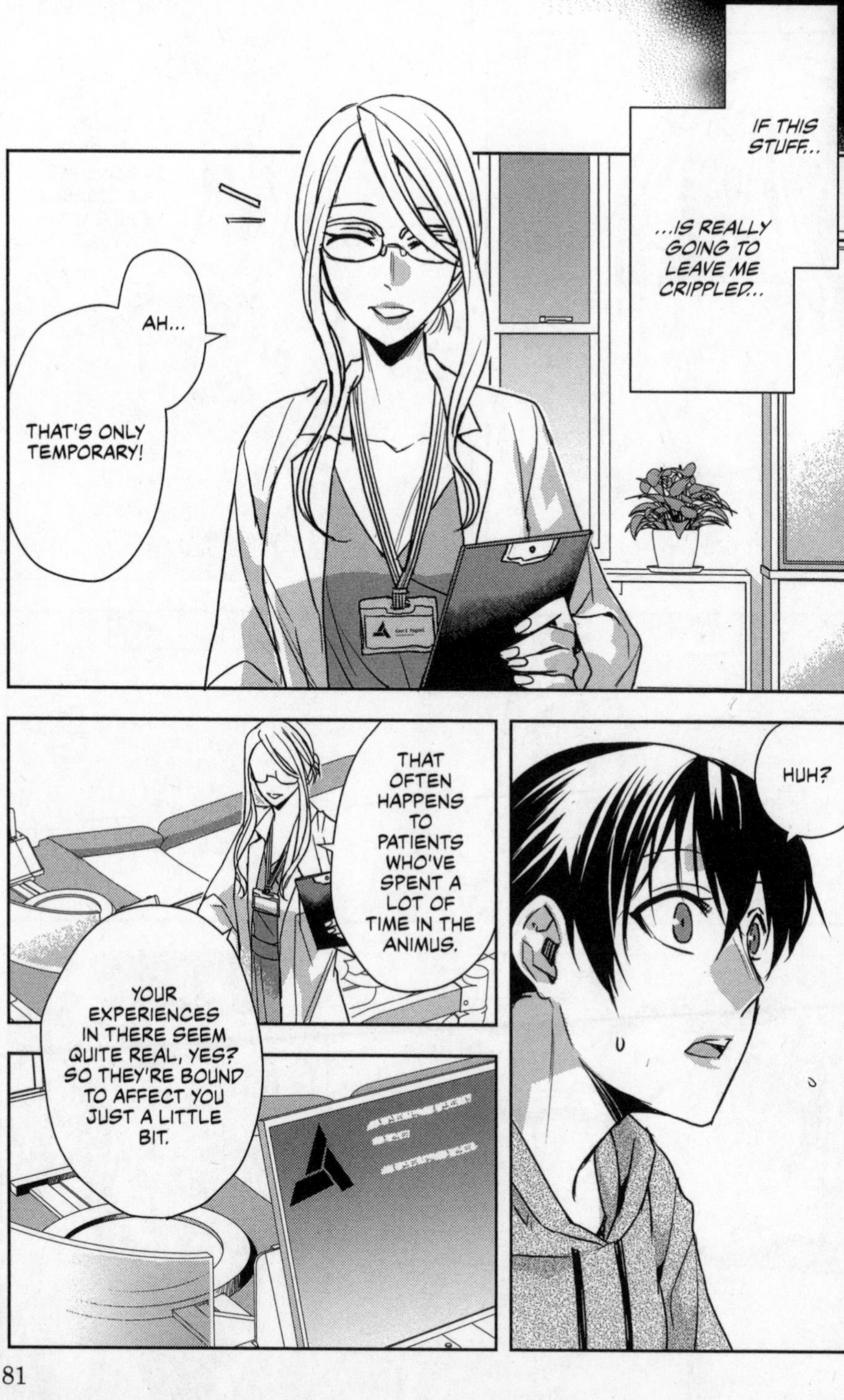
IF THIS STUFF...
...IS REALLY GOING TO LEAVE ME CRIPPLED...
AH...
THAT'S ONLY TEMPORARY!
HUH?
THAT OFTEN HAPPENS TO PATIENTS WHO'VE SPENT A LOT OF TIME IN THE ANIMUS.
YOUR EXPERIENCES IN THERE SEEM QUITE REAL, YES? SO THEY'RE BOUND TO AFFECT YOU JUST A LITTLE BIT.

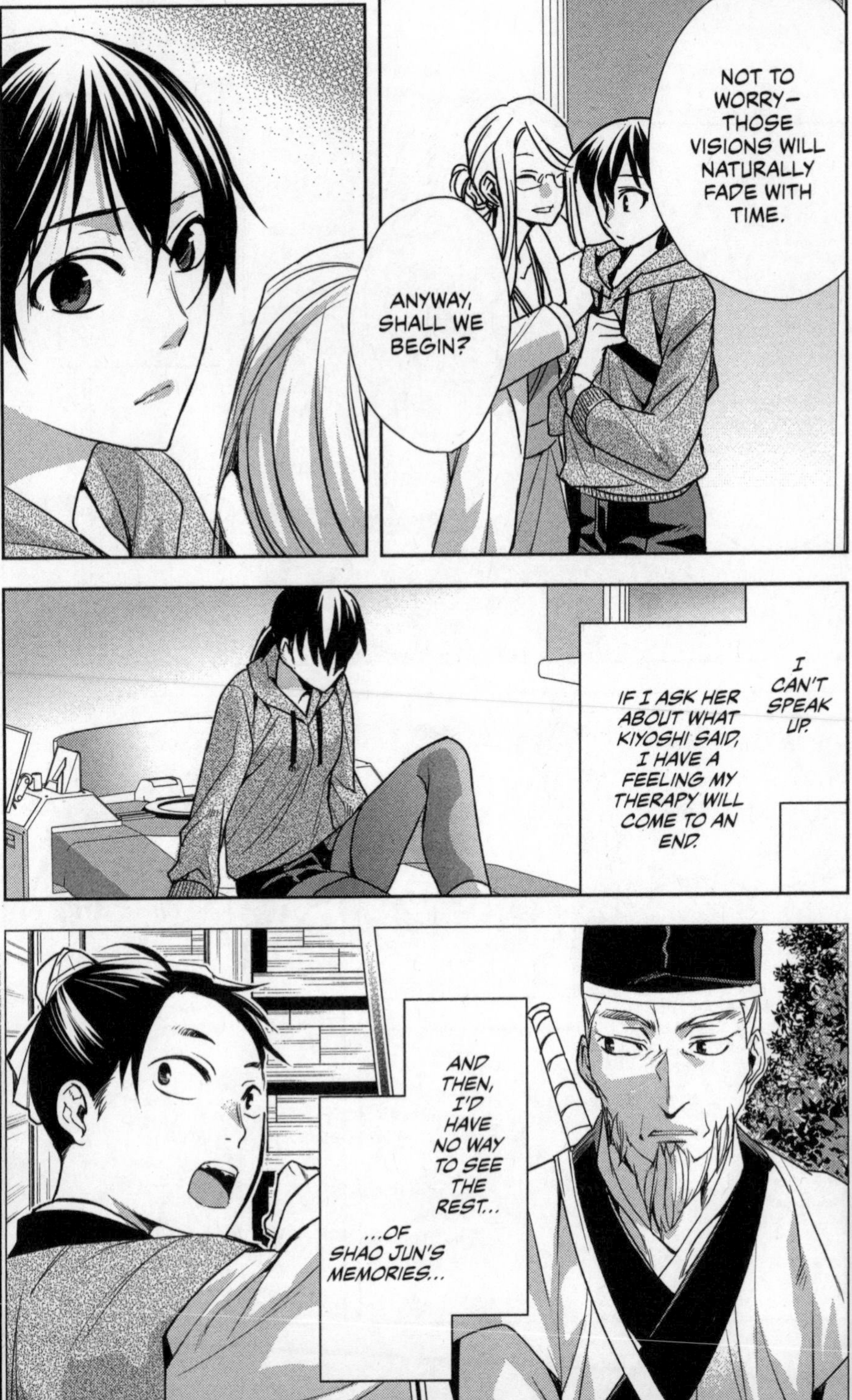
NOT TO WORRY—THOSE VISIONS WILL NATURALLY FADE WITH TIME.
ANYWAY, SHALL WE BEGIN?
I CAN'T SPEAK UP.
IF I ASK HER ABOUT WHAT KIYOSHI SAID, I HAVE A FEELING MY THERAPY WILL COME TO AN END.
AND THEN, I'D HAVE NO WAY TO SEE THE REST...
...OF SHAO JUN'S MEMORIES...

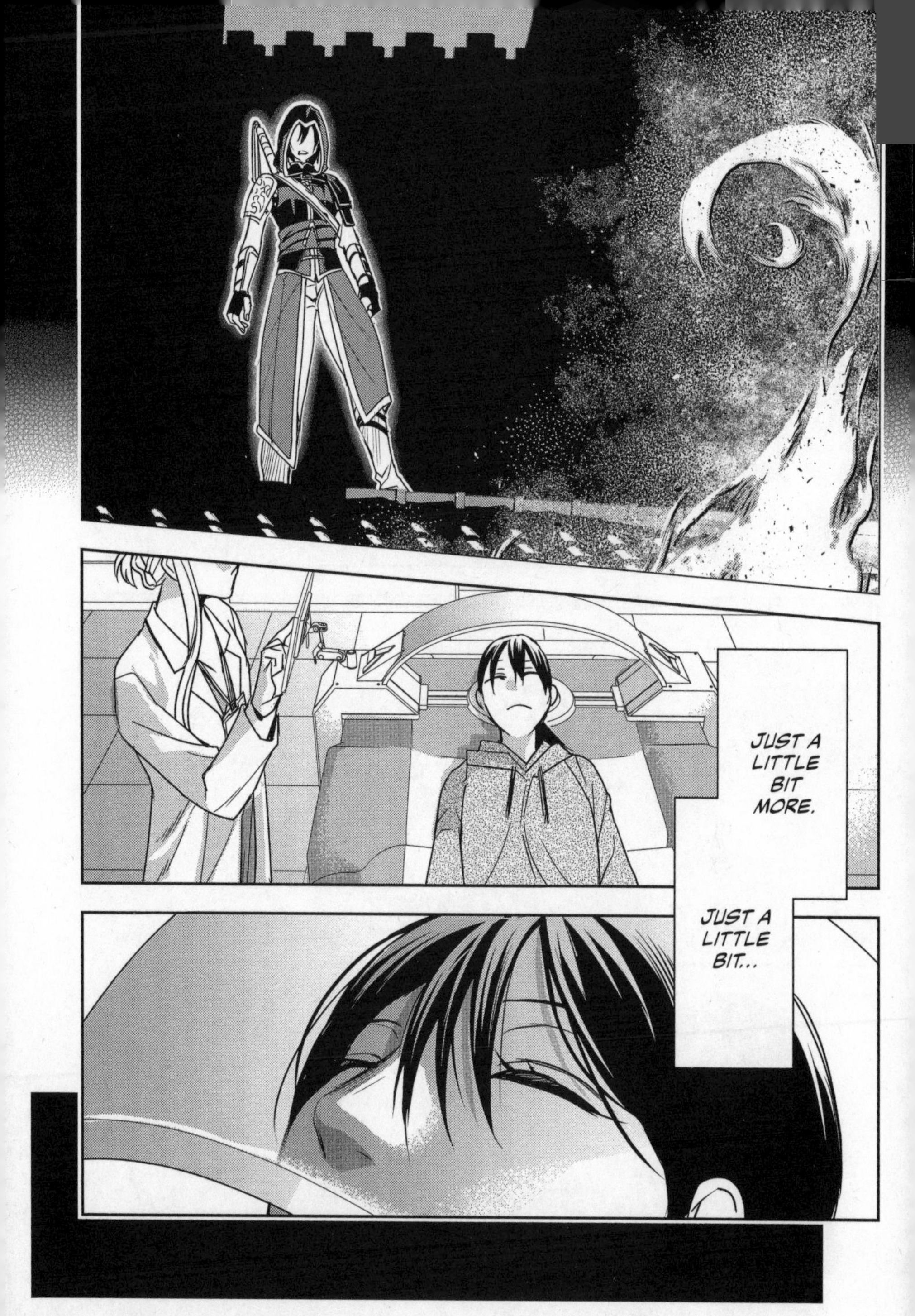
JUST A LITTLE BIT MORE.
JUST A LITTLE BIT...

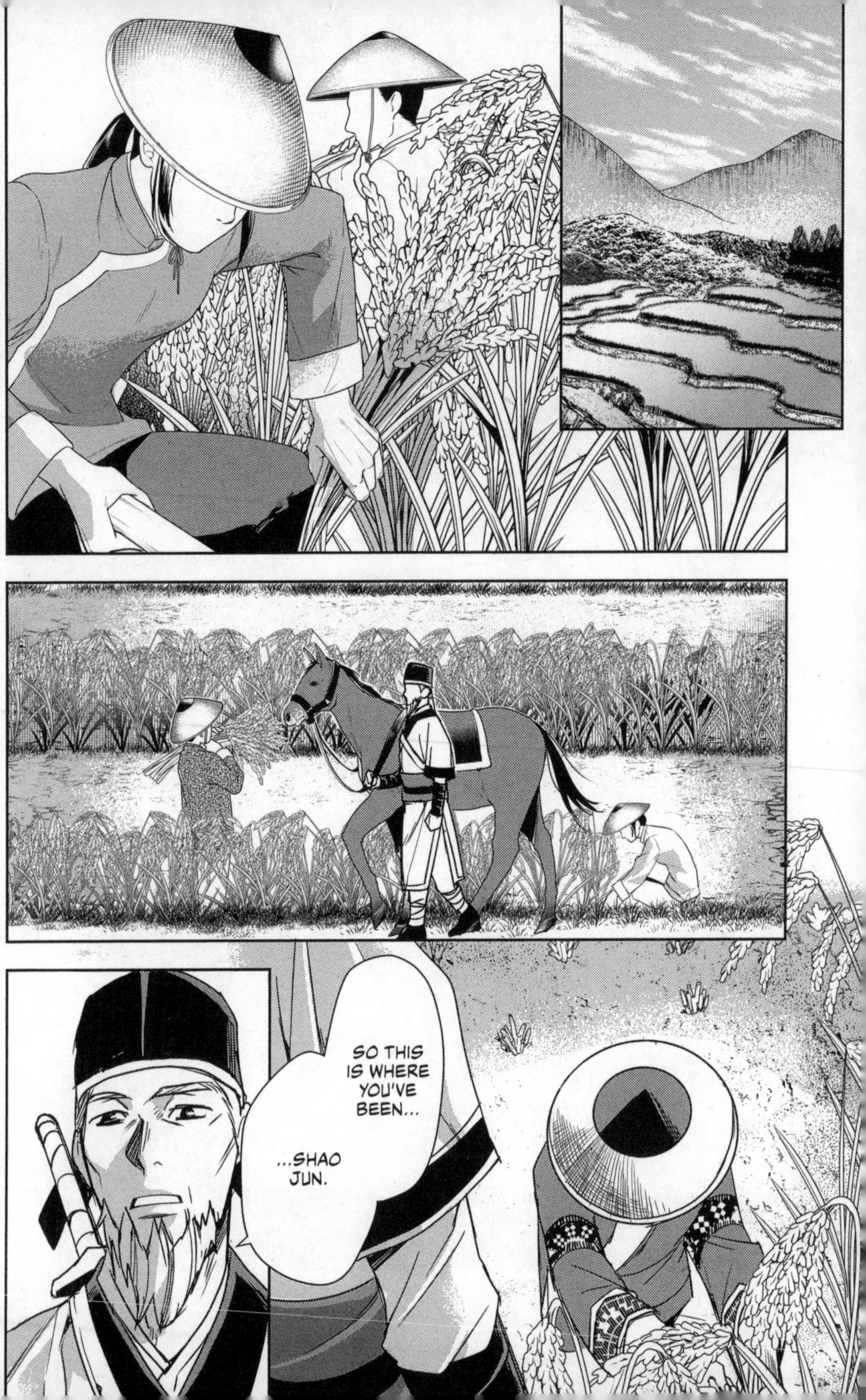
SO THIS IS WHERE YOU'VE BEEN...
...SHAO JUN.

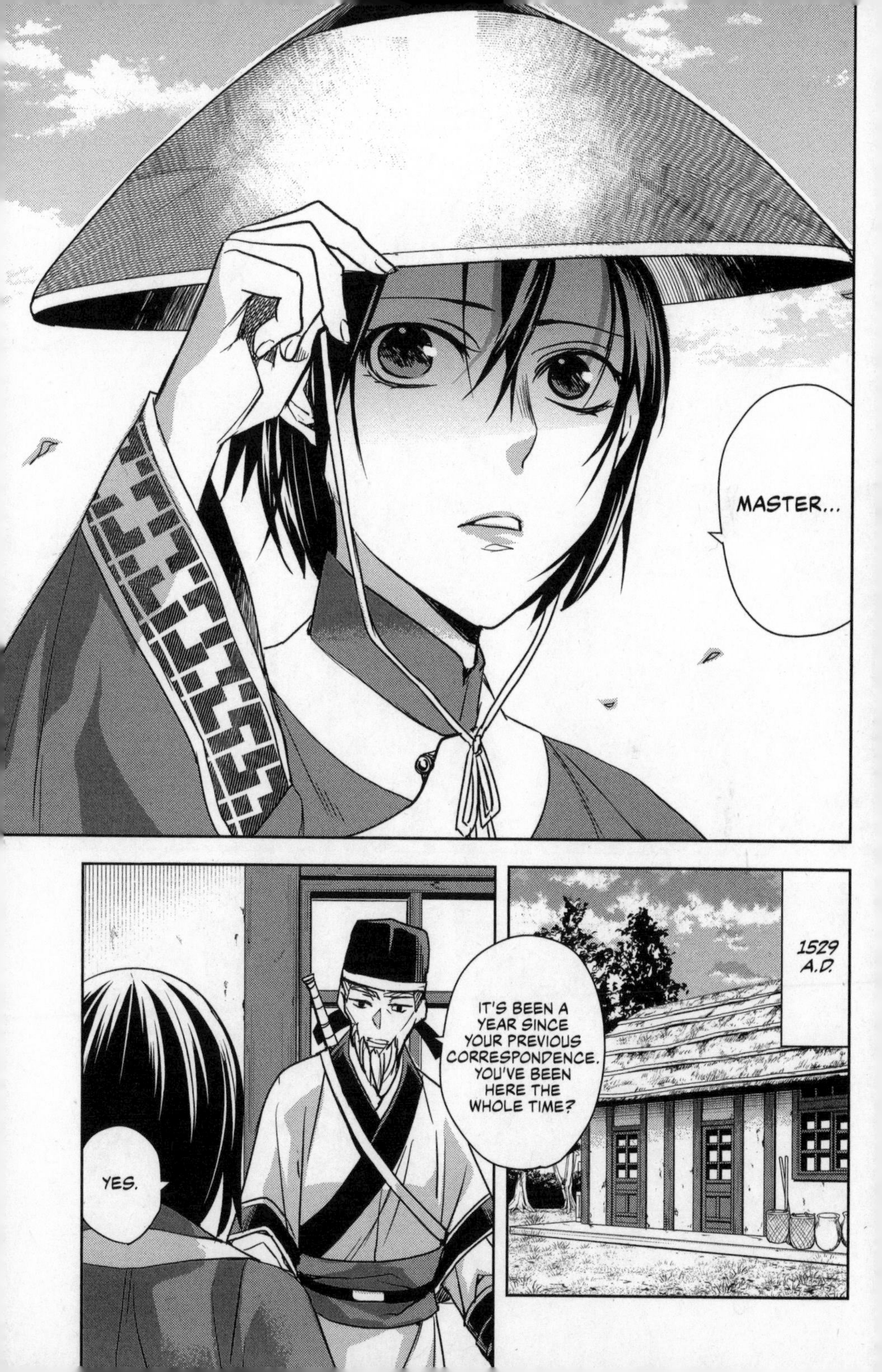
MASTER...
1529 A.D.
IT'S BEEN A YEAR SINCE YOUR PREVIOUS CORRESPONDENCE. YOU'VE BEEN HERE THE WHOLE TIME?
YES.

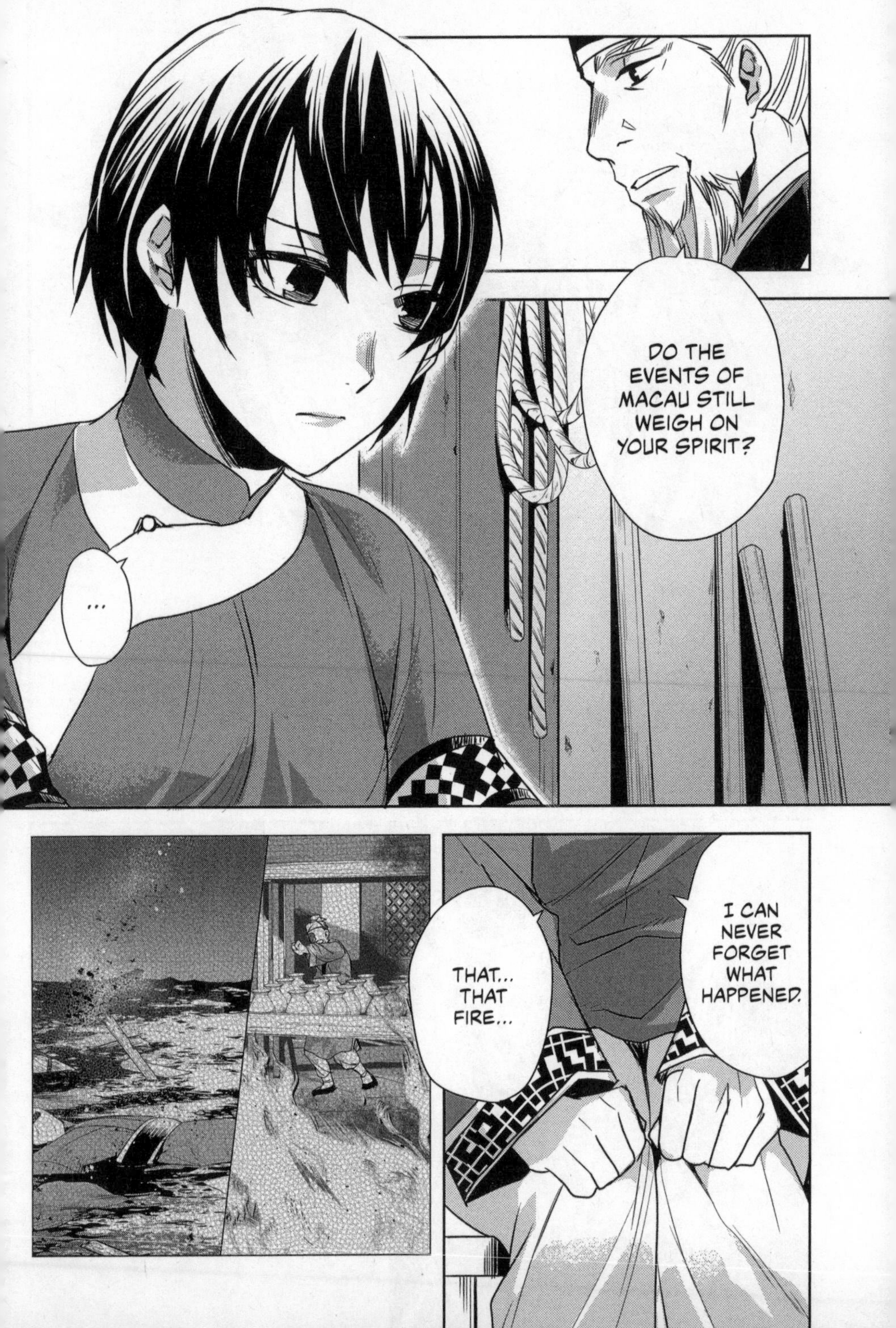
DO THE EVENTS OF MACAU STILL WEIGH ON YOUR SPIRIT?
...
I CAN NEVER FORGET WHAT HAPPENED.
THAT... THAT FIRE...

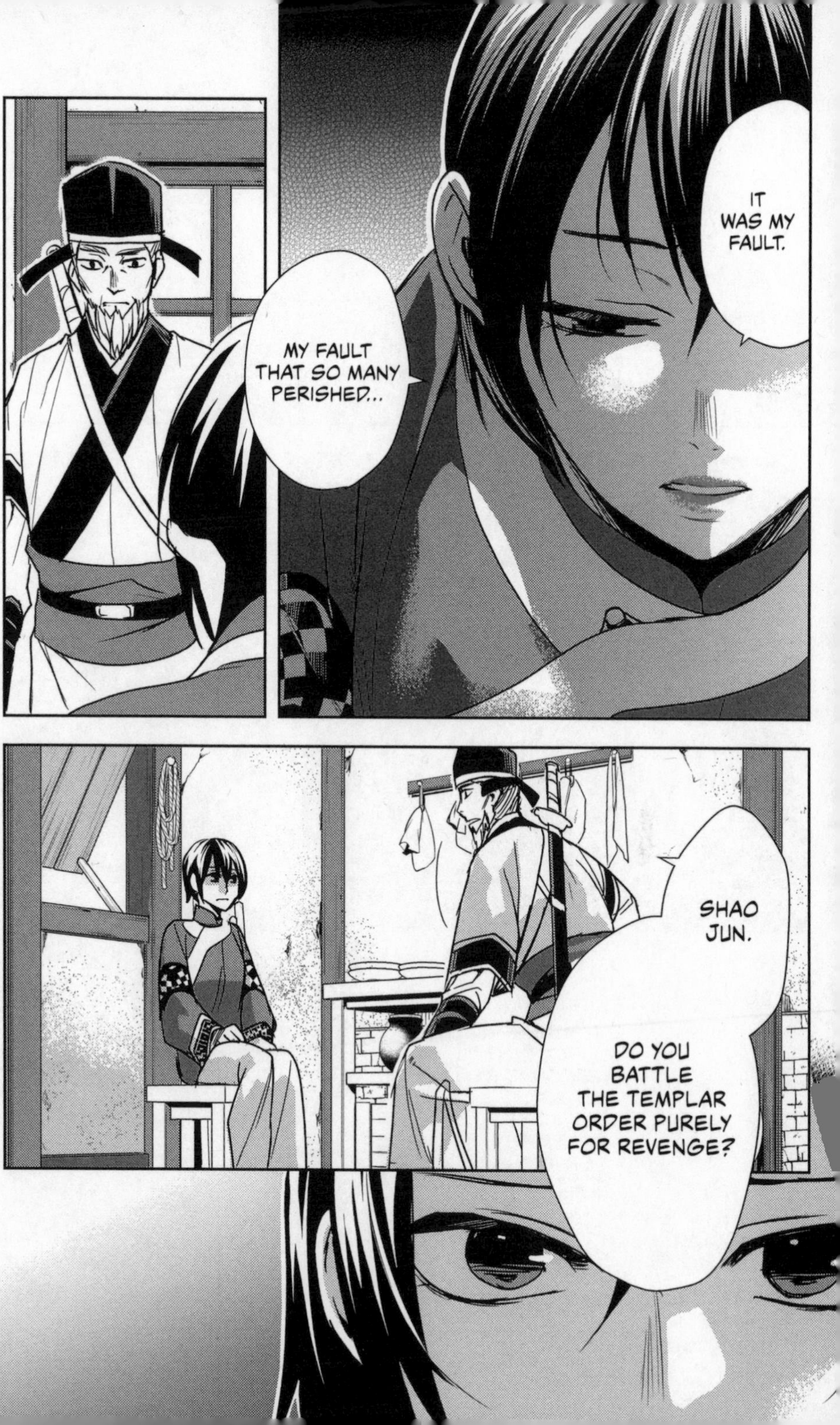
IT WAS MY FAULT.
MY FAULT THAT SO MANY PERISHED...
SHAO JUN.
DO YOU BATTLE THE TEMPLAR ORDER PURELY FOR REVENGE?

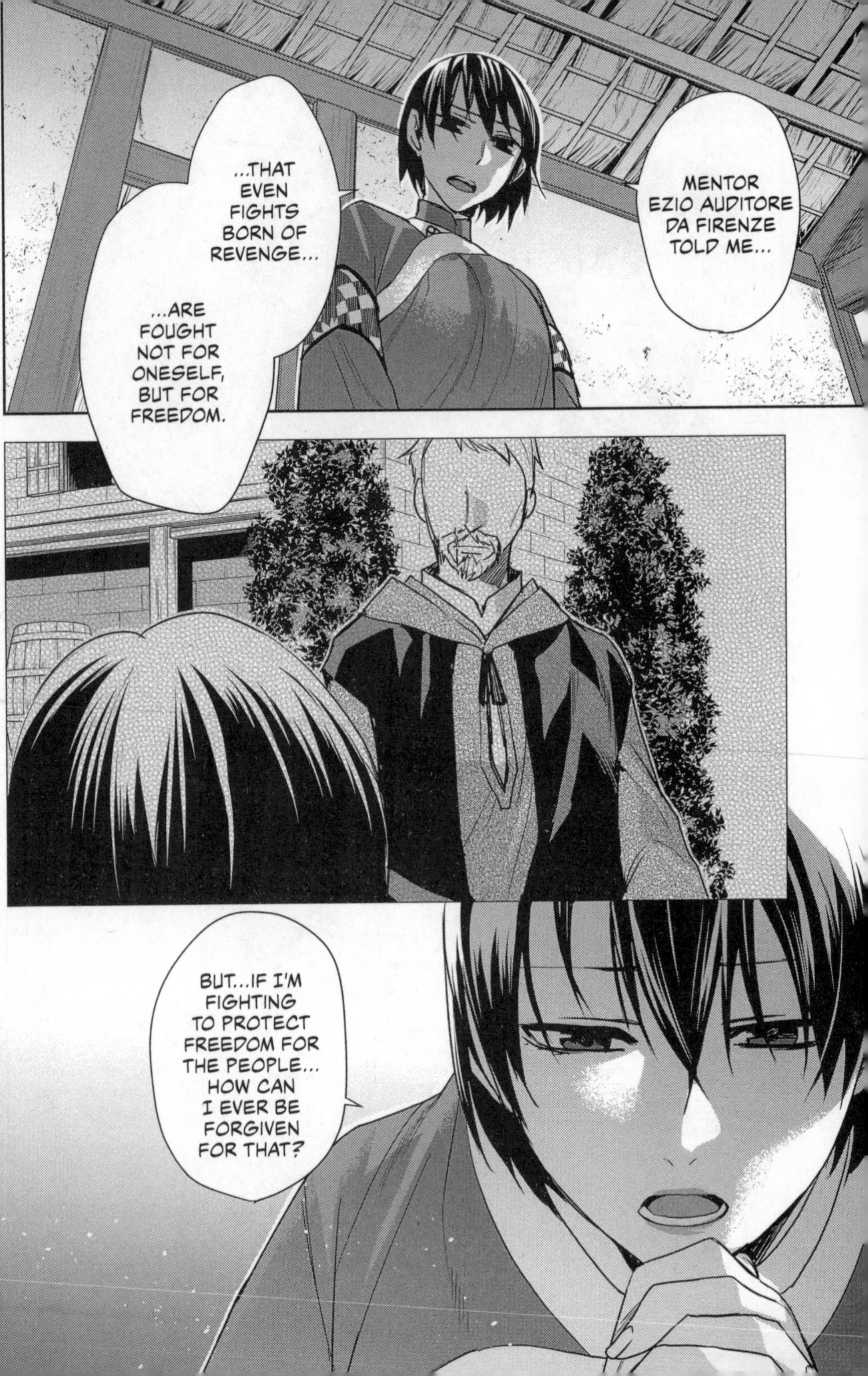
MENTOR EZIO AUDITORE DA FIRENZE TOLD ME...
...THAT EVEN FIGHTS BORN OF REVENGE...
...ARE FOUGHT NOT FOR ONESELF, BUT FOR FREEDOM.
BUT...IF I'M FIGHTING TO PROTECT FREEDOM FOR THE PEOPLE... HOW CAN I EVER BE FORGIVEN FOR THAT?

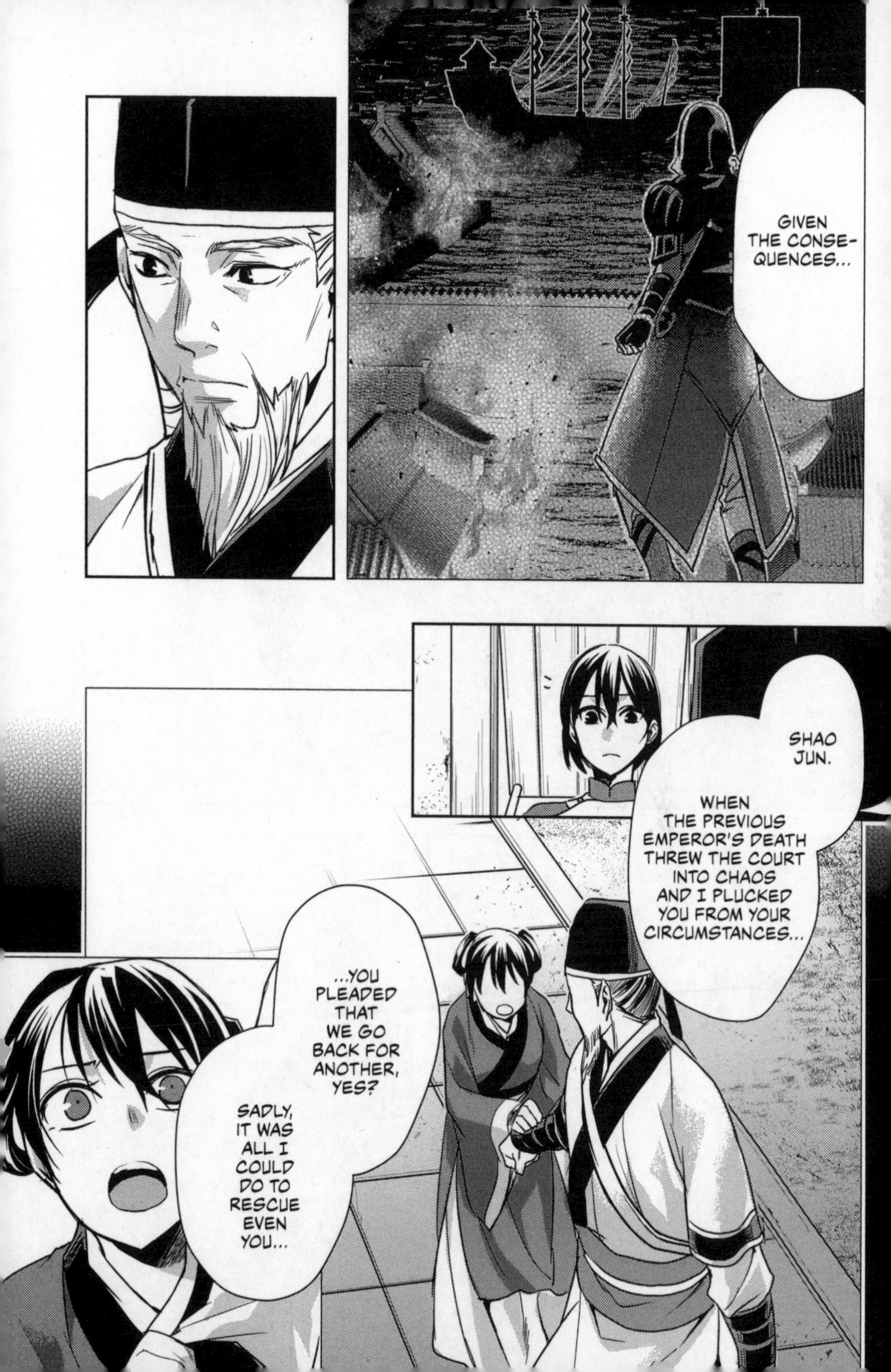

GIVEN THE CONSE-QUENCES...
SHAO JUN.
WHEN THE PREVIOUS EMPEROR'S DEATH THREW THE COURT INTO CHAOS AND I PLUCKED YOU FROM YOUR CIRCUMSTANCES...
...YOU PLEADED THAT WE GO BACK FOR ANOTHER, YES?
SADLY, IT WAS ALL I COULD DO TO RESCUE EVEN YOU...

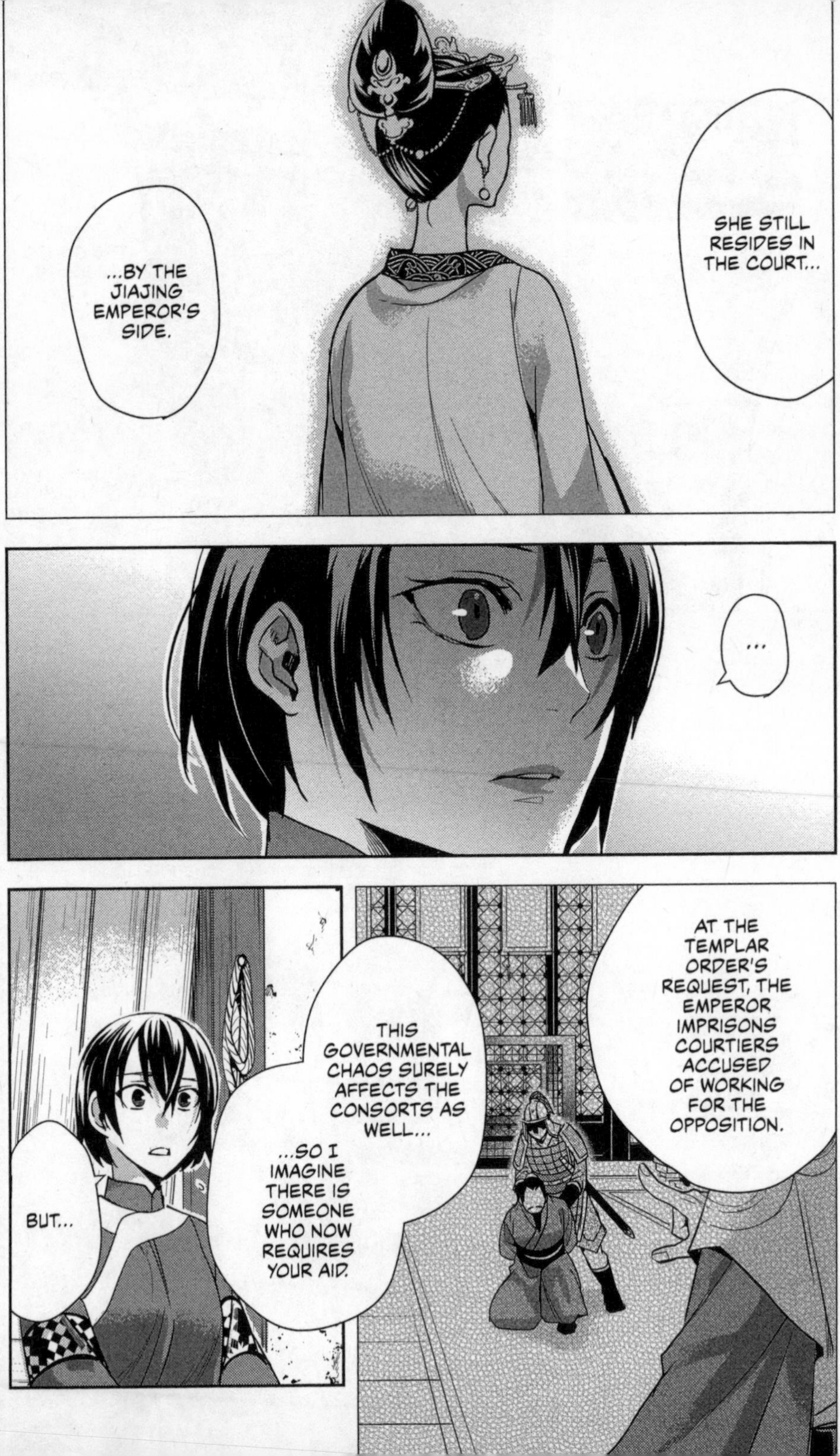
SHE STILL RESIDES IN THE COURT...
...BY THE JIAJING EMPEROR'S SIDE.
...
AT THE TEMPLAR ORDER'S REQUEST, THE EMPEROR IMPRISONS COURTIERS ACCUSED OF WORKING FOR THE OPPOSITION.
THIS GOVERNMENTAL CHAOS SURELY AFFECTS THE CONSORTS AS WELL...
...SO I IMAGINE THERE IS SOMEONE WHO NOW REQUIRES YOUR AID.
BUT...

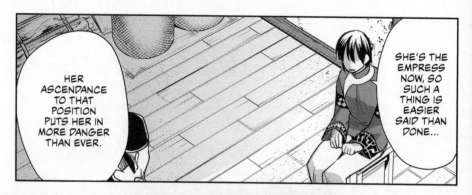

SHE'S THE EMPRESS NOW, SO SUCH A THING IS EASIER SAID THAN DONE...
HER ASCENDANCE TO THAT POSITION PUTS HER IN MORE DANGER THAN EVER.
QIXIE...

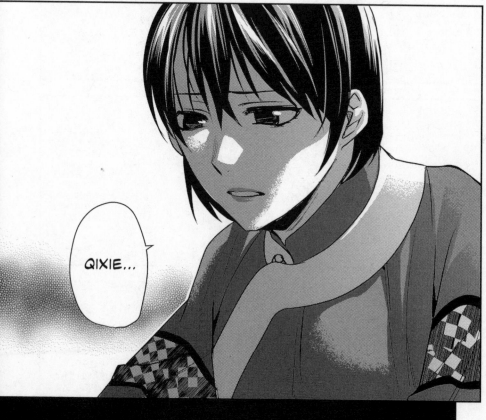

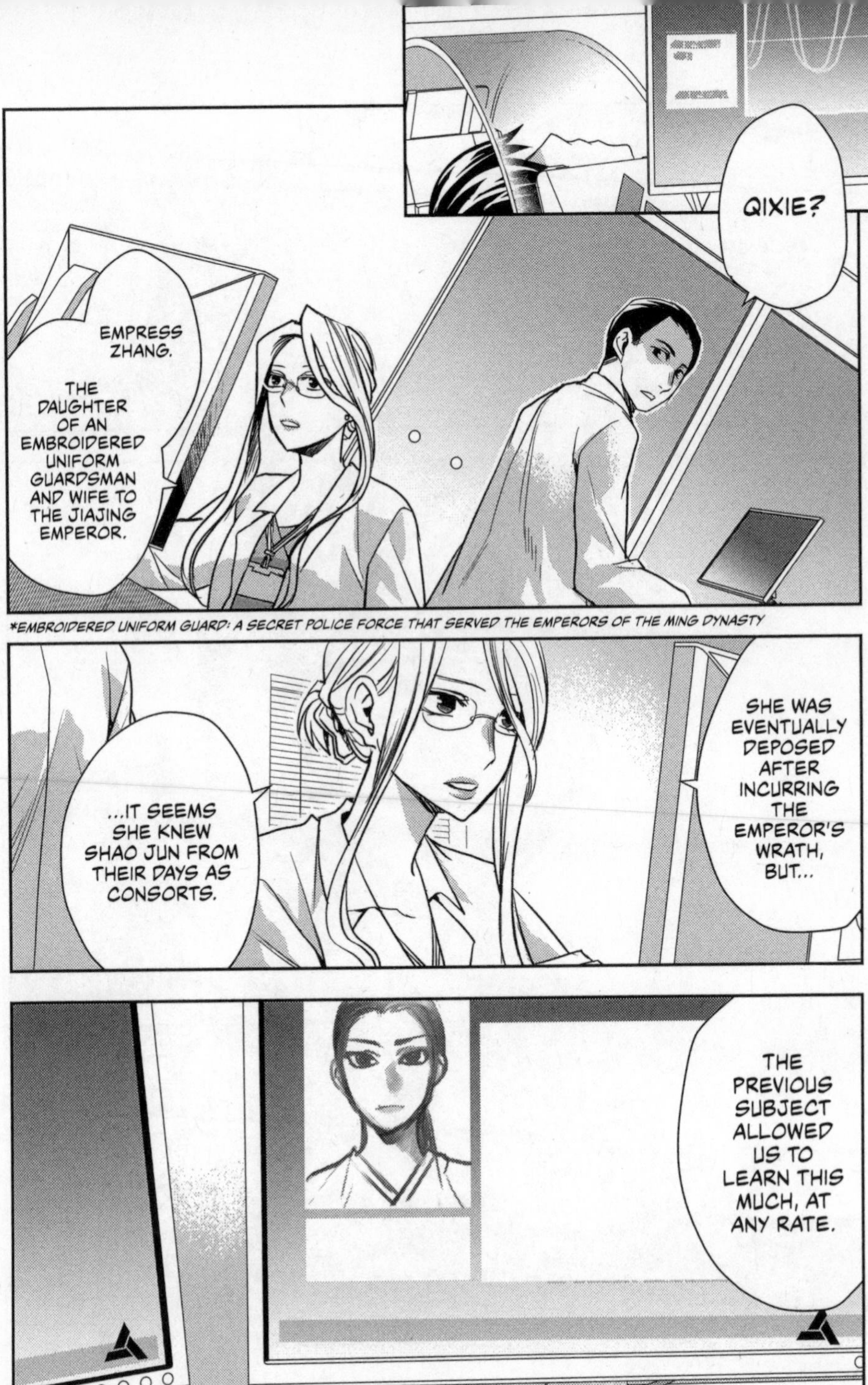
QIXIE?
EMPRESS ZHANG.
THE DAUGHTER OF AN EMBROIDERED UNIFORM GUARDSMAN AND WIFE TO THE JIAJING EMPEROR.
*EMBROIDERED UNIFORM GUARD: A SECRET POLICE FORCE THAT SERVED THE EMPERORS OF THE MING DYNASTY
SHE WAS EVENTUALLY DEPOSED AFTER INCURRING THE EMPEROR'S WRATH, BUT...
...IT SEEMS SHE KNEW SHAO JUN FROM THEIR DAYS AS CONSORTS.
THE PREVIOUS SUBJECT ALLOWED US TO LEARN THIS MUCH, AT ANY RATE.

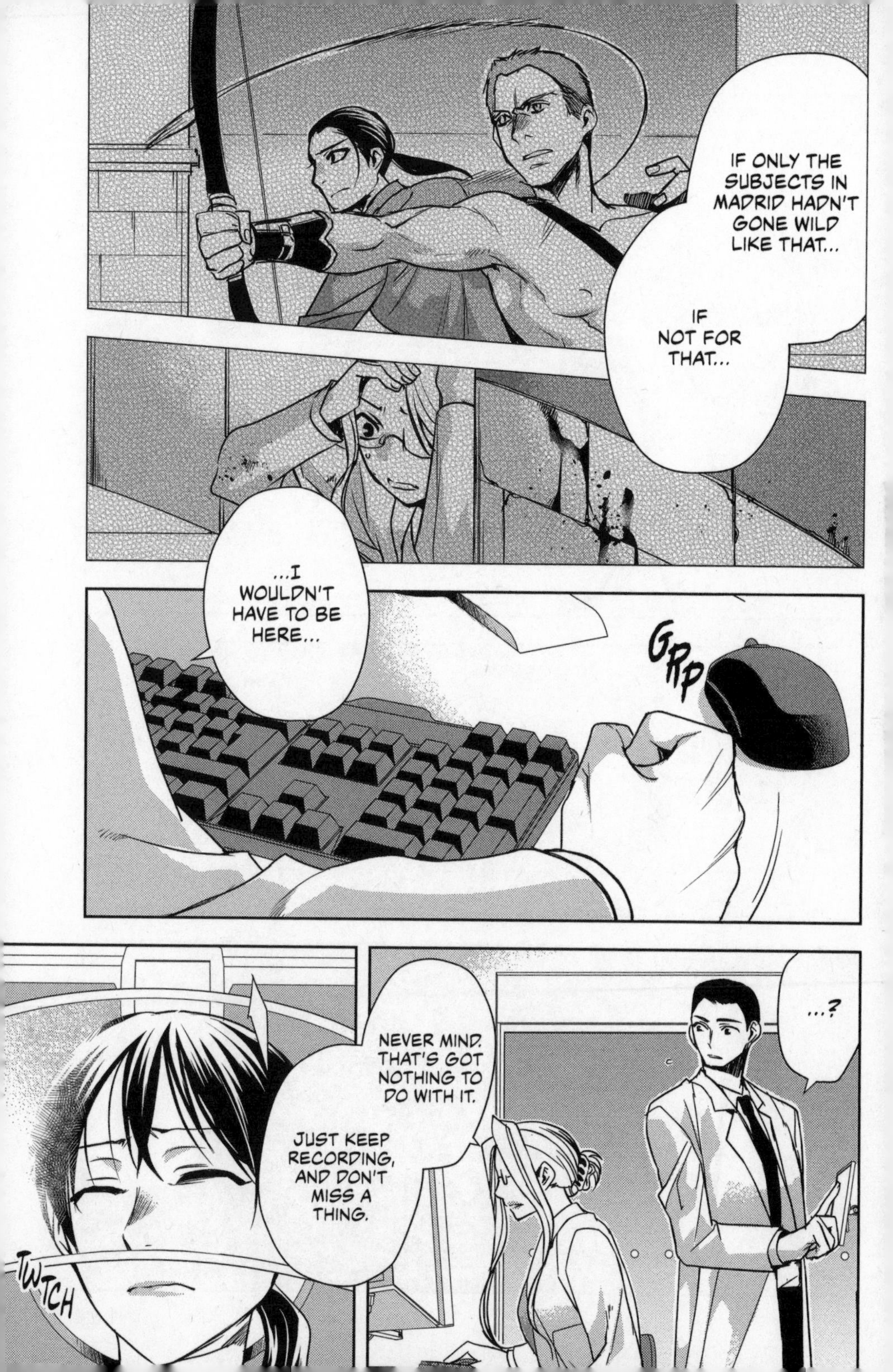
IF ONLY THE SUBJECTS IN MADRID HADN'T GONE WILD LIKE THAT...
IF NOT FOR THAT...
...I WOULDN'T HAVE TO BE HERE...
GRP
...?
NEVER MIND. THAT'S GOT NOTHING TO DO WITH IT.
JUST KEEP RECORDING, AND DON'T MISS A THING.
TWTCH

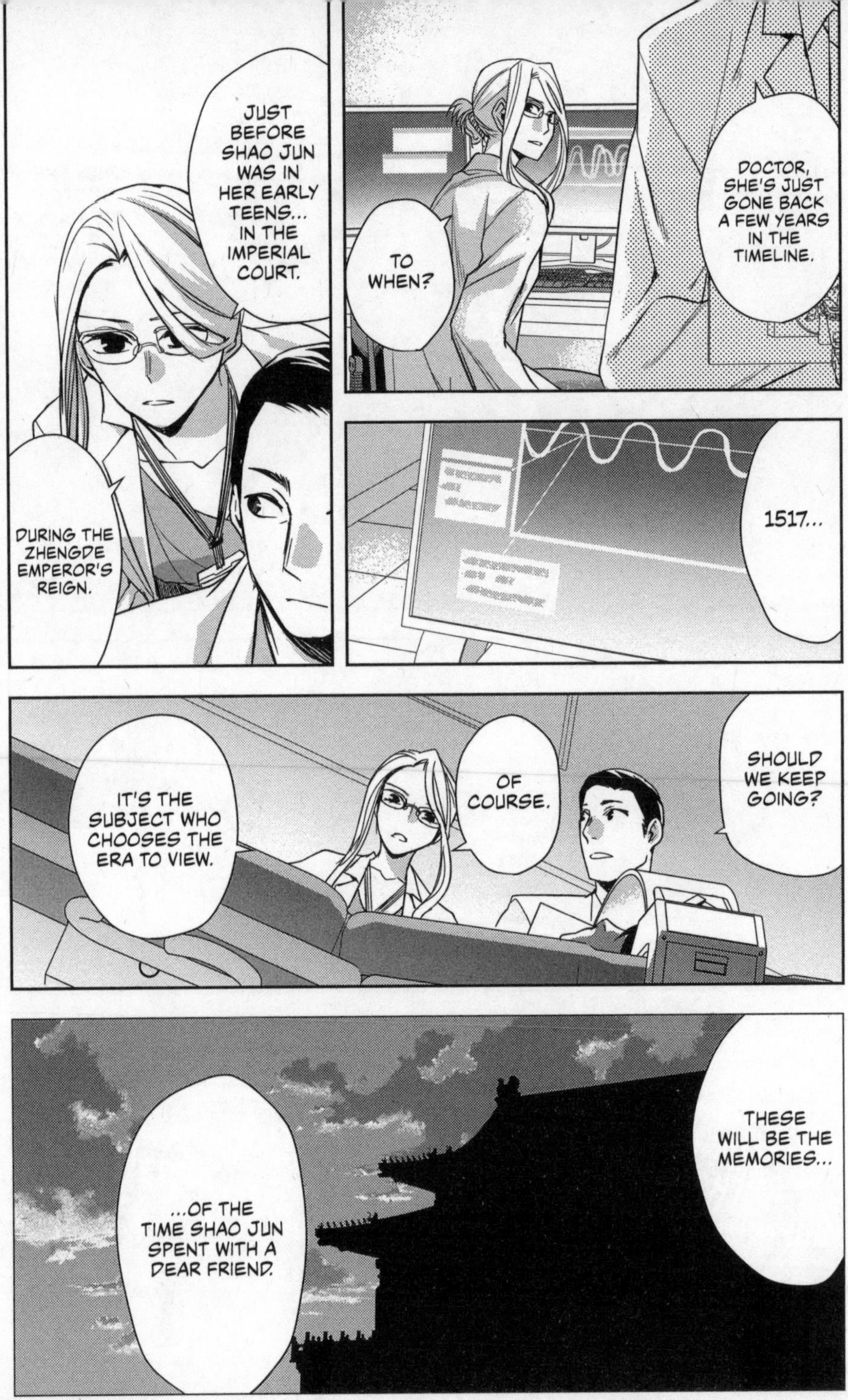
DOCTOR, SHE'S JUST GONE BACK A FEW YEARS IN THE TIMELINE.
TO WHEN?
1517...
JUST BEFORE SHAO JUN WAS IN HER EARLY TEENS... IN THE IMPERIAL COURT.
DURING THE ZHENGDE EMPEROR'S REIGN.
SHOULD WE KEEP GOING?
OF COURSE.
IT'S THE SUBJECT WHO CHOOSES THE ERA TO VIEW.
THESE WILL BE THE MEMORIES...
...OF THE TIME SHAO JUN SPENT WITH A DEAR FRIEND.

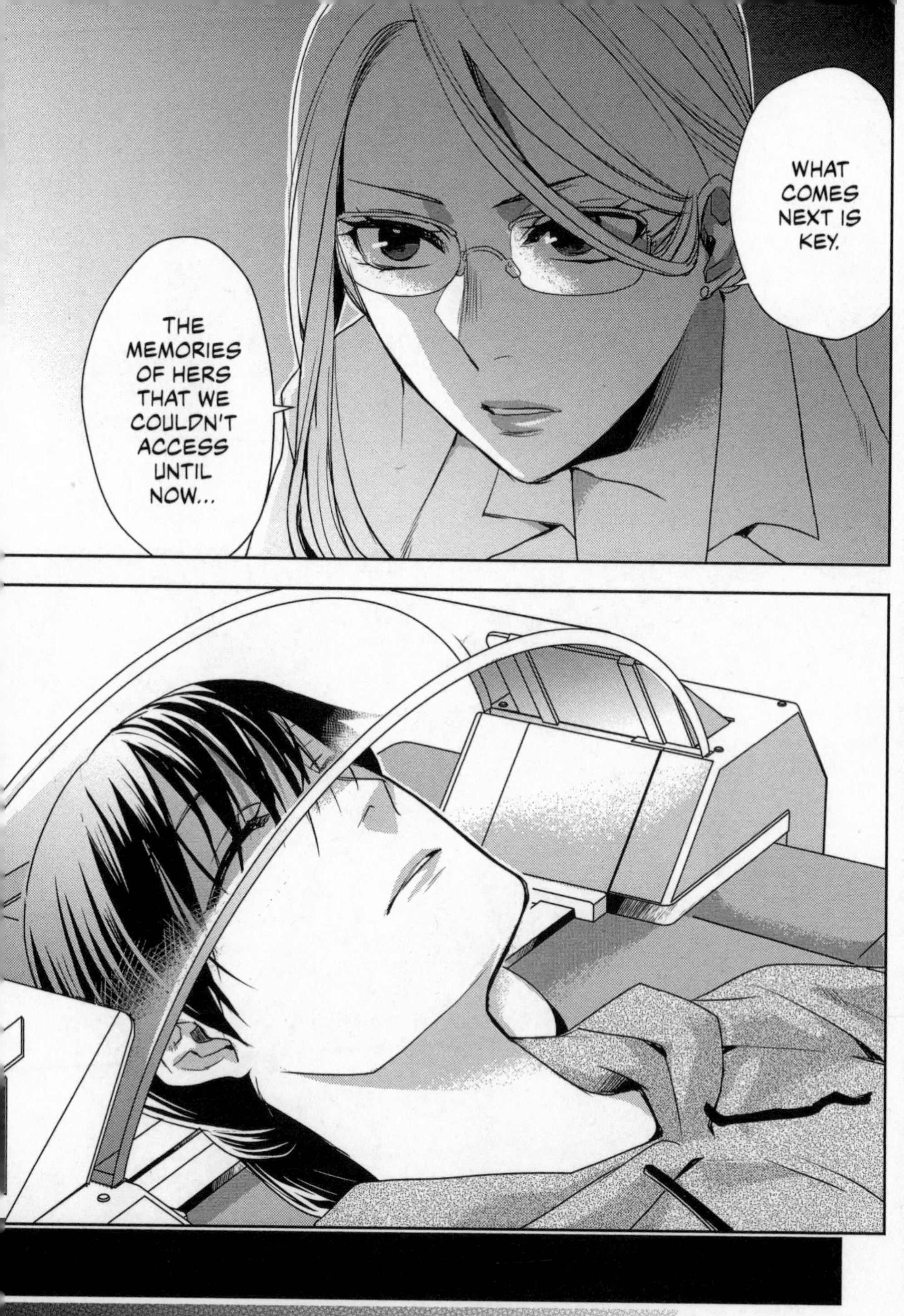
WHAT COMES NEXT IS KEY.
THE MEMORIES OF HERS THAT WE COULDN'T ACCESS UNTIL NOW...

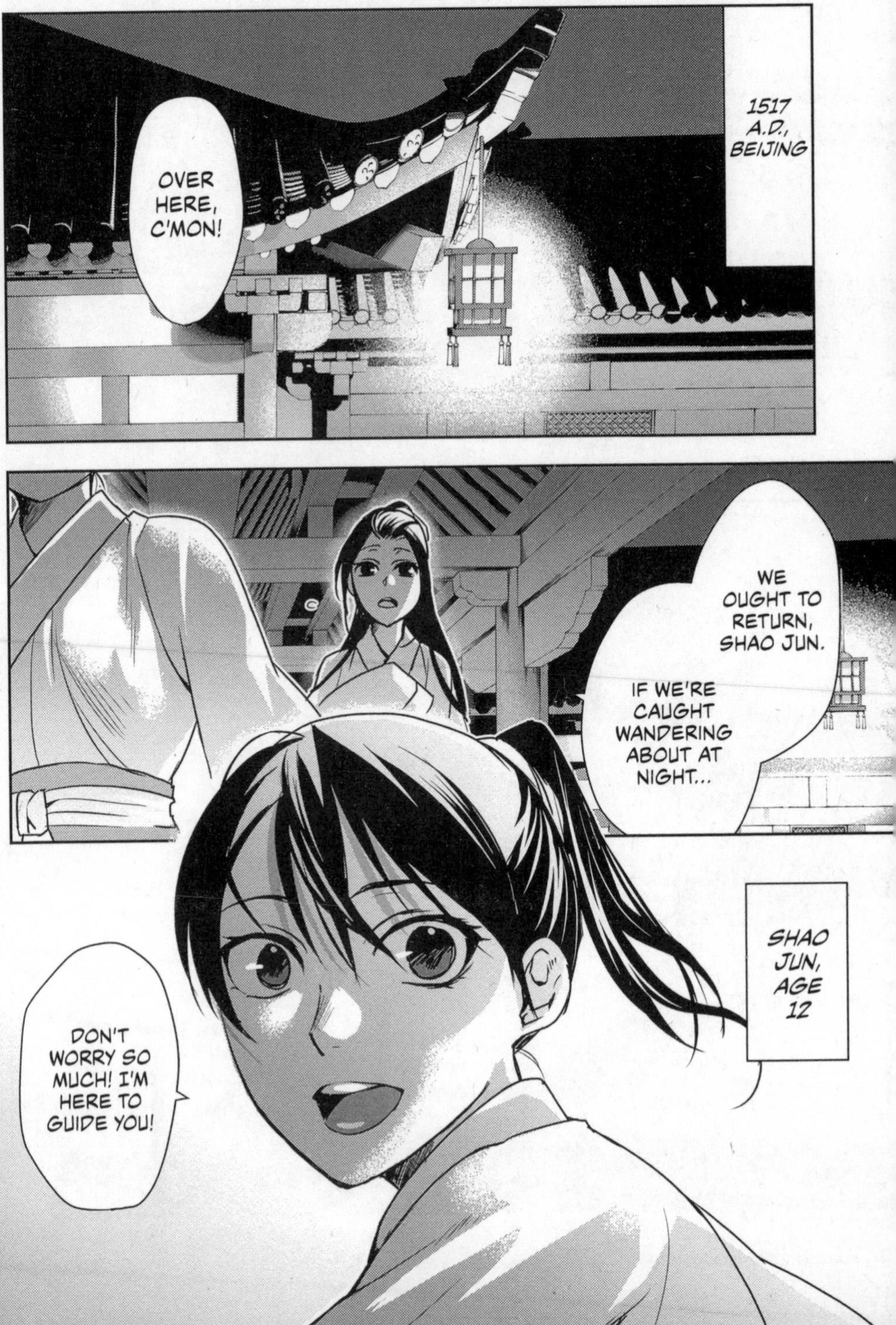
1517 A.D., BEIJING
OVER HERE, C'MON!
WE OUGHT TO RETURN, SHAO JUN.
IF WE'RE CAUGHT WANDERING ABOUT AT NIGHT...
SHAO JUN, AGE 12
DON'T WORRY SO MUCH! I'M HERE TO GUIDE YOU!

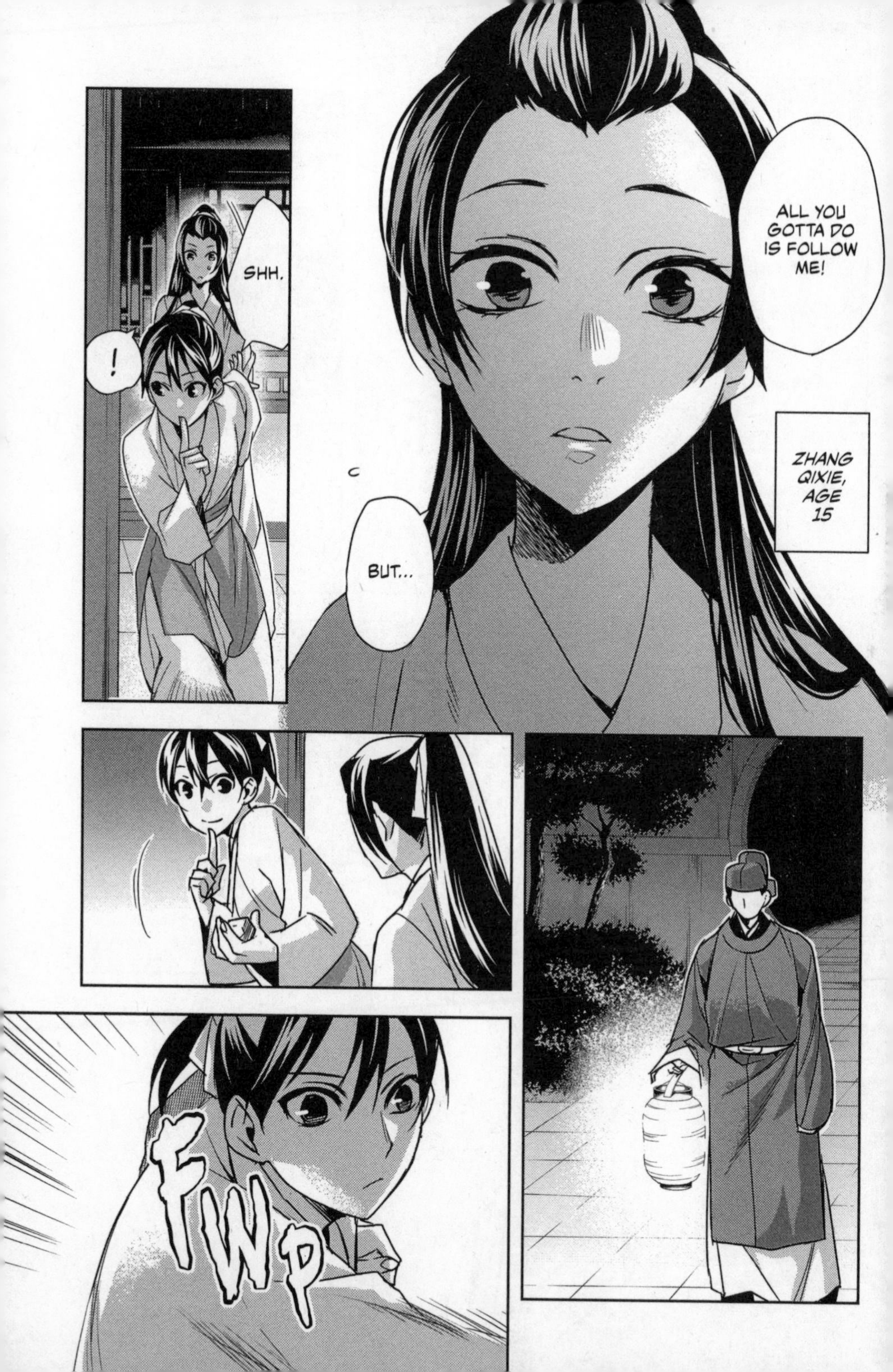
ALL YOU GOTTA DO IS FOLLOW ME!
ZHANG QIXIE, AGE 15
BUT...
SHH.
!
FWP

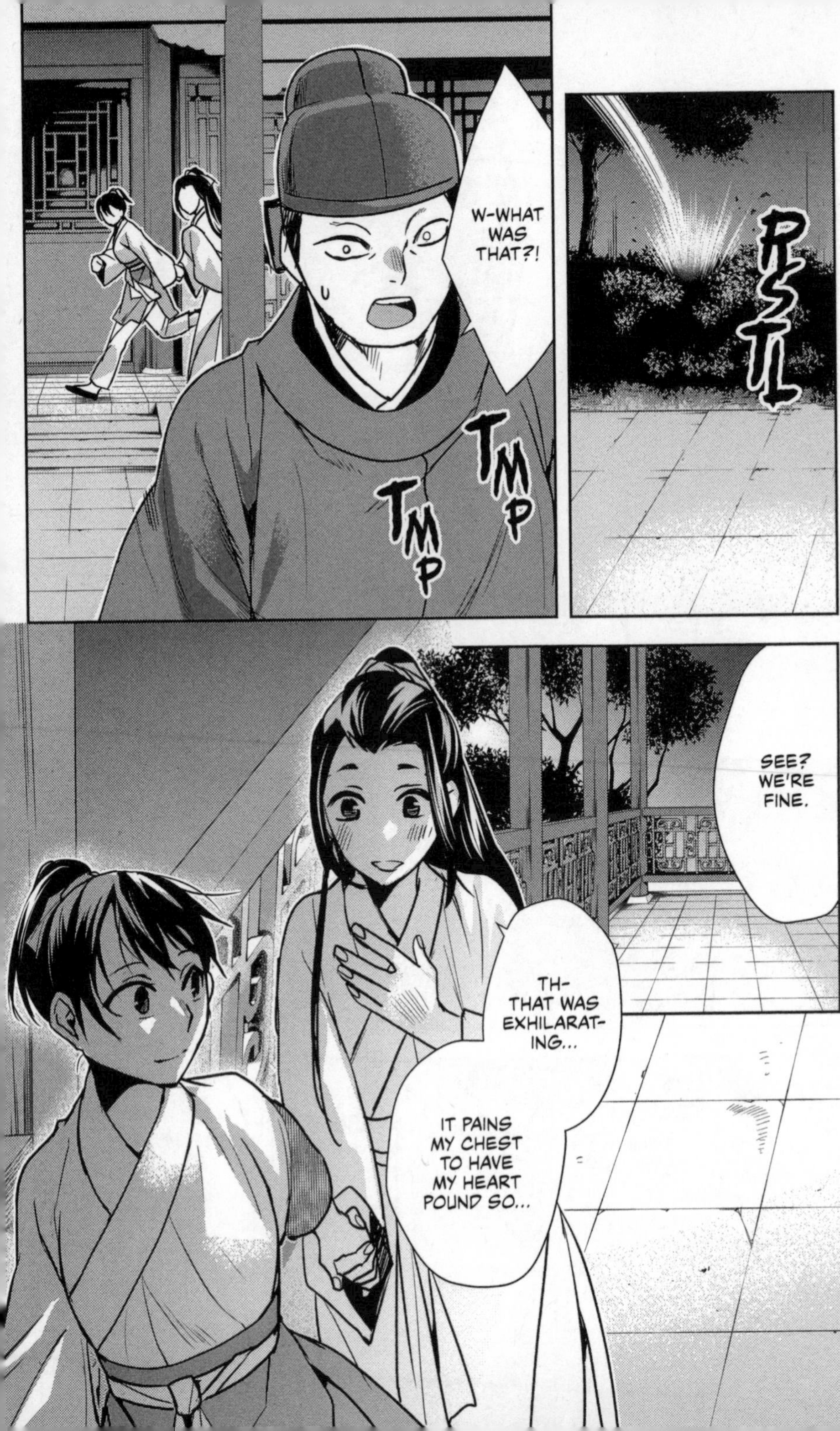
RSTL
W-WHAT WAS THAT?!
TMP
TMP
SEE? WE'RE FINE.
TH-THAT WAS EXHILARATING...
IT PAINS MY CHEST TO HAVE MY HEART POUND SO...

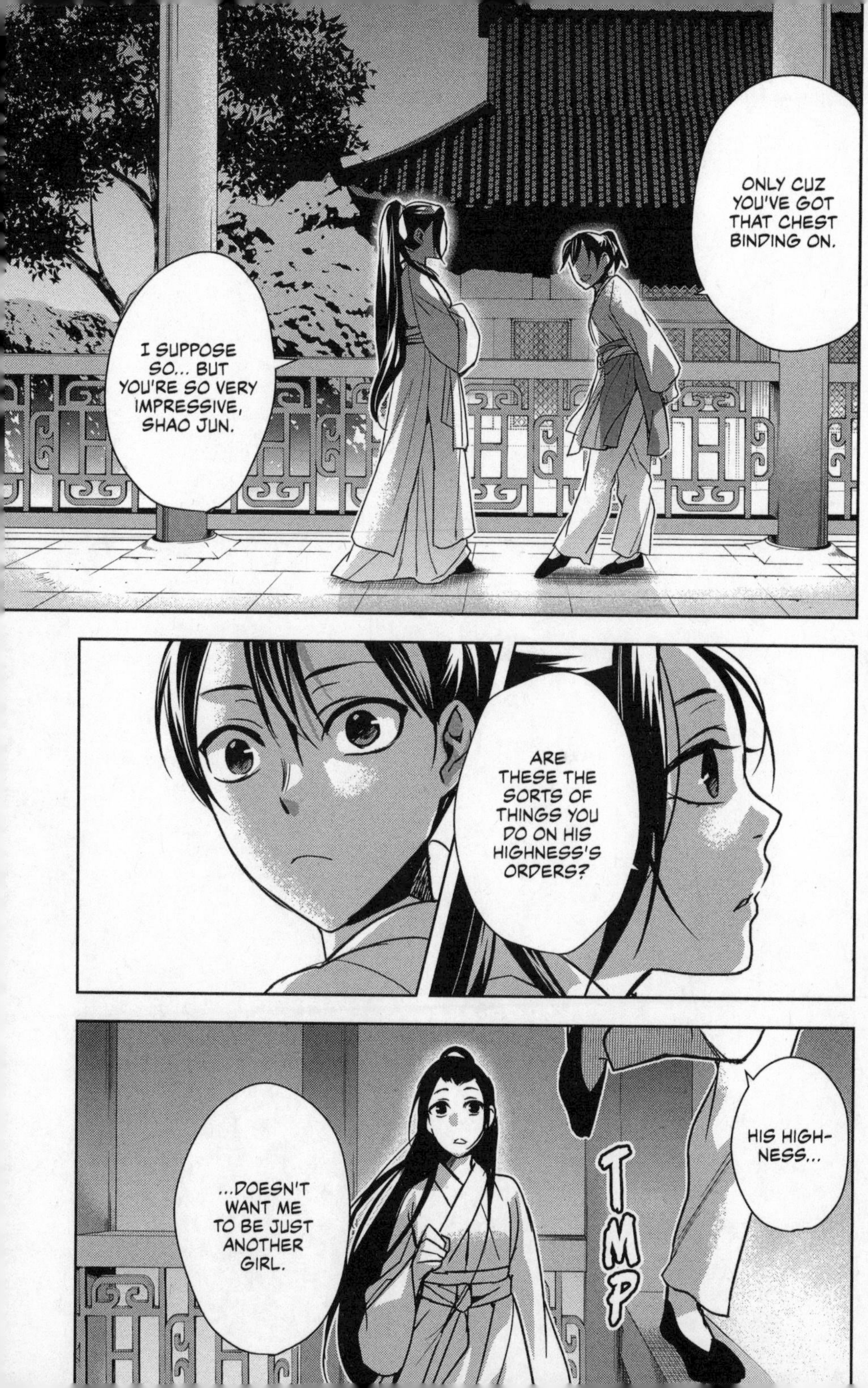
ONLY CUZ YOU'VE GOT THAT CHEST BINDING ON.
I SUPPOSE SO... BUT YOU'RE SO VERY IMPRESSIVE, SHAO JUN.
ARE THESE THE SORTS OF THINGS YOU DO ON HIS HIGHNESS'S ORDERS?
HIS HIGH-NESS...
TMP
...DOESN'T WANT ME TO BE JUST ANOTHER GIRL.

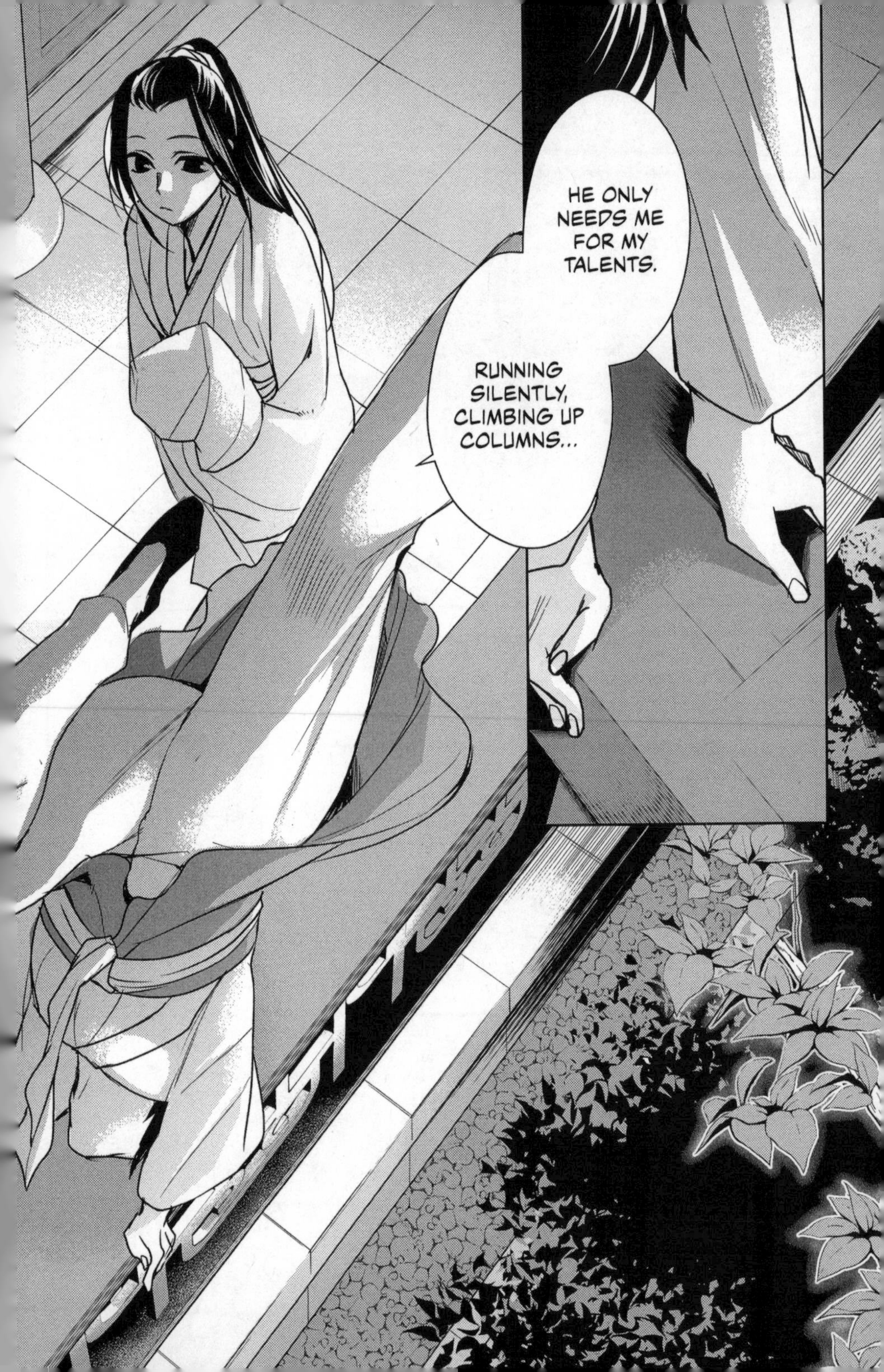
HE ONLY NEEDS ME FOR MY TALENTS.
RUNNING SILENTLY, CLIMBING UP COLUMNS...

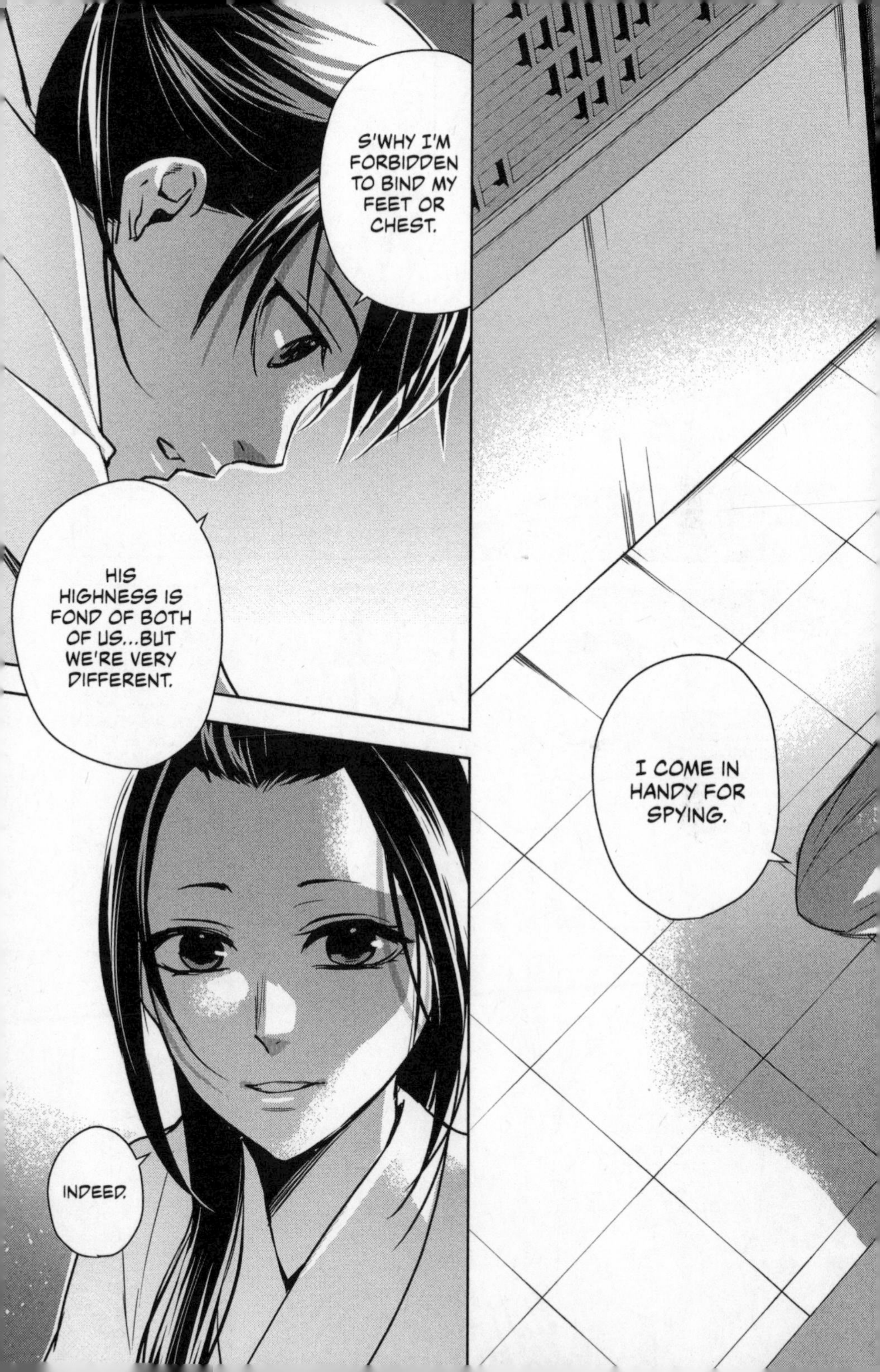
I COME IN HANDY FOR SPYING.
S'WHY I'M FORBIDDEN TO BIND MY FEET OR CHEST.
HIS HIGHNESS IS FOND OF BOTH OF US...BUT WE'RE VERY DIFFERENT.
INDEED.

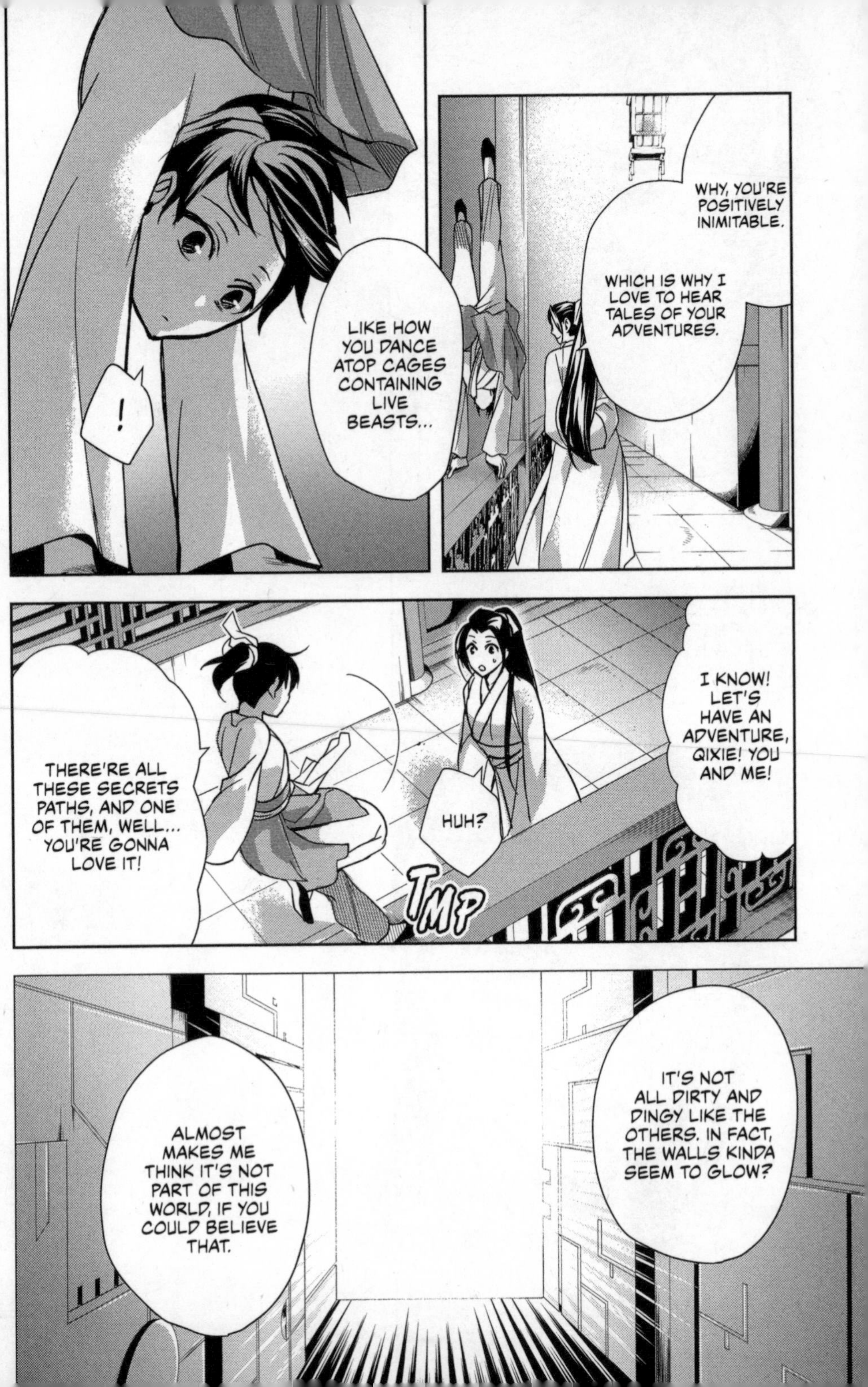
WHY, YOU'RE POSITIVELY INIMITABLE.
WHICH IS WHY I LOVE TO HEAR TALES OF YOUR ADVENTURES.
LIKE HOW YOU DANCE ATOP CAGES CONTAINING LIVE BEASTS...
!
I KNOW! LET'S HAVE AN ADVENTURE, QIXIE! YOU AND ME!
HUH?
TMP
THERE'RE ALL THESE SECRETS PATHS, AND ONE OF THEM, WELL... YOU'RE GONNA LOVE IT!
IT'S NOT ALL DIRTY AND DINGY LIKE THE OTHERS. IN FACT, THE WALLS KINDA SEEM TO GLOW?
ALMOST MAKES ME THINK IT'S NOT PART OF THIS WORLD, IF YOU COULD BELIEVE THAT.

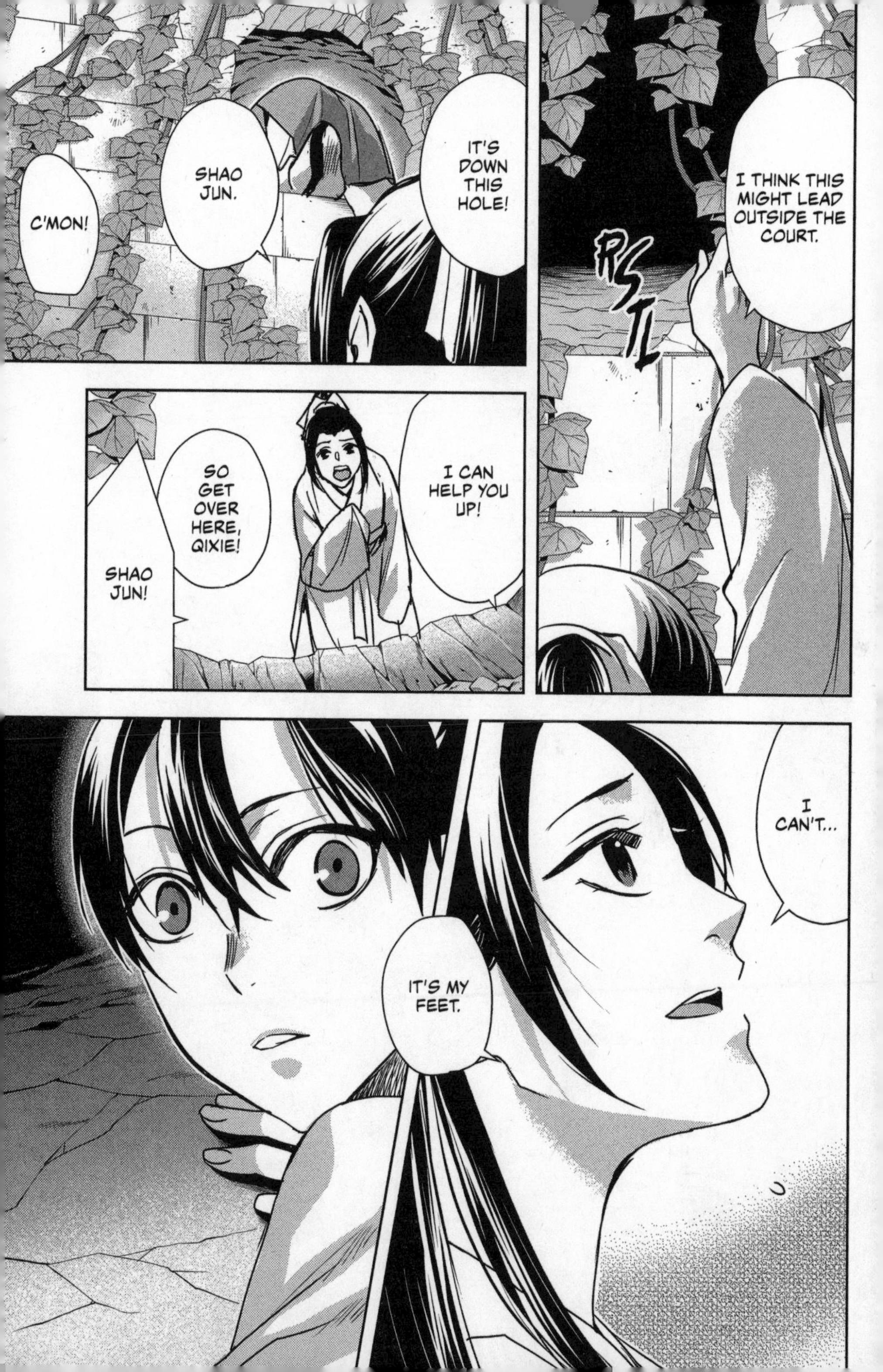
I THINK THIS MIGHT LEAD OUTSIDE THE COURT.
RSTL
IT'S DOWN THIS HOLE!
SHAO JUN.
C'MON!
I CAN HELP YOU UP!
SO GET OVER HERE, QIXIE!
SHAO JUN!
I CAN'T...
IT'S MY FEET.

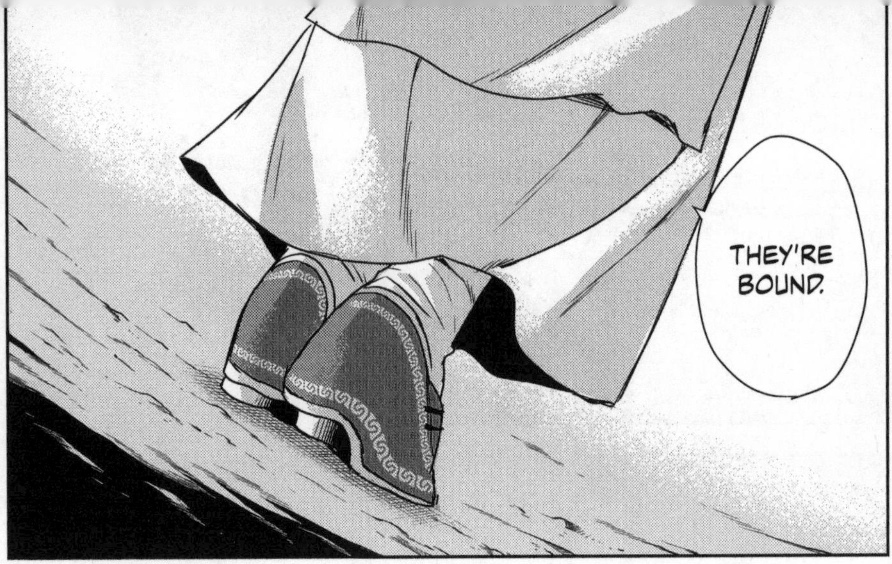
THEY'RE BOUND.

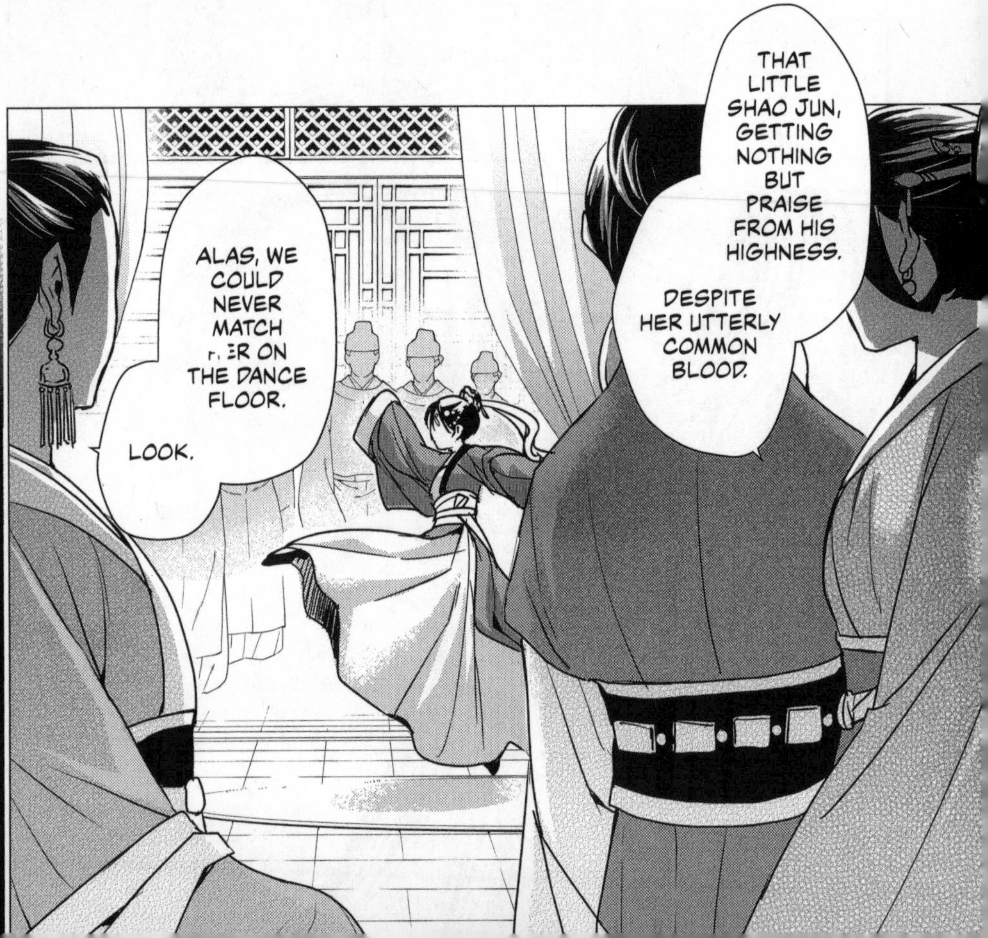
THAT LITTLE SHAO JUN, GETTING NOTHING BUT PRAISE FROM HIS HIGHNESS.
DESPITE HER UTTERLY COMMON BLOOD.
ALAS, WE COULD NEVER MATCH HER ON THE DANCE FLOOR.
LOOK.

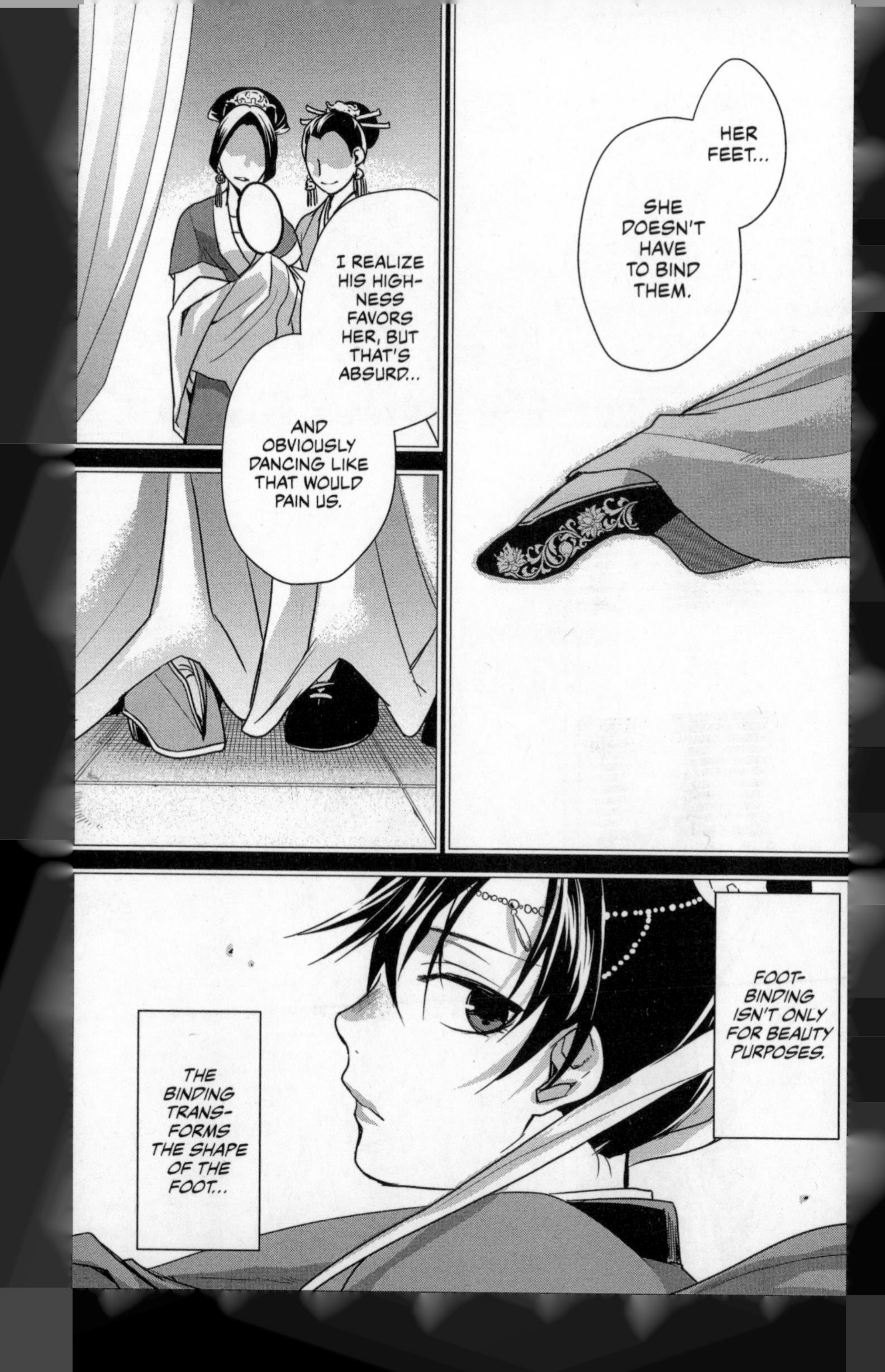
HER FEET...
SHE DOESN'T HAVE TO BIND THEM.
I REALIZE HIS HIGHNESS FAVORS HER, BUT THAT'S ABSURD...
AND OBVIOUSLY DANCING LIKE THAT WOULD PAIN US.
FOOT-BINDING ISN'T ONLY FOR BEAUTY PURPOSES.
THE BINDING TRANSFORMS THE SHAPE OF THE FOOT...

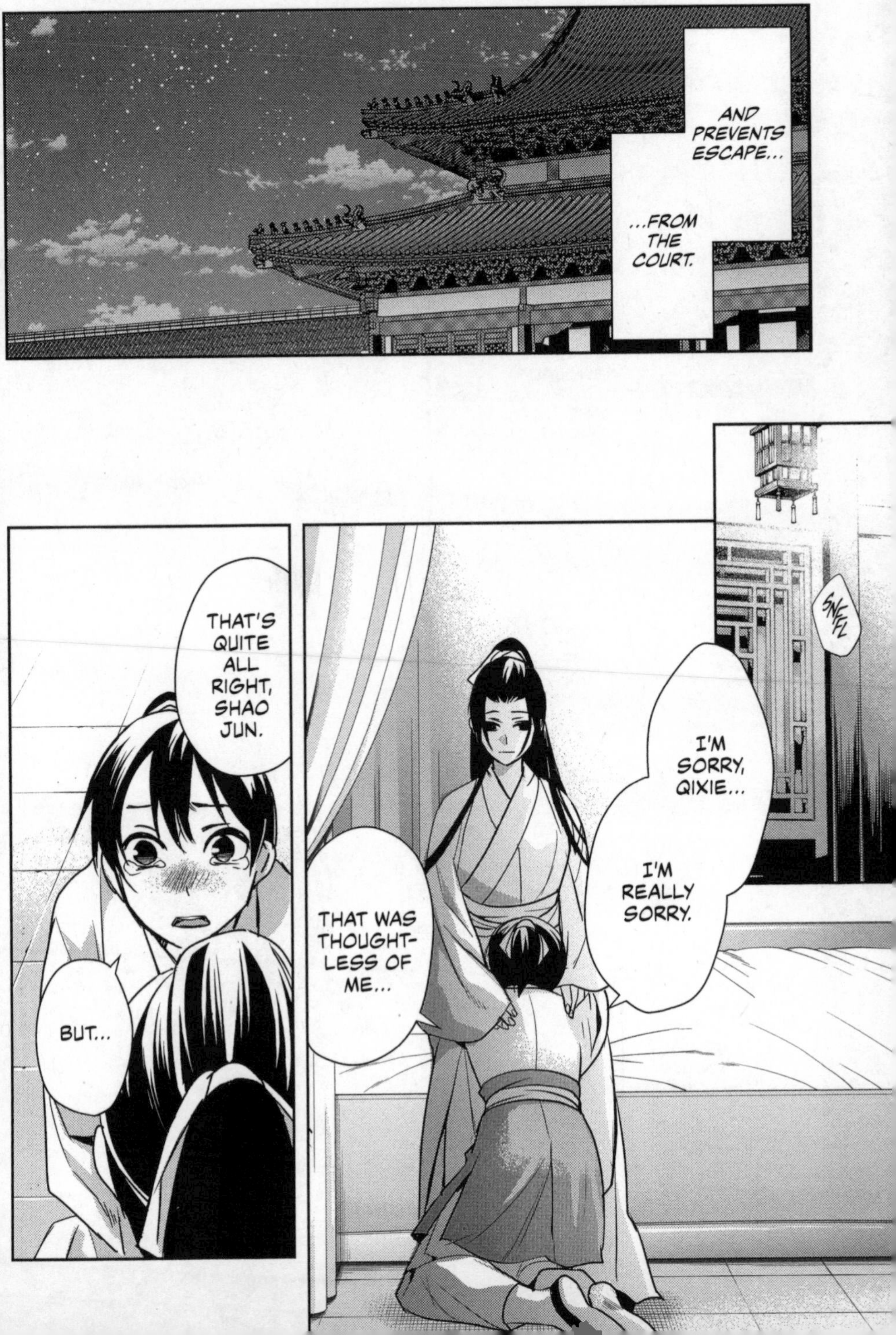
AND PREVENTS ESCAPE...
...FROM THE COURT.
SNFFL
I'M SORRY, QIXIE...
I'M REALLY SORRY.
THAT WAS THOUGHTLESS OF ME...
THAT'S QUITE ALL RIGHT, SHAO JUN.
BUT...

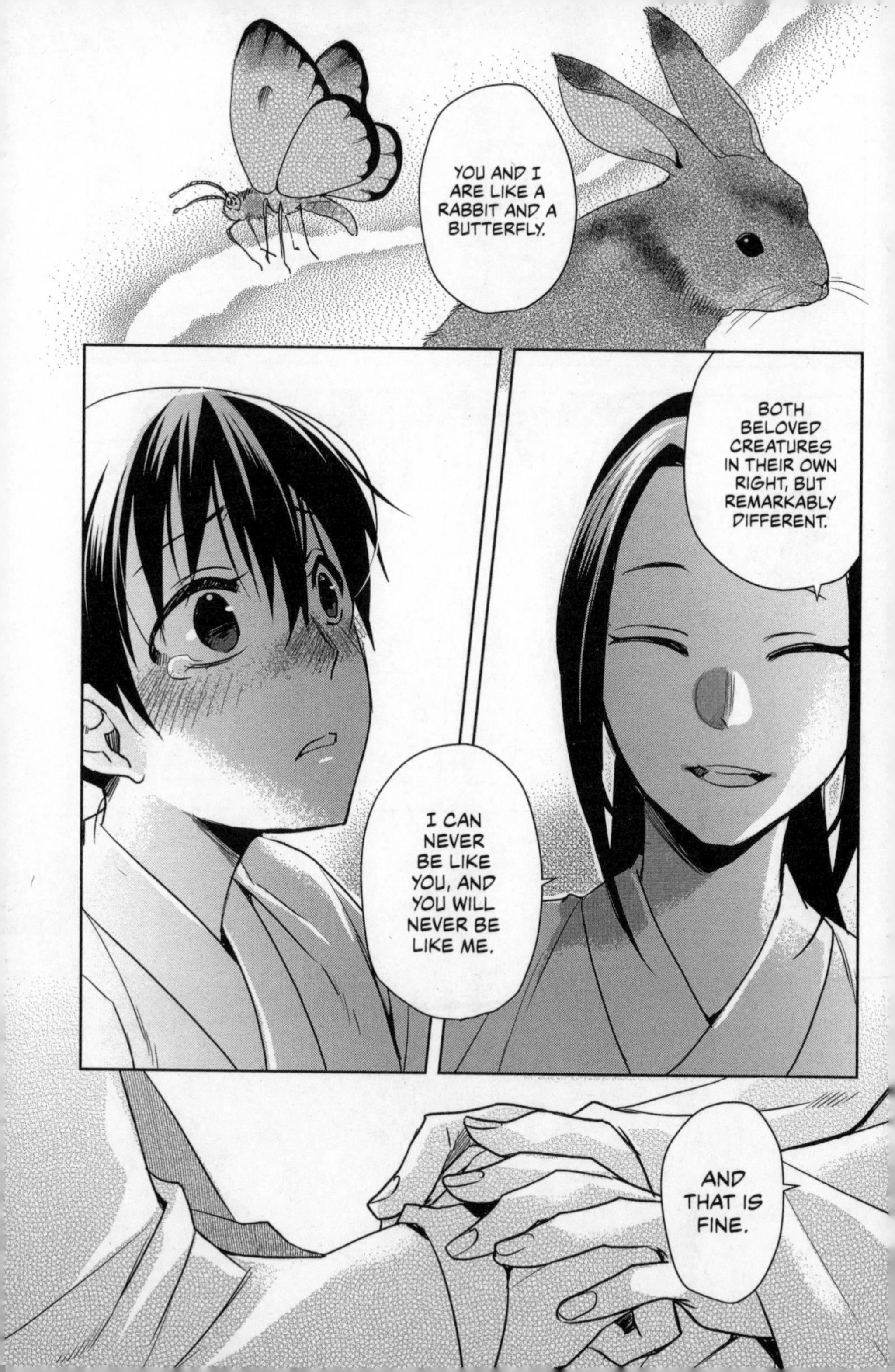
YOU AND I ARE LIKE A RABBIT AND A BUTTERFLY.
BOTH BELOVED CREATURES IN THEIR OWN RIGHT, BUT REMARKABLY DIFFERENT.
I CAN NEVER BE LIKE YOU, AND YOU WILL NEVER BE LIKE ME.
AND THAT IS FINE.

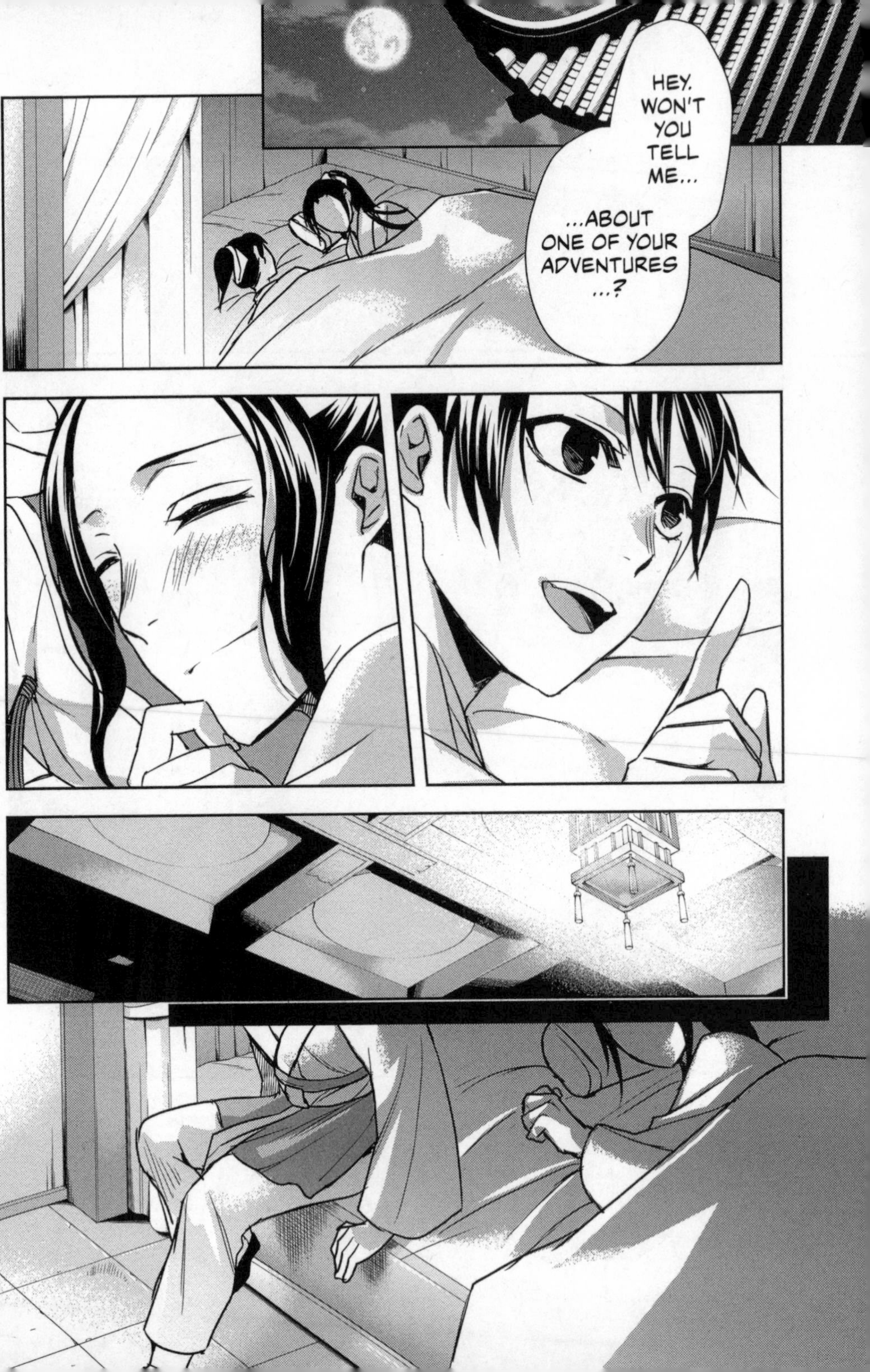
HEY. WON'T YOU TELL ME...
...ABOUT ONE OF YOUR ADVENTURES ...?

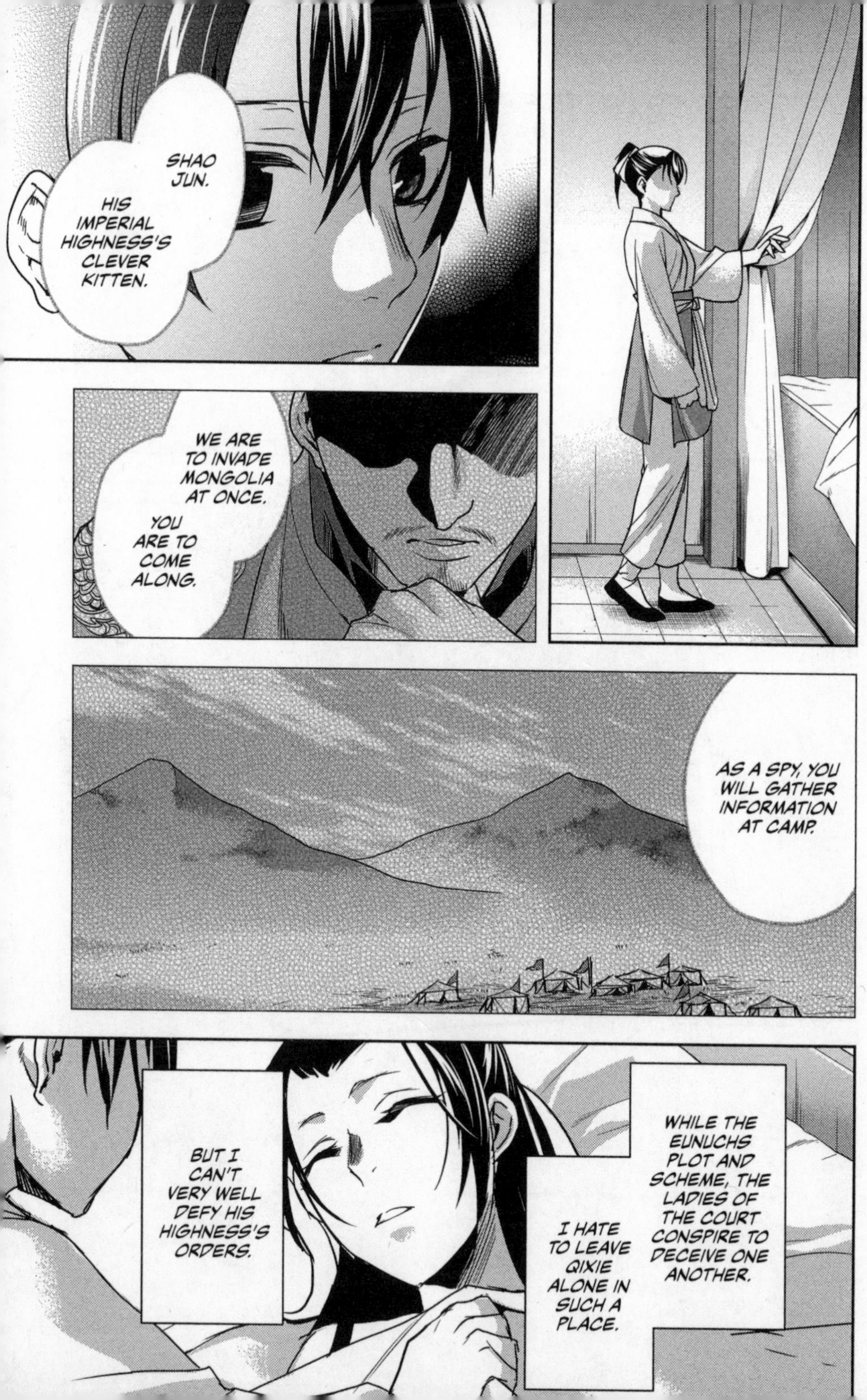
SHAO JUN.
HIS IMPERIAL HIGHNESS'S CLEVER KITTEN.
WE ARE TO INVADE MONGOLIA AT ONCE.
YOU ARE TO COME ALONG.
AS A SPY, YOU WILL GATHER INFORMATION AT CAMP.
WHILE THE EUNUCHS PLOT AND SCHEME, THE LADIES OF THE COURT CONSPIRE TO DECEIVE ONE ANOTHER.
I HATE TO LEAVE QIXIE ALONE IN SUCH A PLACE.
BUT I CAN'T VERY WELL DEFY HIS HIGHNESS'S ORDERS.

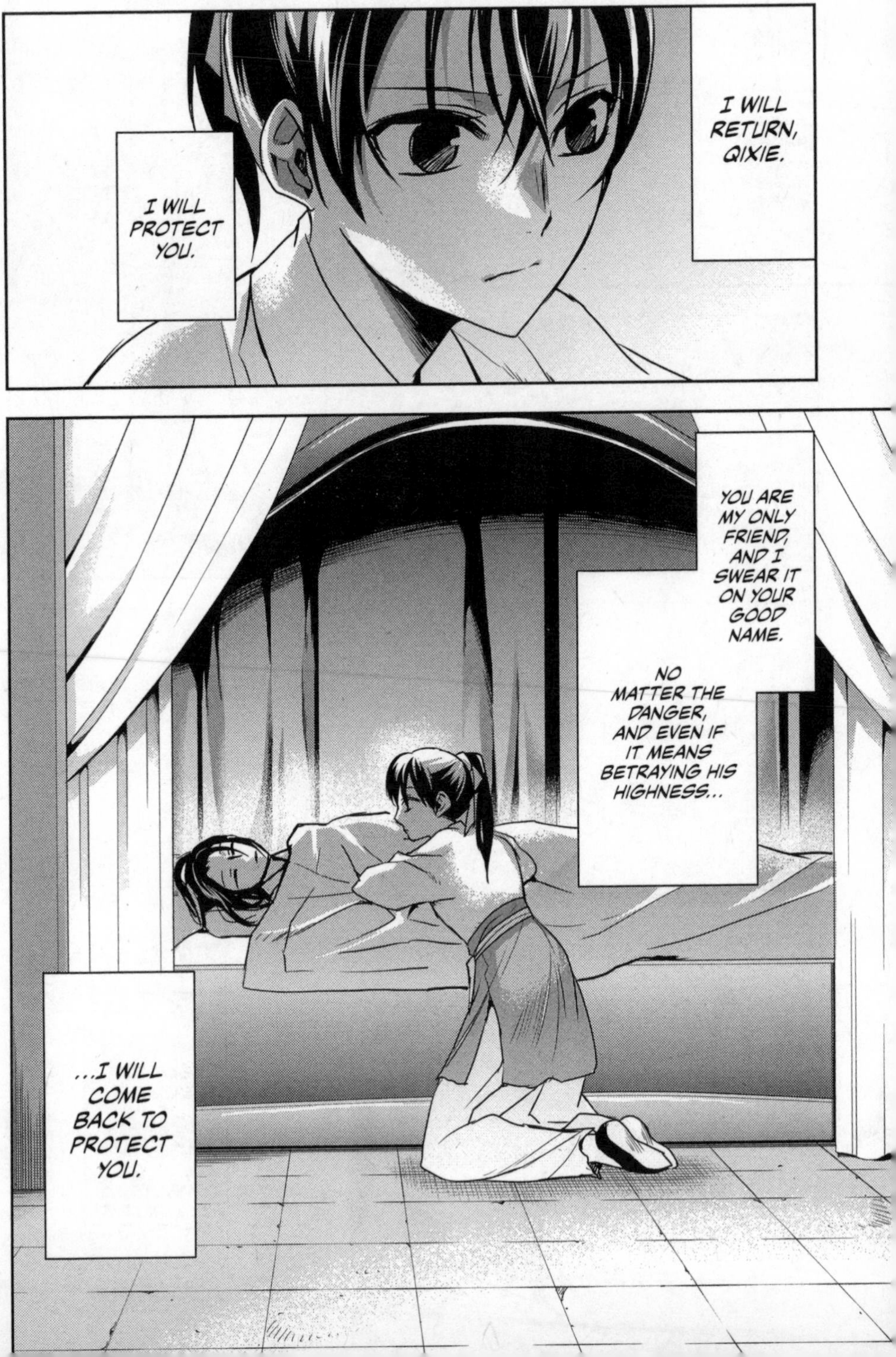
I WILL RETURN, QIXIE.
I WILL PROTECT YOU.
YOU ARE MY ONLY FRIEND, AND I SWEAR IT ON YOUR GOOD NAME.
NO MATTER THE DANGER, AND EVEN IF IT MEANS BETRAYING HIS HIGHNESS...
...I WILL COME BACK TO PROTECT YOU.

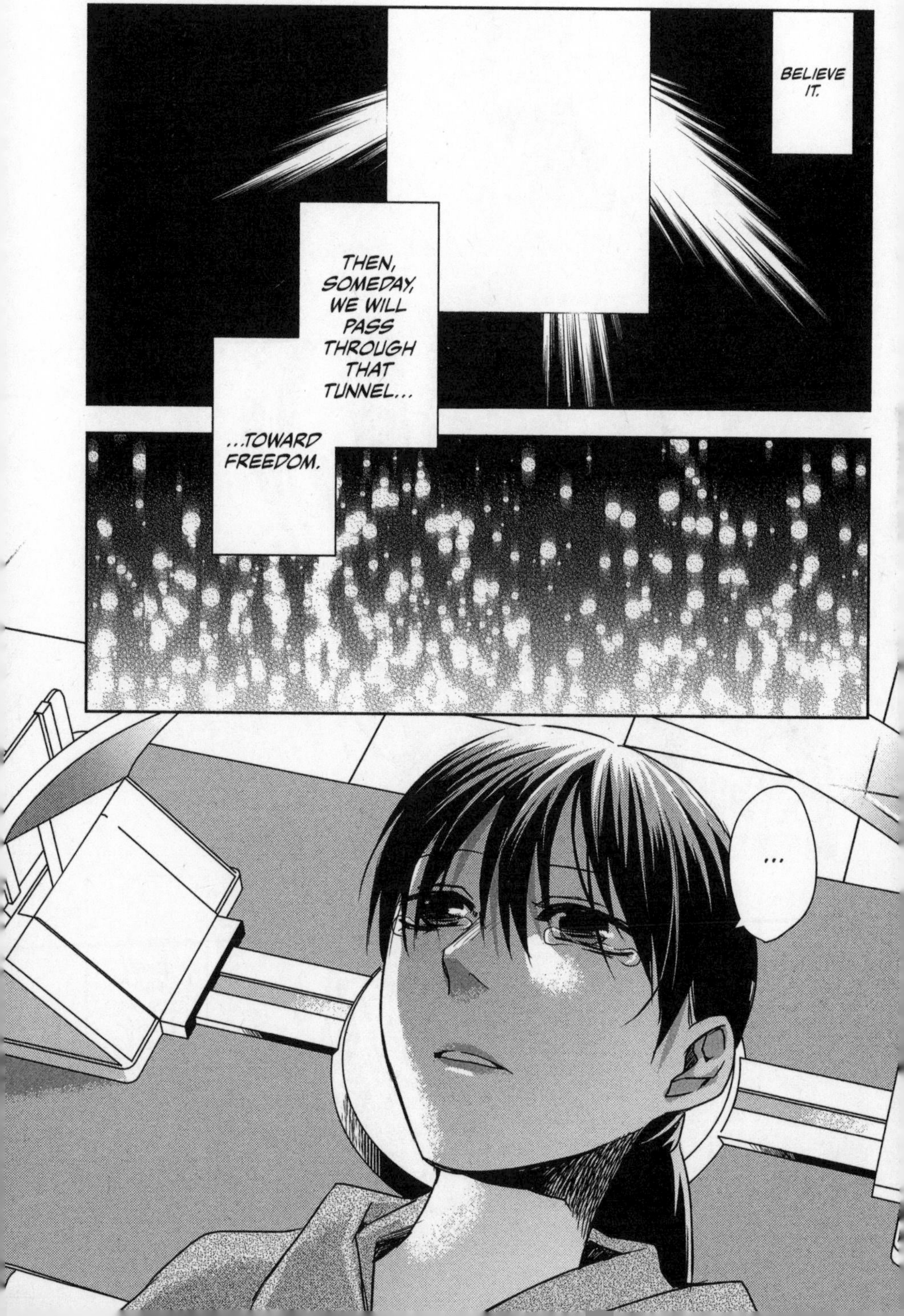
BELIEVE IT.
THEN, SOMEDAY, WE WILL PASS THROUGH THAT TUNNEL...
...TOWARD FREEDOM.
...

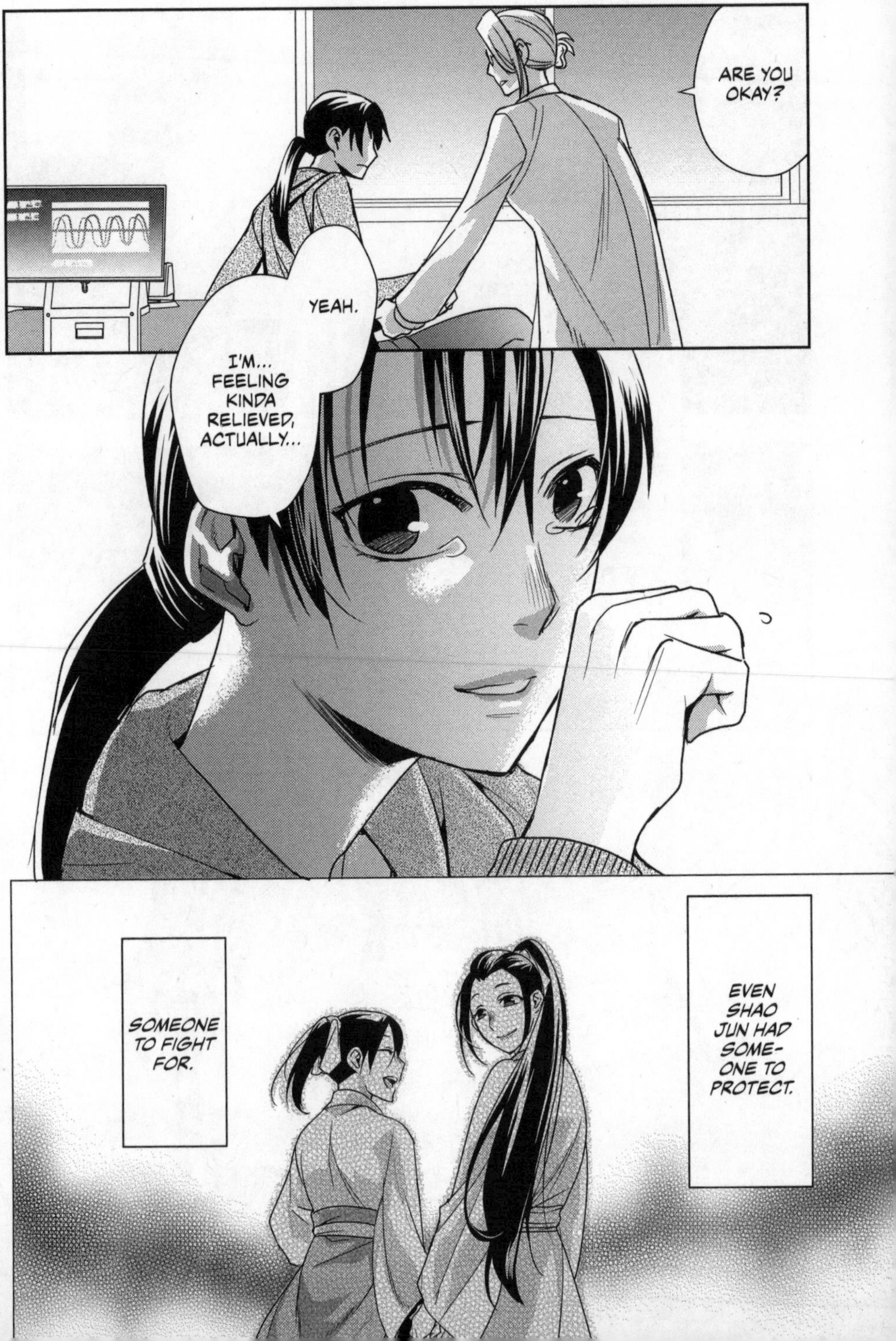
ARE YOU OKAY?
YEAH.
I'M... FEELING KINDA RELIEVED, ACTUALLY...
EVEN SHAO JUN HAD SOME-ONE TO PROTECT.
SOMEONE TO FIGHT FOR.

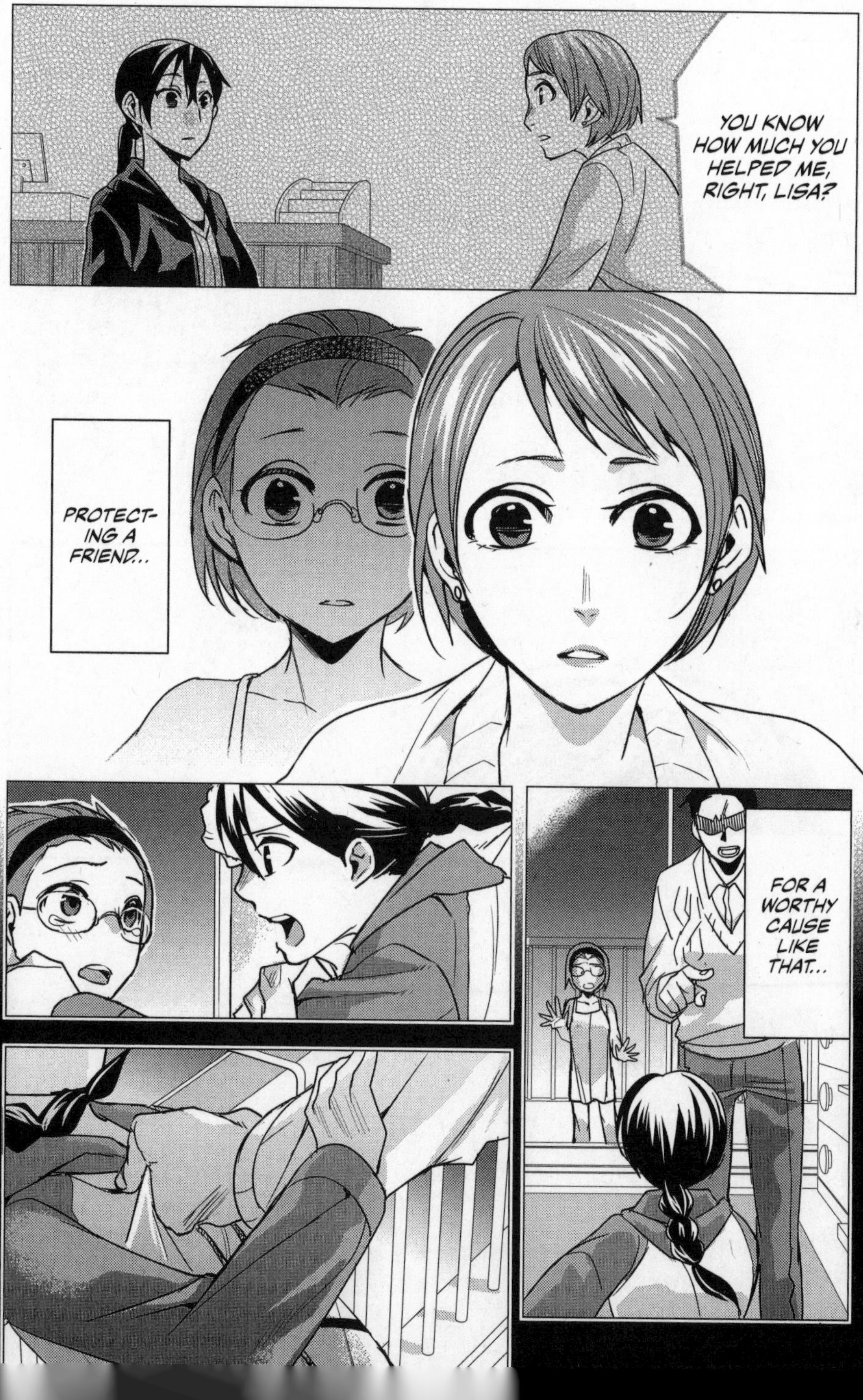
YOU KNOW HOW MUCH YOU HELPED ME, RIGHT, LISA?
PROTECT-ING A FRIEND...
FOR A WORTHY CAUSE LIKE THAT...

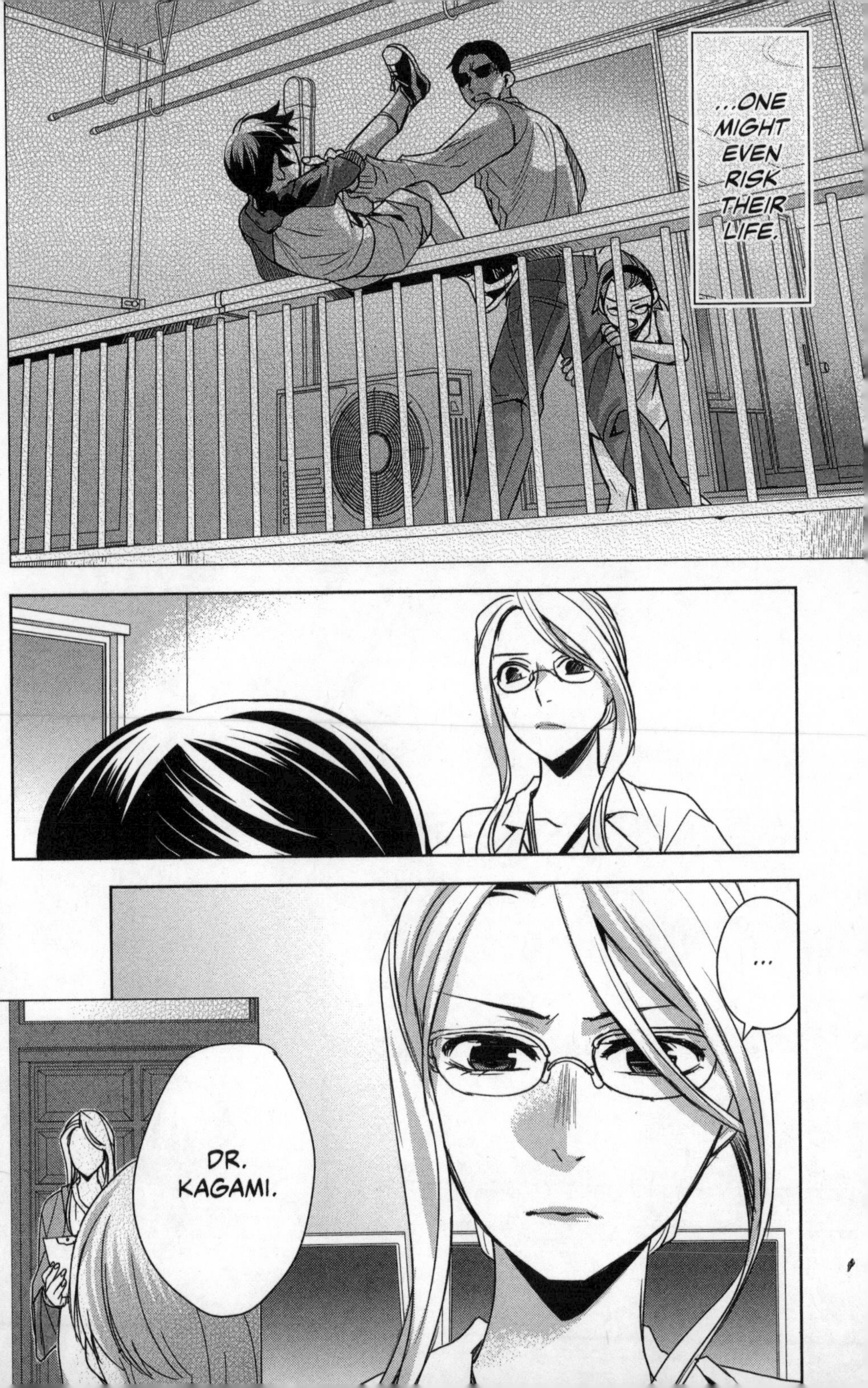
...ONE MIGHT EVEN RISK THEIR LIFE.
...
DR. KAGAMI.

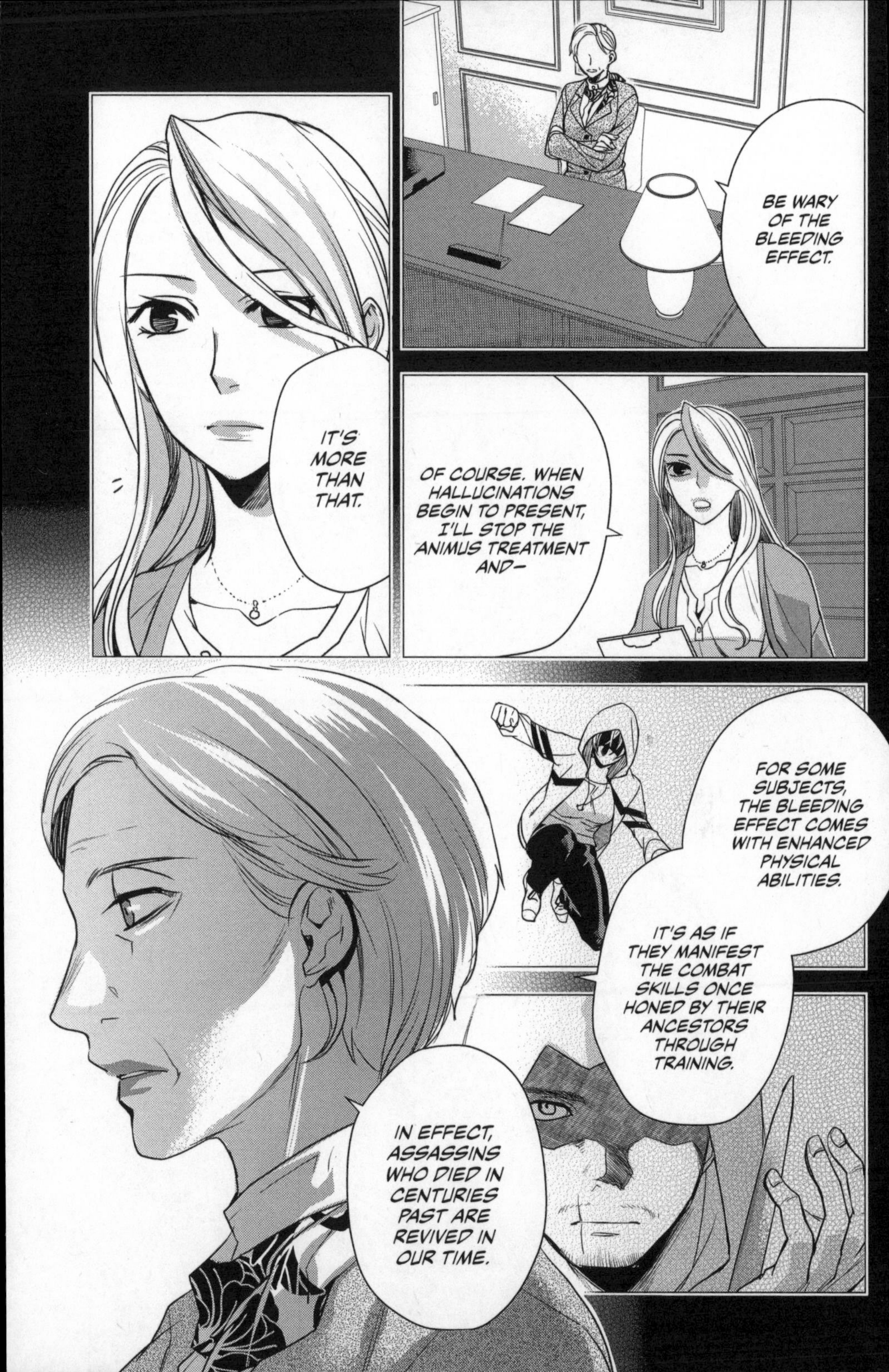
BE WARY OF THE BLEEDING EFFECT.
OF COURSE. WHEN HALLUCINATIONS BEGIN TO PRESENT, I'LL STOP THE ANIMUS TREATMENT AND—
IT'S MORE THAN THAT.
FOR SOME SUBJECTS, THE BLEEDING EFFECT COMES WITH ENHANCED PHYSICAL ABILITIES.
IT'S AS IF THEY MANIFEST THE COMBAT SKILLS ONCE HONED BY THEIR ANCESTORS THROUGH TRAINING.
IN EFFECT, ASSASSINS WHO DIED IN CENTURIES PAST ARE REVIVED IN OUR TIME.

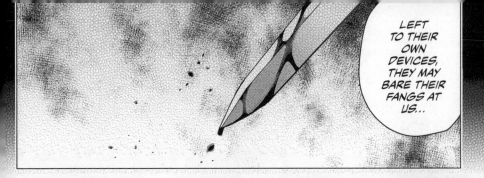

LEFT TO THEIR OWN DEVICES, THEY MAY BARE THEIR FANGS AT US...

...

THIS GIRL... SHE...

...MAY BECOME ONE OF THOSE DANGEROUS SUBJECTS.

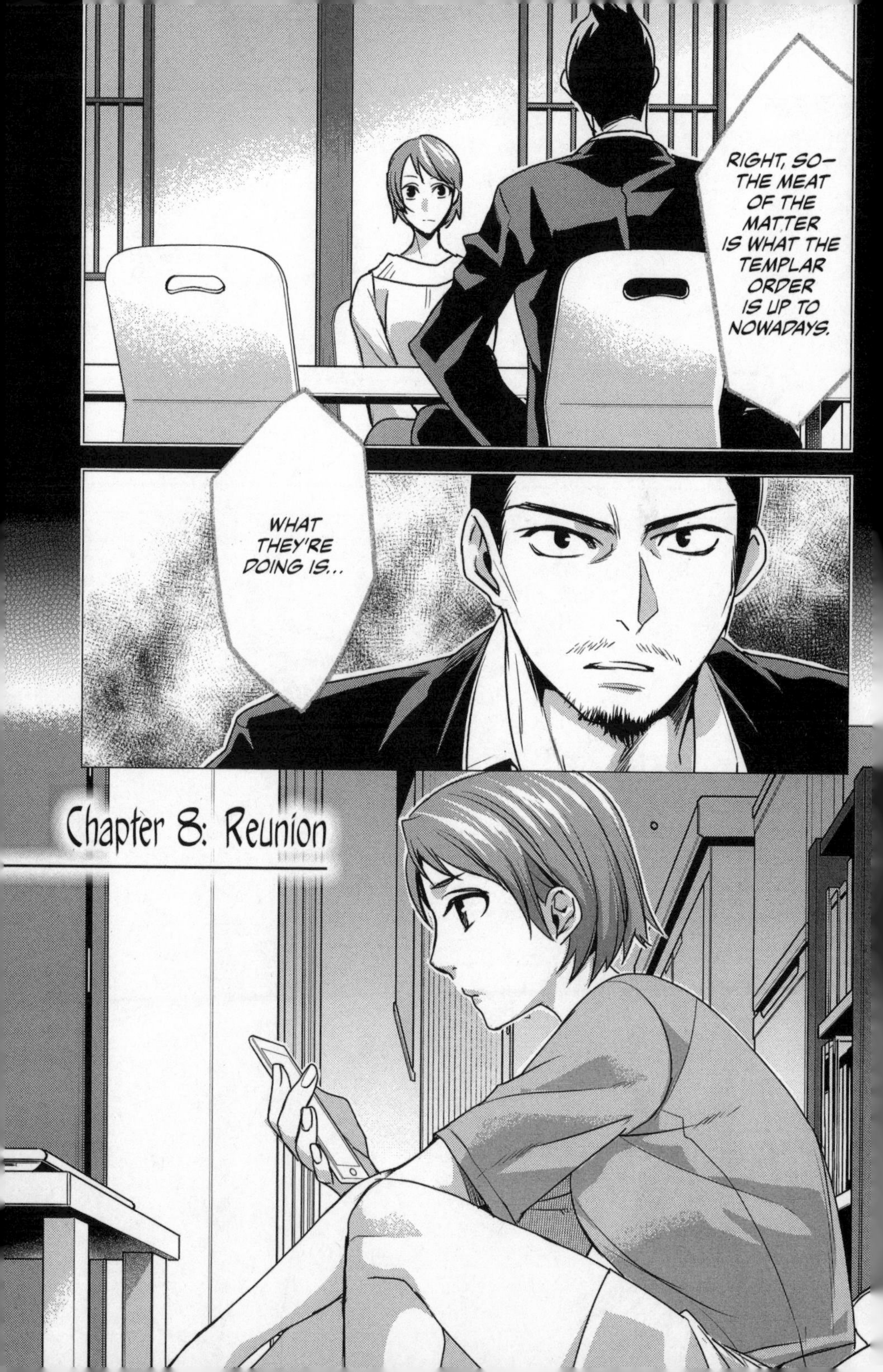
RIGHT, SO— THE MEAT OF THE MATTER IS WHAT THE TEMPLAR ORDER IS UP TO NOWADAYS.
WHAT THEY'RE DOING IS...
Chapter 8: Reunion

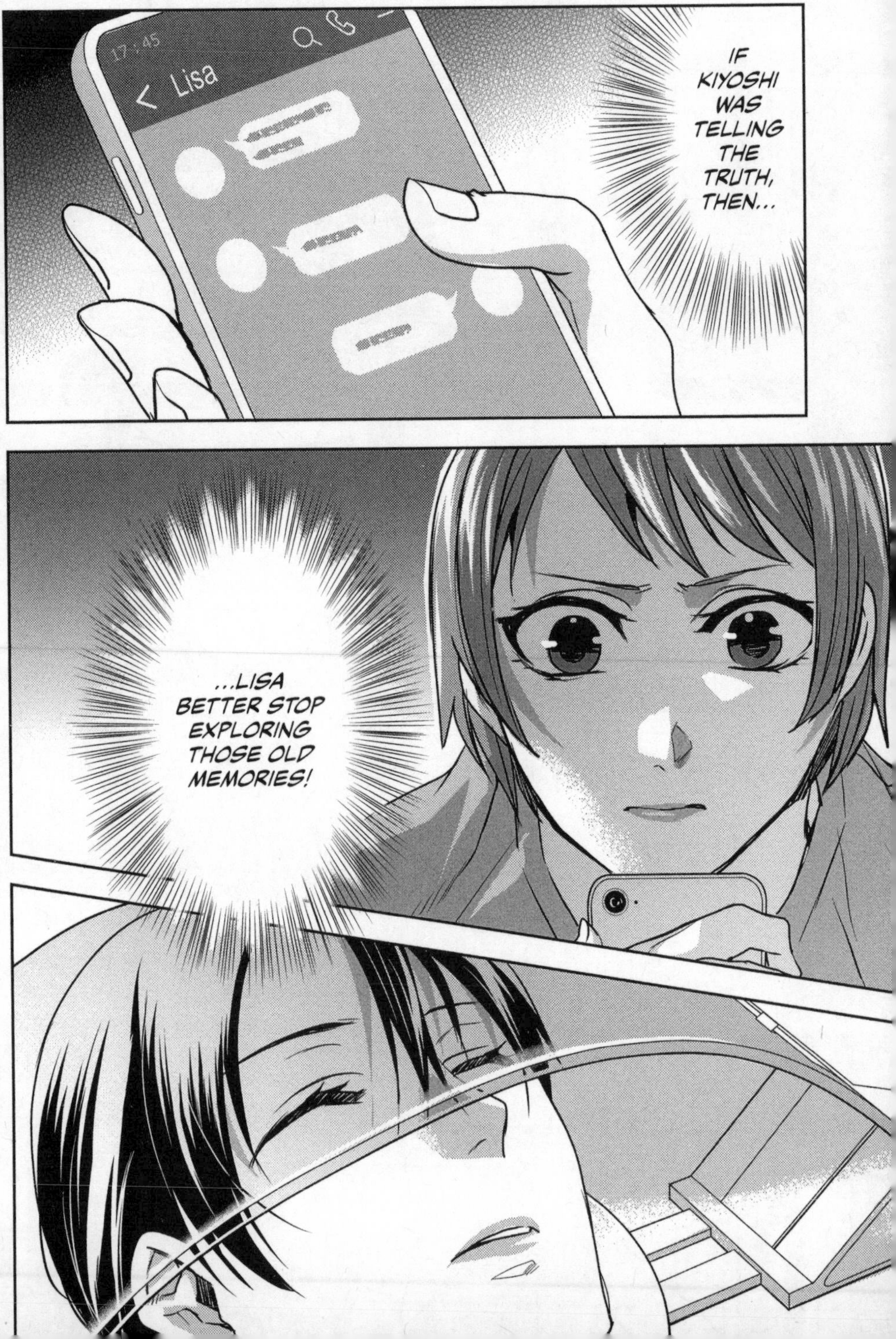
17:45
Lisa
IF KIYOSHI WAS TELLING THE TRUTH, THEN...
...LISA BETTER STOP EXPLORING THOSE OLD MEMORIES!

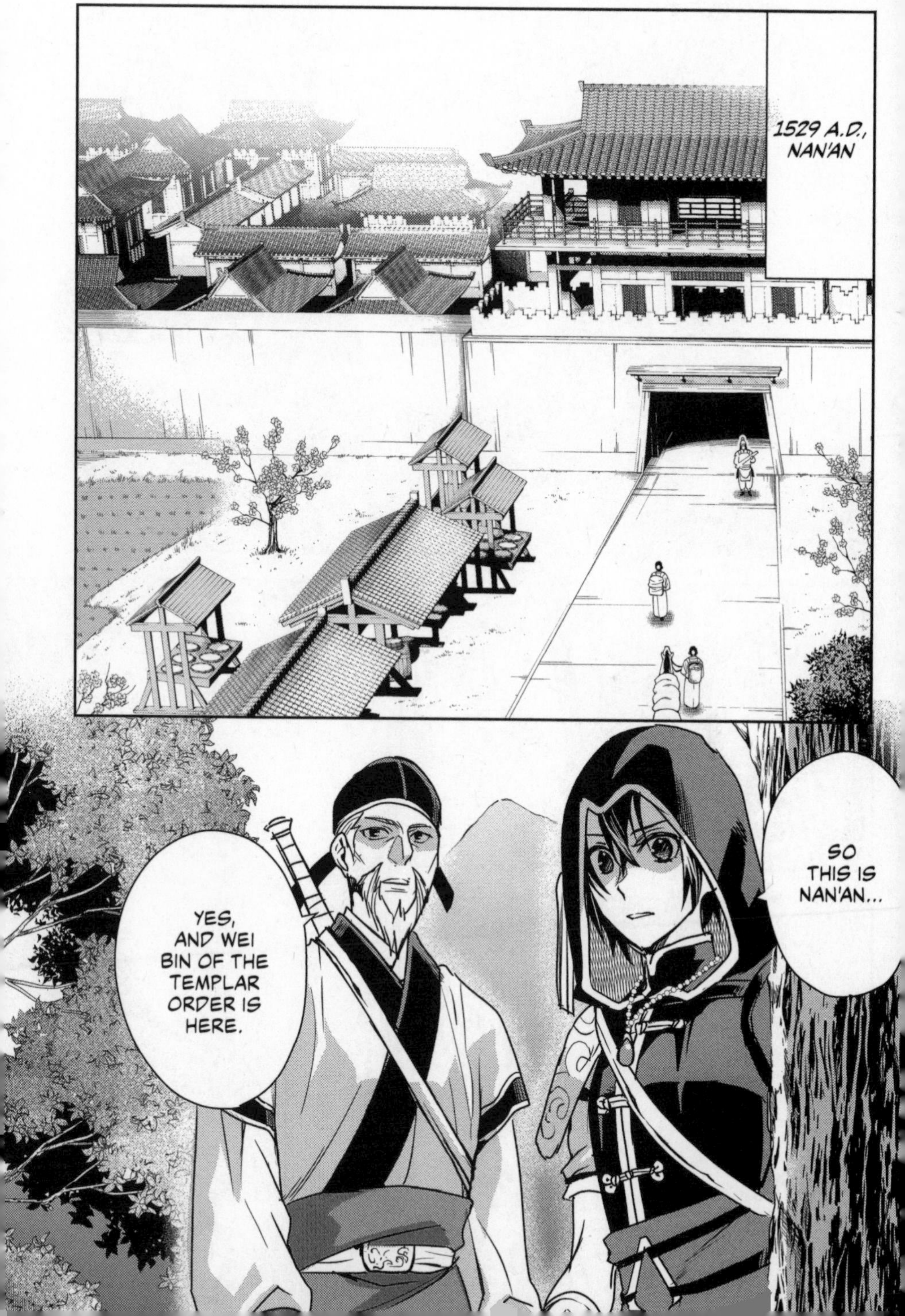
1529 A.D., NAN'AN
SO THIS IS NAN'AN...
YES, AND WEI BIN OF THE TEMPLAR ORDER IS HERE.

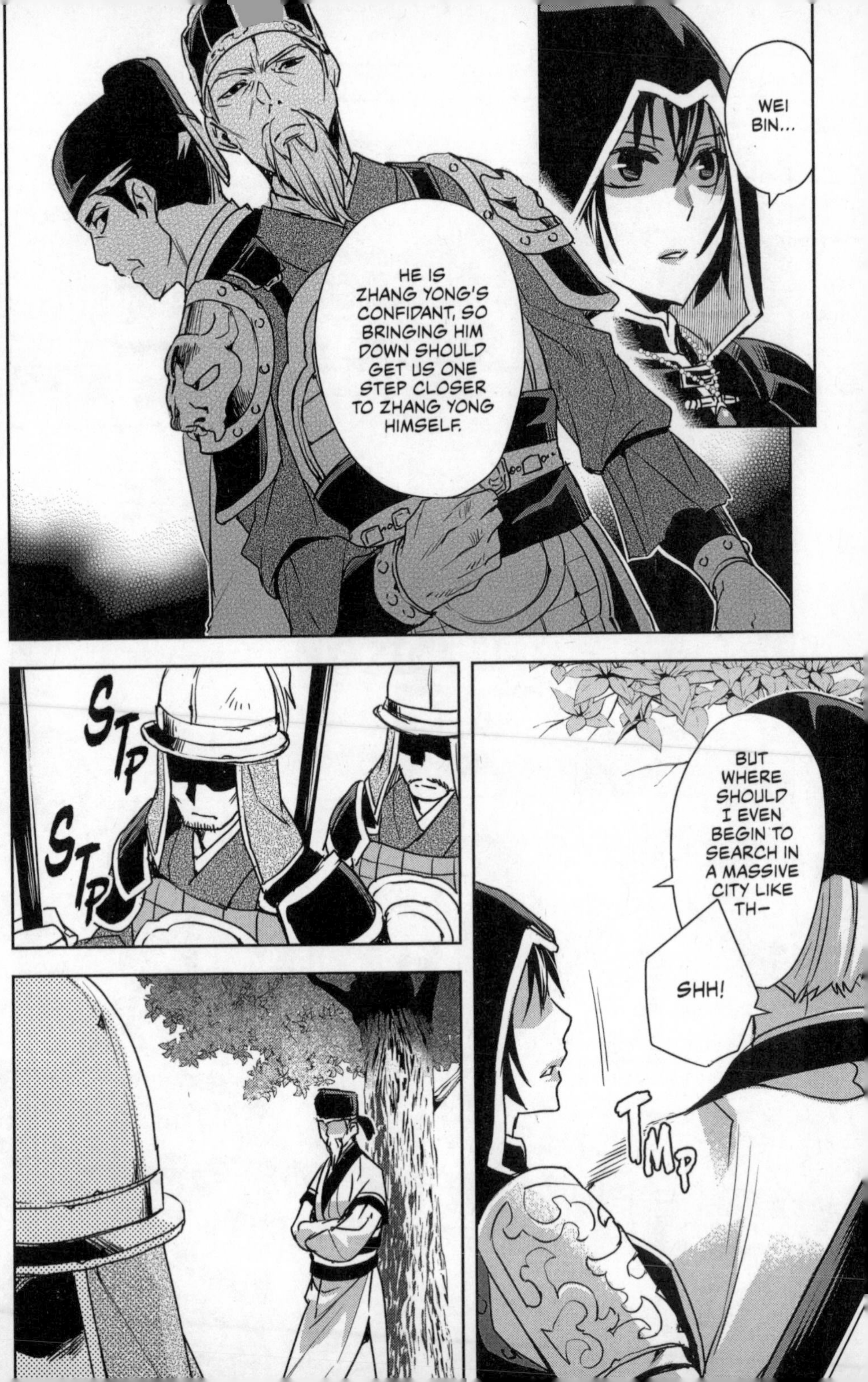

WEI BIN...
HE IS ZHANG YONG'S CONFIDANT, SO BRINGING HIM DOWN SHOULD GET US ONE STEP CLOSER TO ZHANG YONG HIMSELF.
BUT WHERE SHOULD I EVEN BEGIN TO SEARCH IN A MASSIVE CITY LIKE TH—
SHH!
TMP
STP
STP

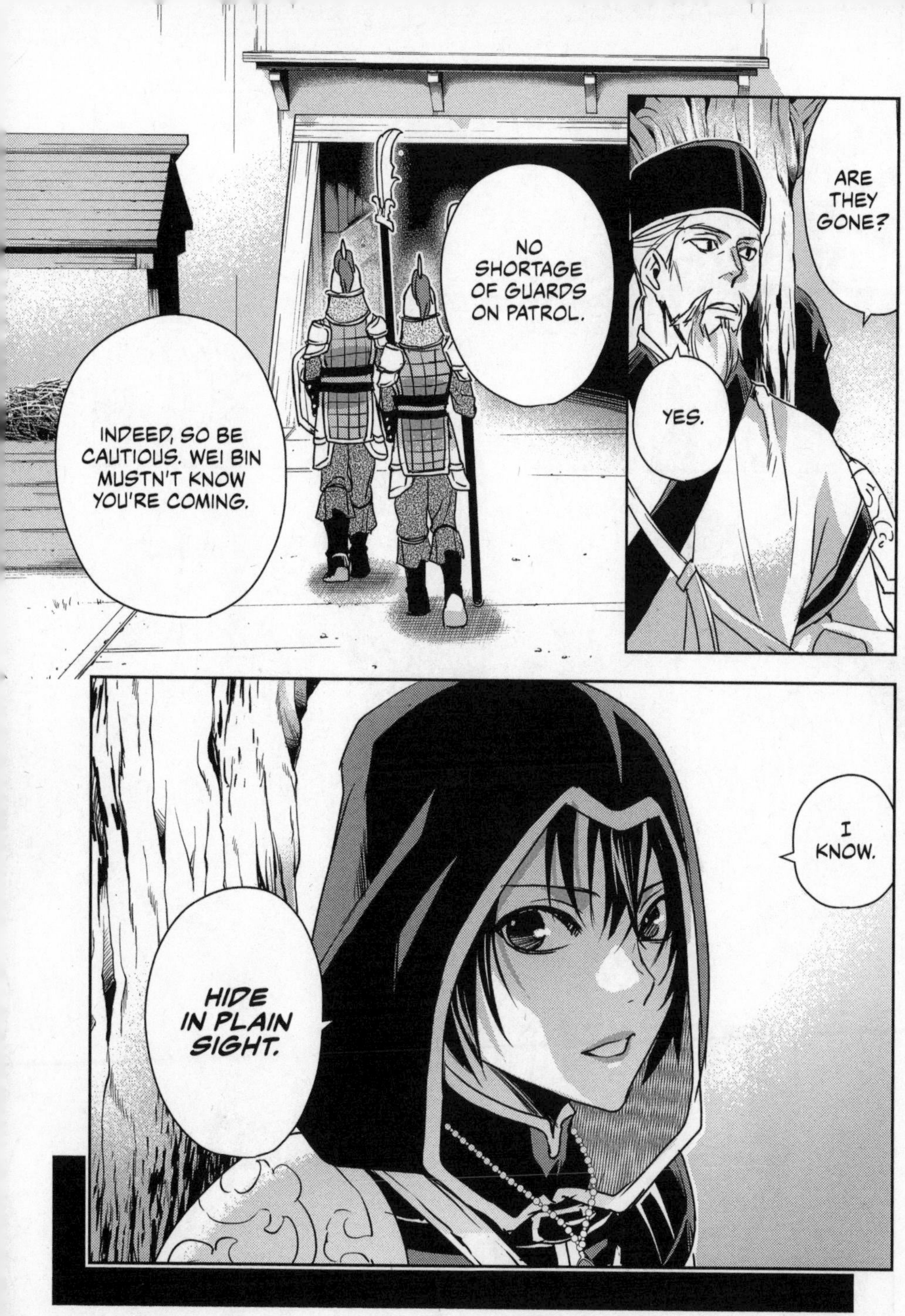
ARE THEY GONE?
YES.
NO SHORTAGE OF GUARDS ON PATROL.
INDEED, SO BE CAUTIOUS. WEI BIN MUSTN'T KNOW YOU'RE COMING.
I KNOW.
HIDE IN PLAIN SIGHT.

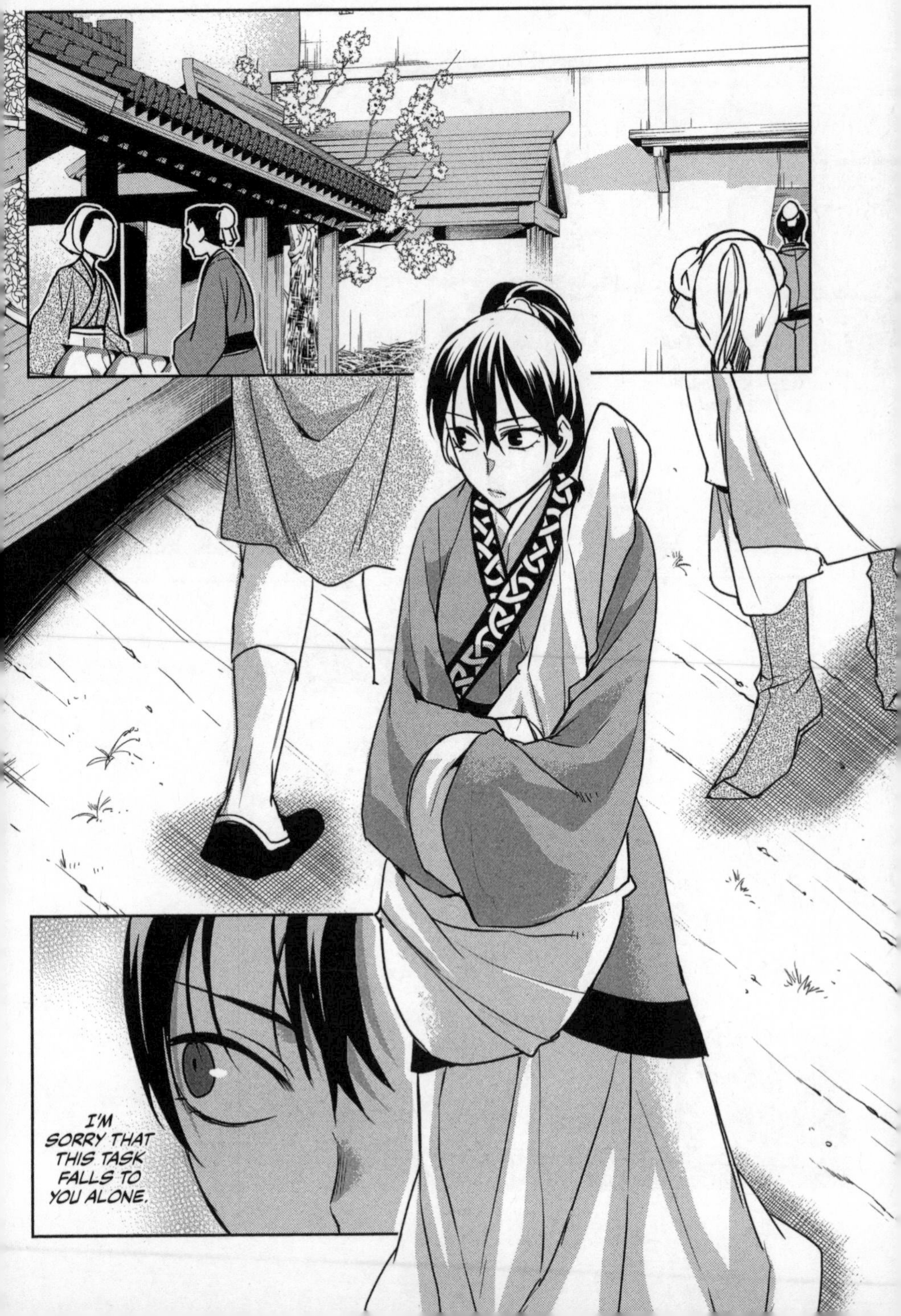
I'M SORRY THAT THIS TASK FALLS TO YOU ALONE.

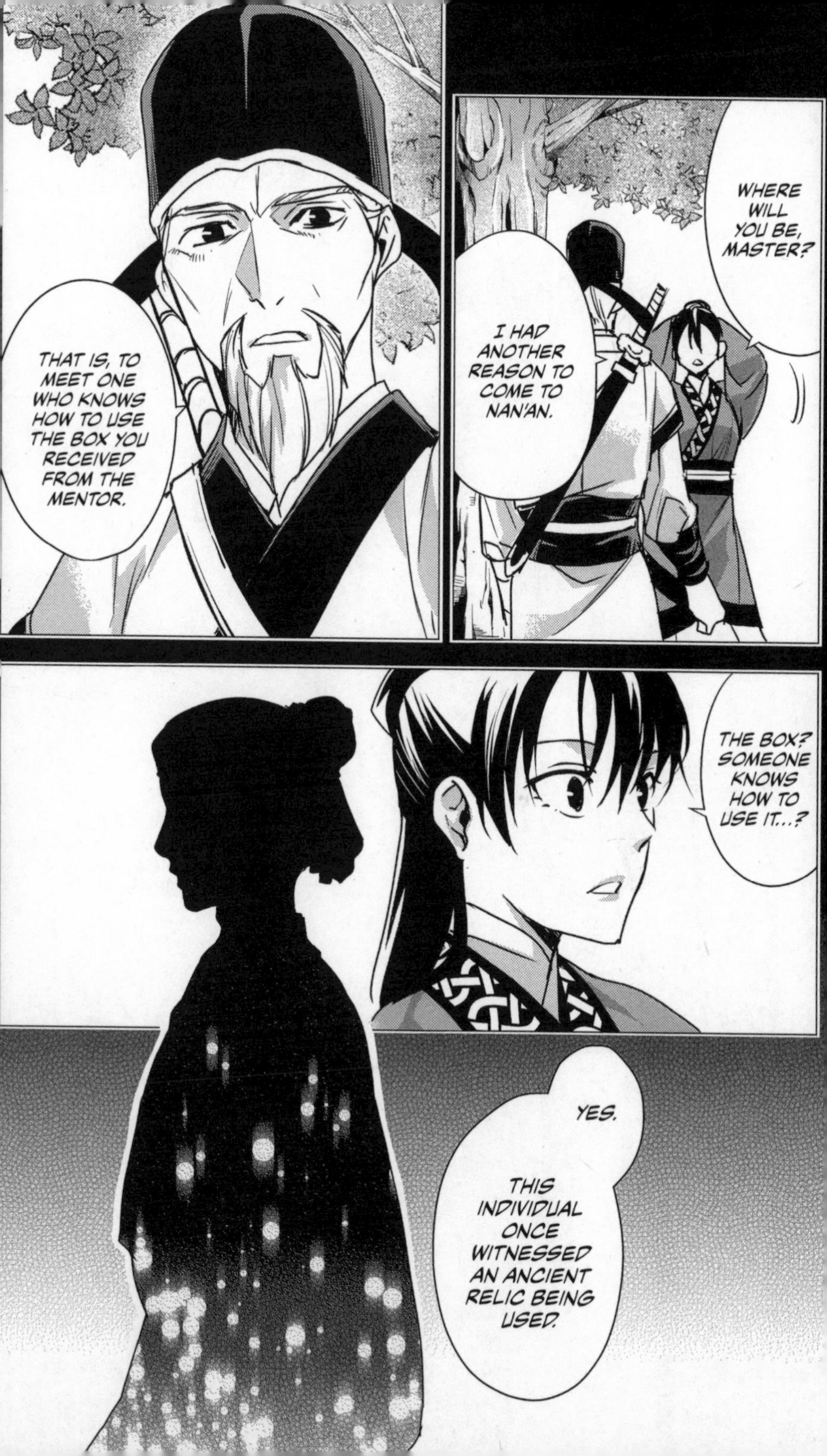
WHERE WILL YOU BE, MASTER?
I HAD ANOTHER REASON TO COME TO NAN'AN.
THAT IS, TO MEET ONE WHO KNOWS HOW TO USE THE BOX YOU RECEIVED FROM THE MENTOR.
THE BOX? SOMEONE KNOWS HOW TO USE IT...?
YES.
THIS INDIVIDUAL ONCE WITNESSED AN ANCIENT RELIC BEING USED.

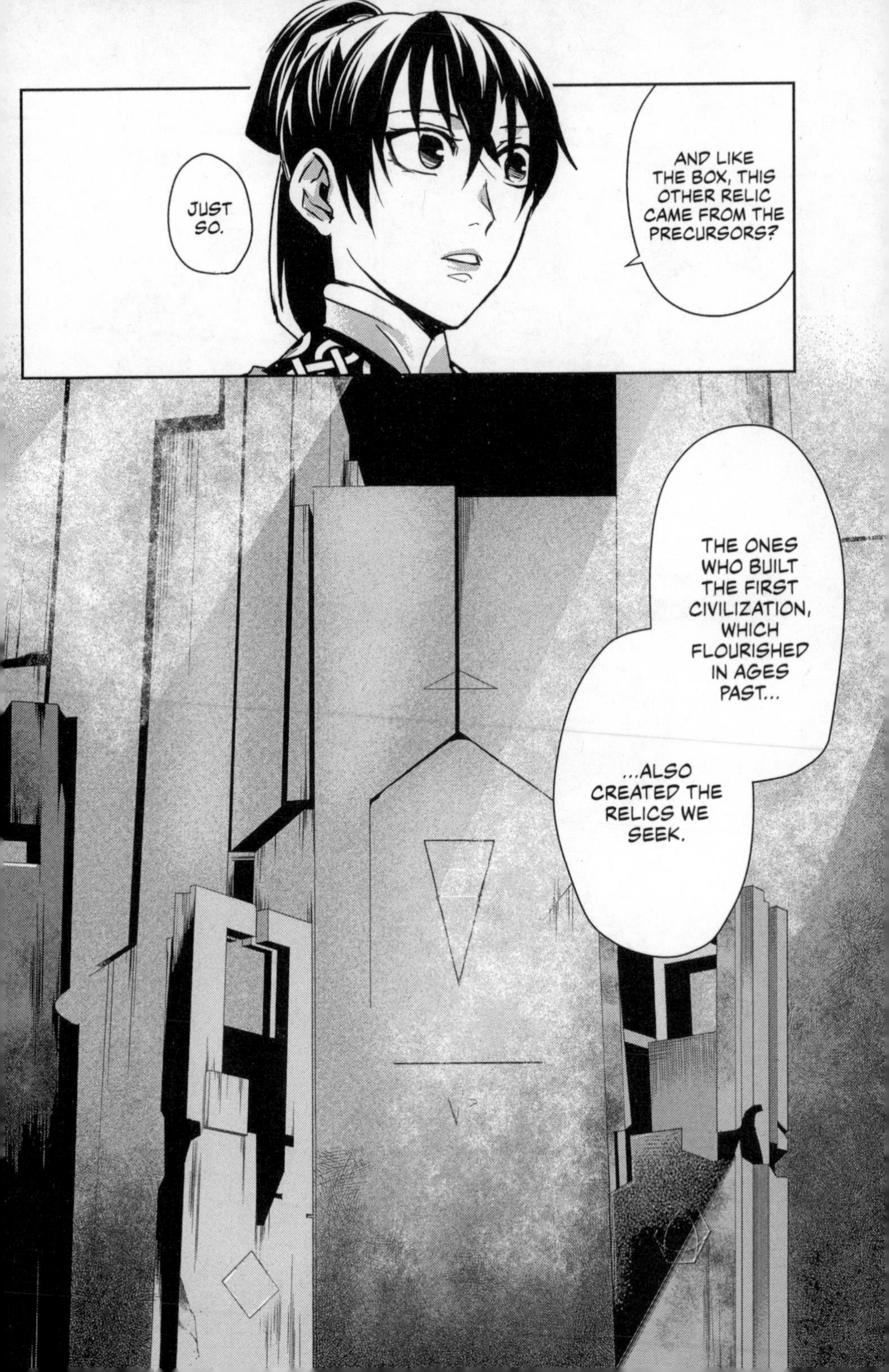
AND LIKE THE BOX, THIS OTHER RELIC CAME FROM THE PRECURSORS?
JUST SO.
THE ONES WHO BUILT THE FIRST CIVILIZATION, WHICH FLOURISHED IN AGES PAST...
...ALSO CREATED THE RELICS WE SEEK.

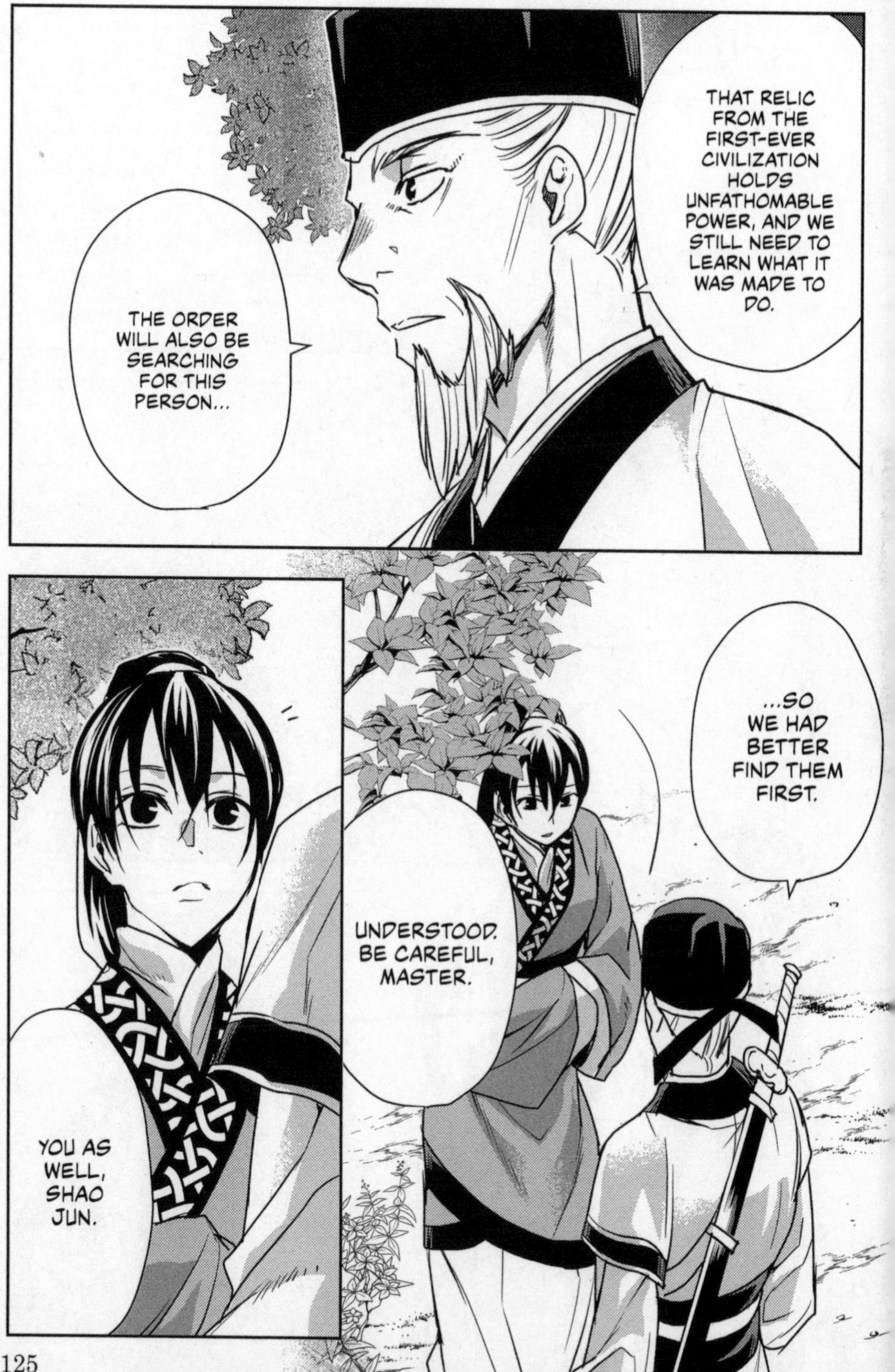
THAT RELIC FROM THE FIRST-EVER CIVILIZATION HOLDS UNFATHOMABLE POWER, AND WE STILL NEED TO LEARN WHAT IT WAS MADE TO DO.
THE ORDER WILL ALSO BE SEARCHING FOR THIS PERSON...
...SO WE HAD BETTER FIND THEM FIRST.
UNDERSTOOD. BE CAREFUL, MASTER.
YOU AS WELL, SHAO JUN.

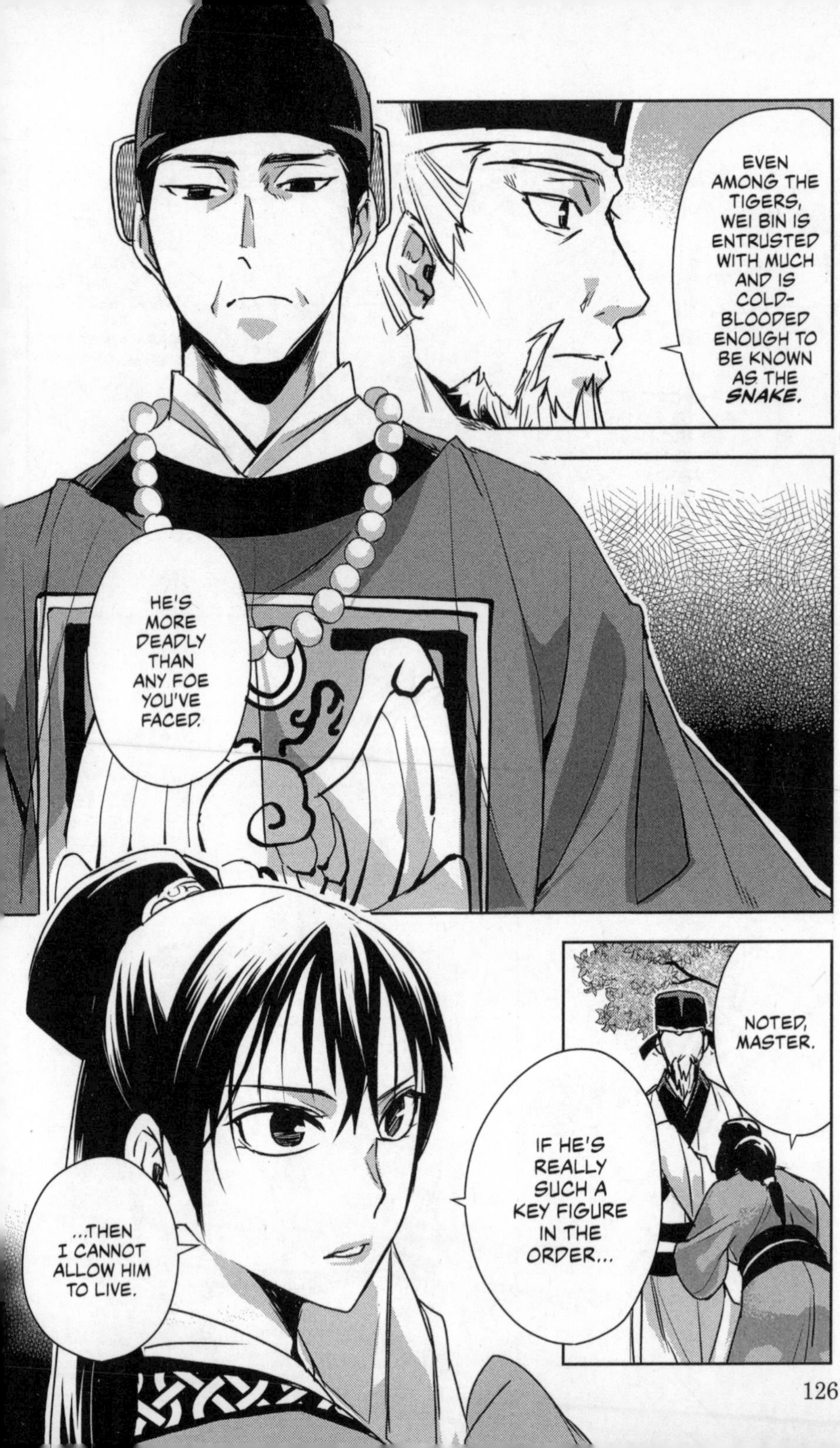
EVEN AMONG THE TIGERS, WEI BIN IS ENTRUSTED WITH MUCH AND IS COLD-BLOODED ENOUGH TO BE KNOWN AS THE *SNAKE.*
HE'S MORE DEADLY THAN ANY FOE YOU'VE FACED.
NOTED, MASTER.
IF HE'S REALLY SUCH A KEY FIGURE IN THE ORDER...
...THEN I CANNOT ALLOW HIM TO LIVE.

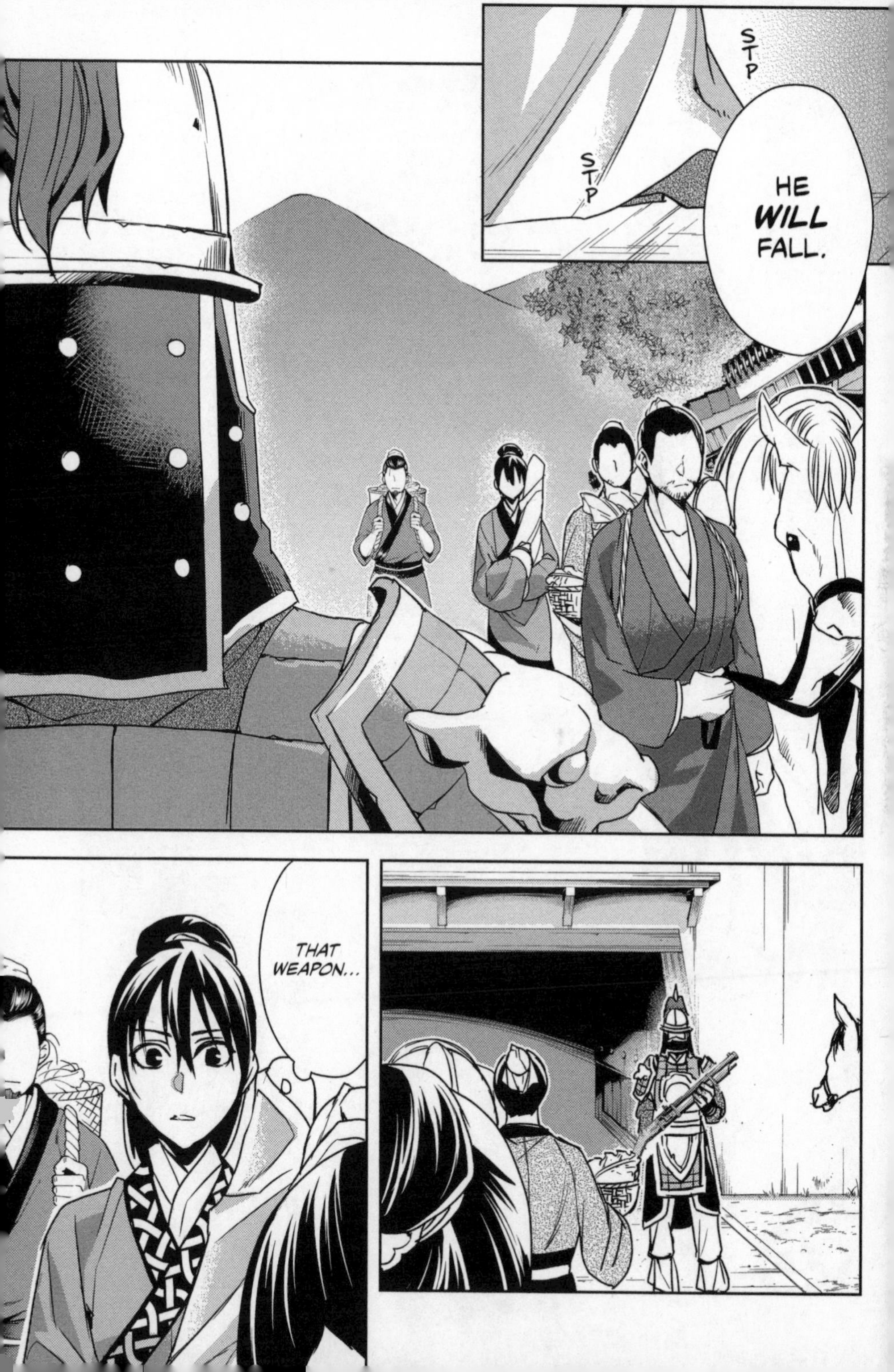
STP
STP
HE WILL FALL.
THAT WEAPON...

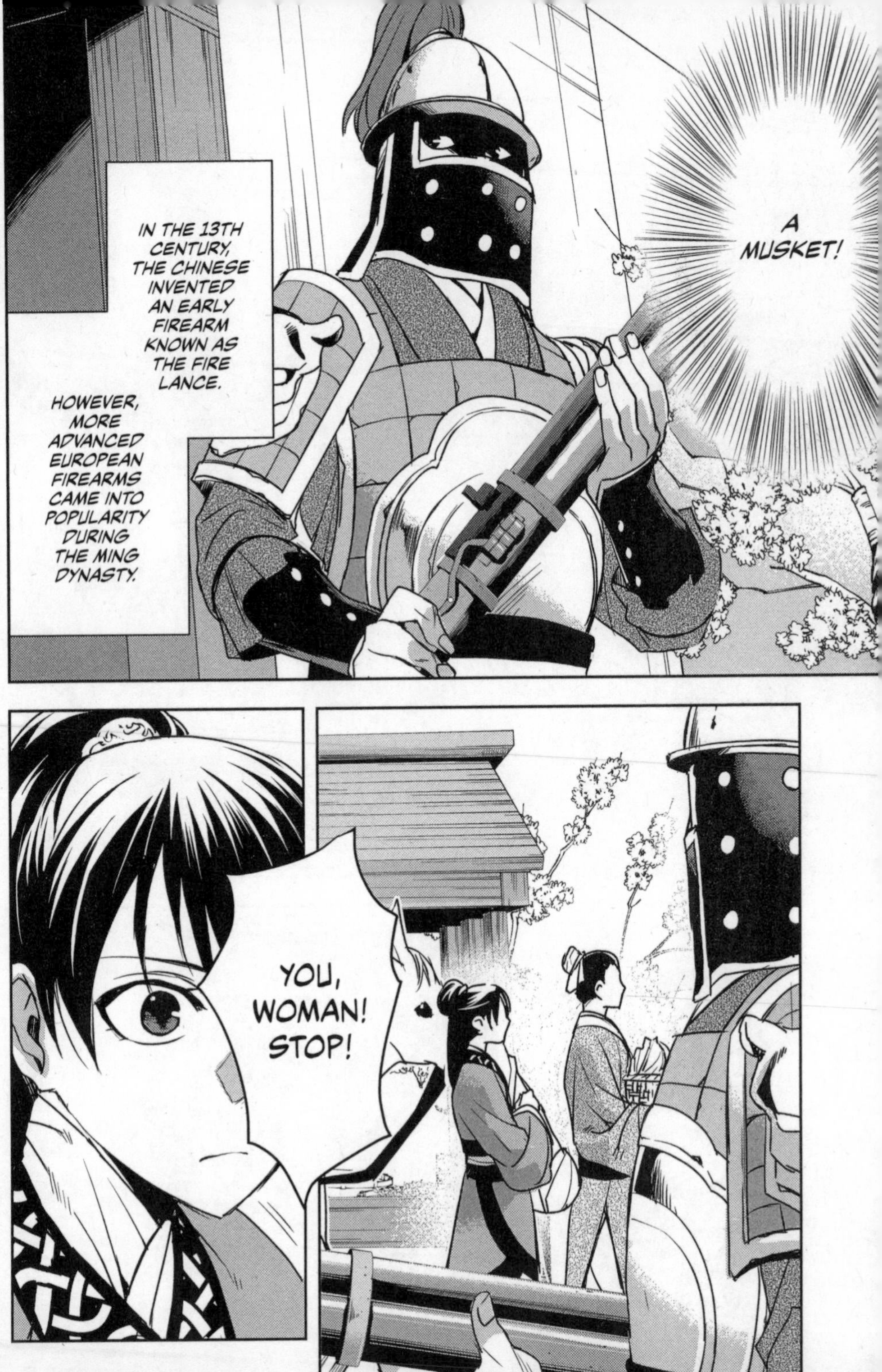
A MUSKET!
IN THE 13TH CENTURY, THE CHINESE INVENTED AN EARLY FIREARM KNOWN AS THE FIRE LANCE.
HOWEVER, MORE ADVANCED EUROPEAN FIREARMS CAME INTO POPULARITY DURING THE MING DYNASTY.
YOU, WOMAN! STOP!

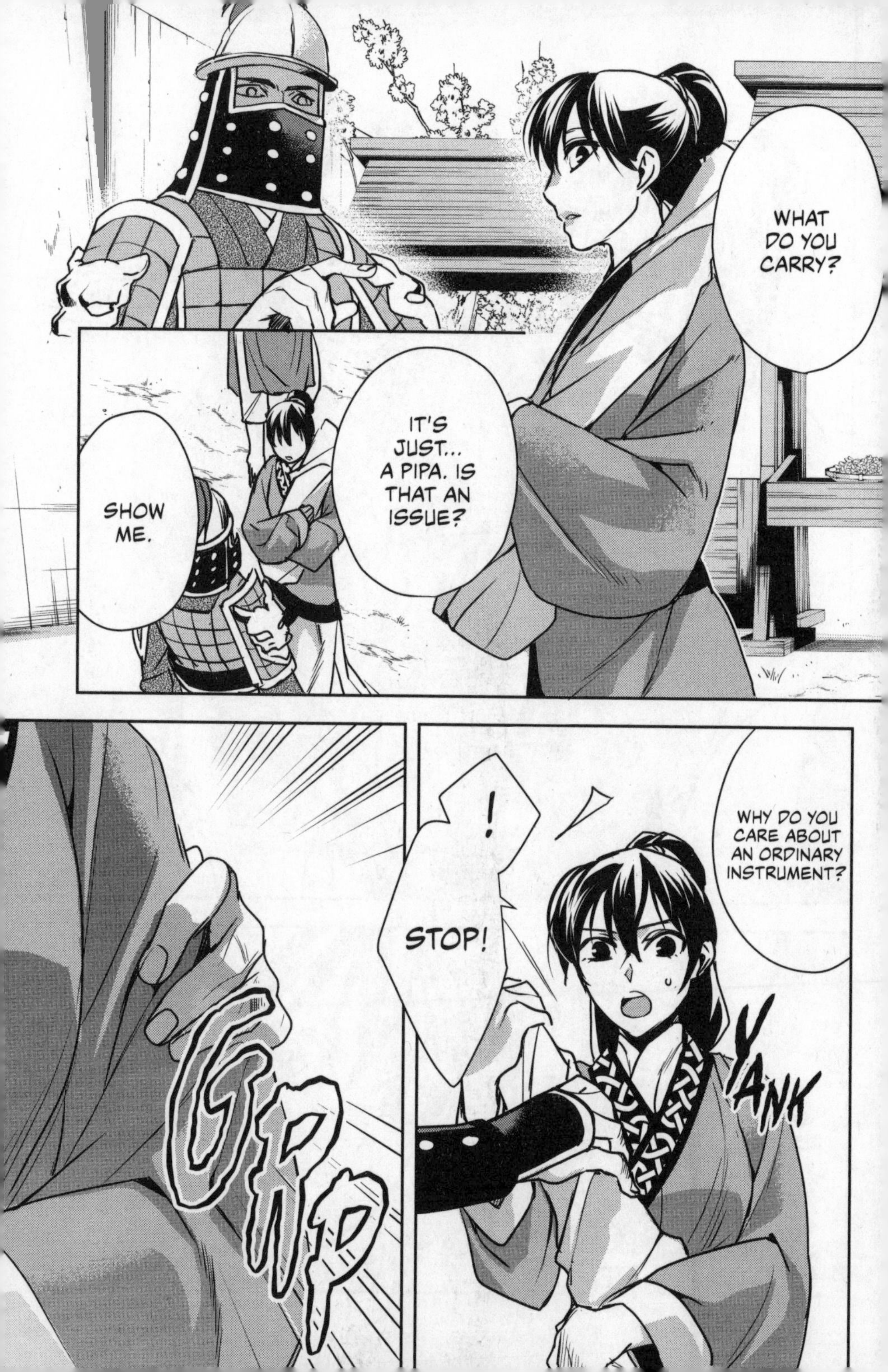
WHAT DO YOU CARRY?
IT'S JUST... A PIPA. IS THAT AN ISSUE?
SHOW ME.
WHY DO YOU CARE ABOUT AN ORDINARY INSTRUMENT?
!
STOP!
YANK
GRIP

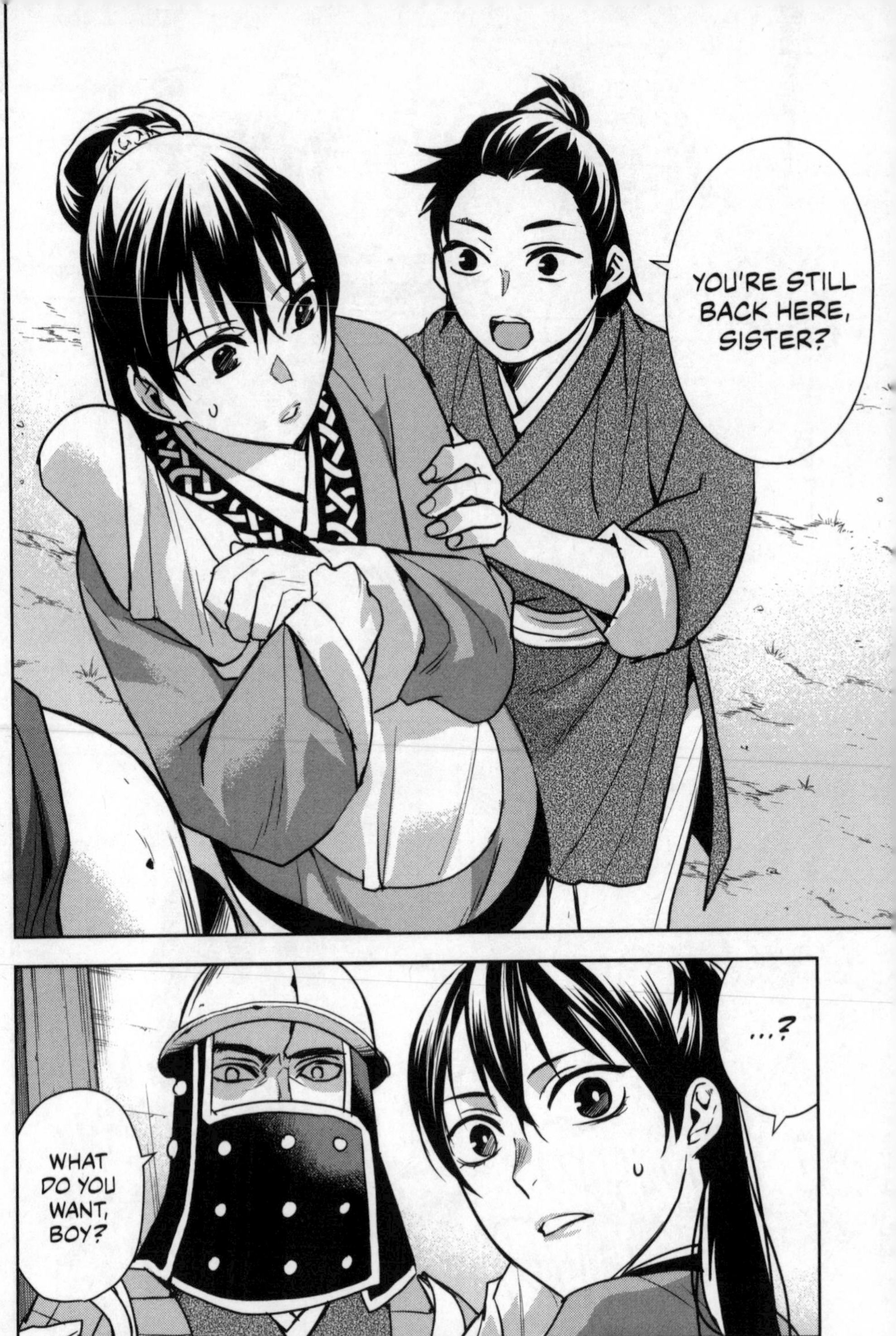
YOU'RE STILL BACK HERE, SISTER?
...?
WHAT DO YOU WANT, BOY?

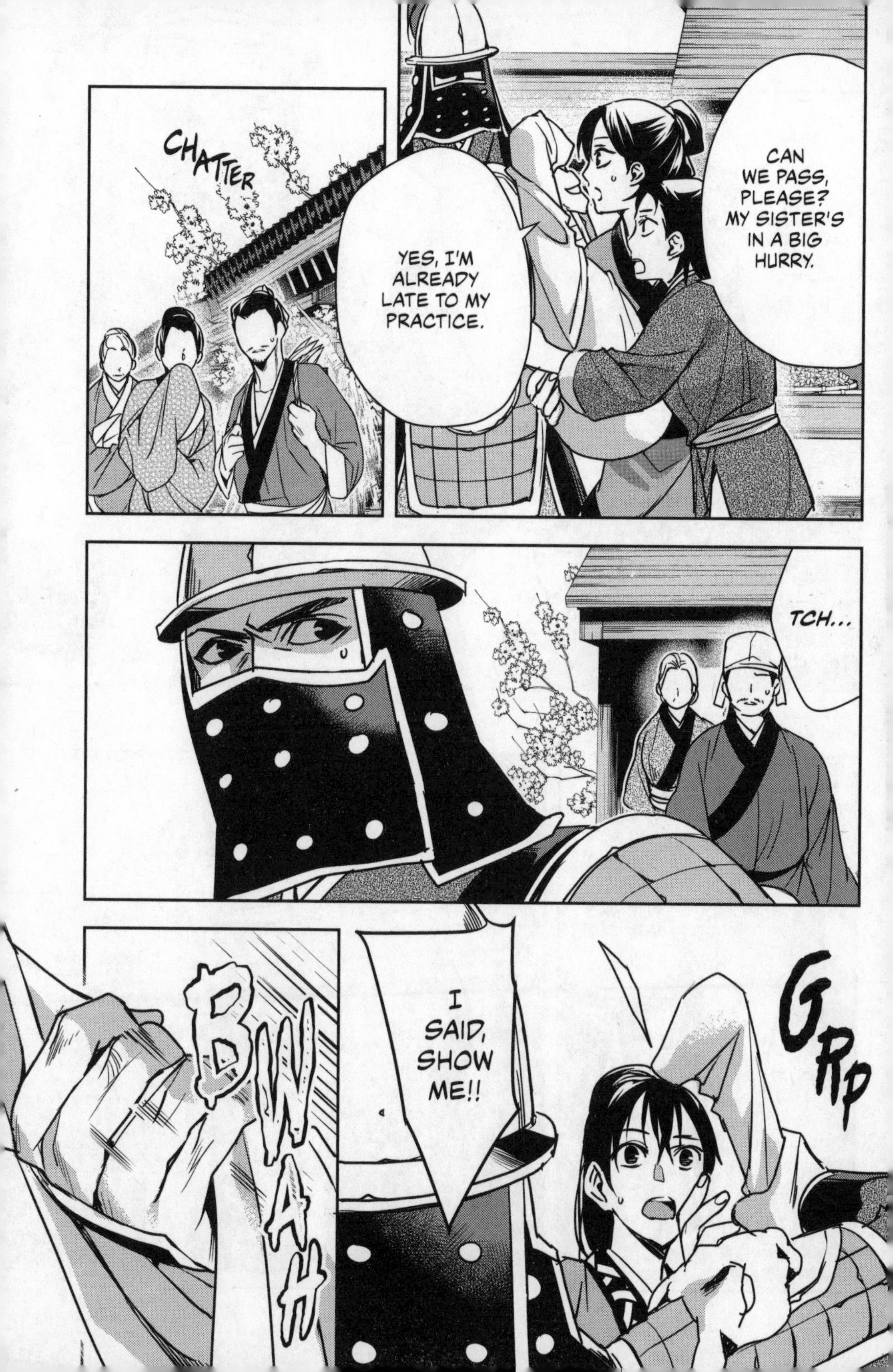
CAN WE PASS, PLEASE? MY SISTER'S IN A BIG HURRY.
YES, I'M ALREADY LATE TO MY PRACTICE.
CHATTER
TCH...
GRP
I SAID, SHOW ME!!
BWAH

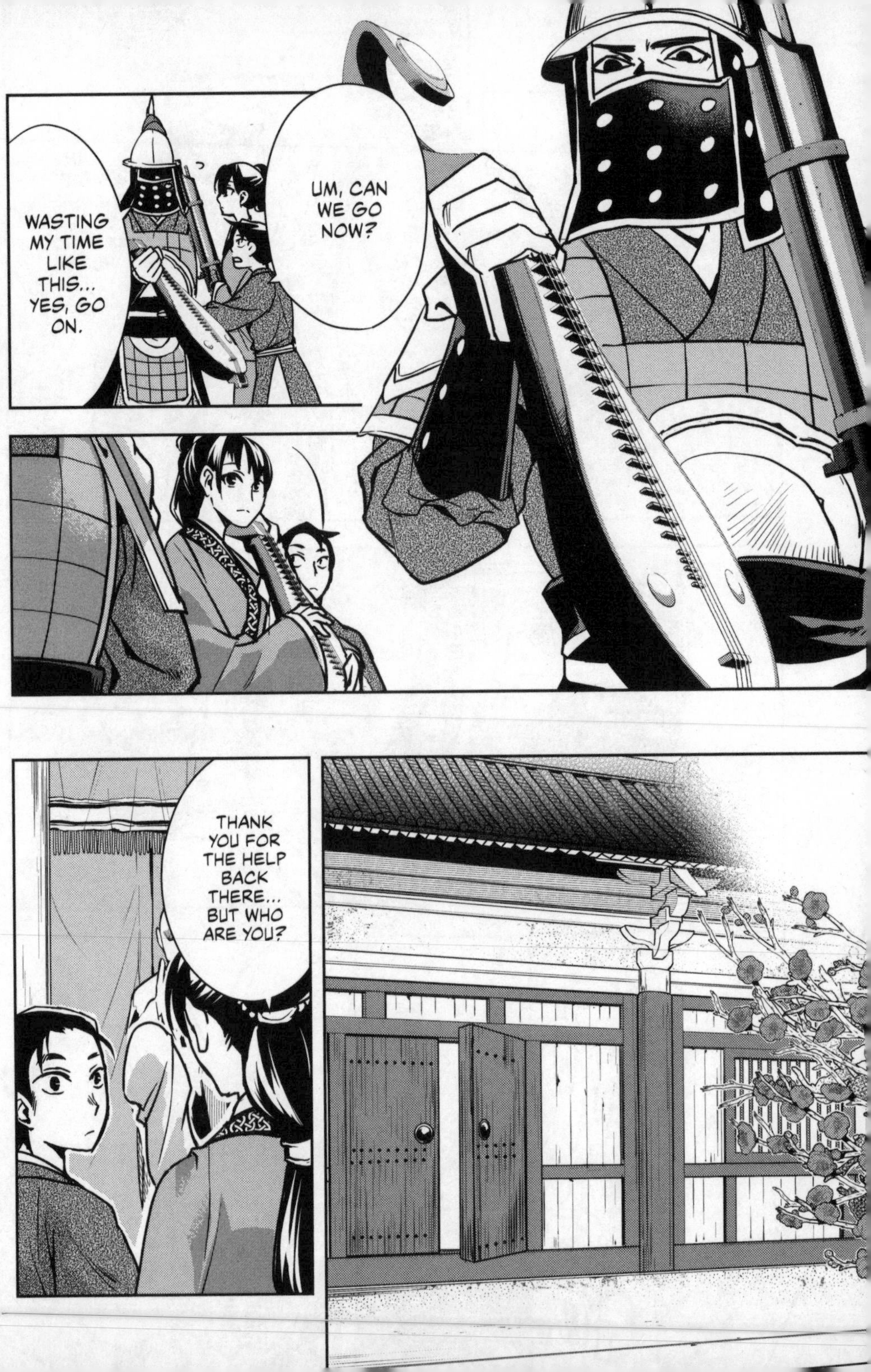
UM, CAN WE GO NOW?
WASTING MY TIME LIKE THIS... YES, GO ON.
THANK YOU FOR THE HELP BACK THERE... BUT WHO ARE YOU?

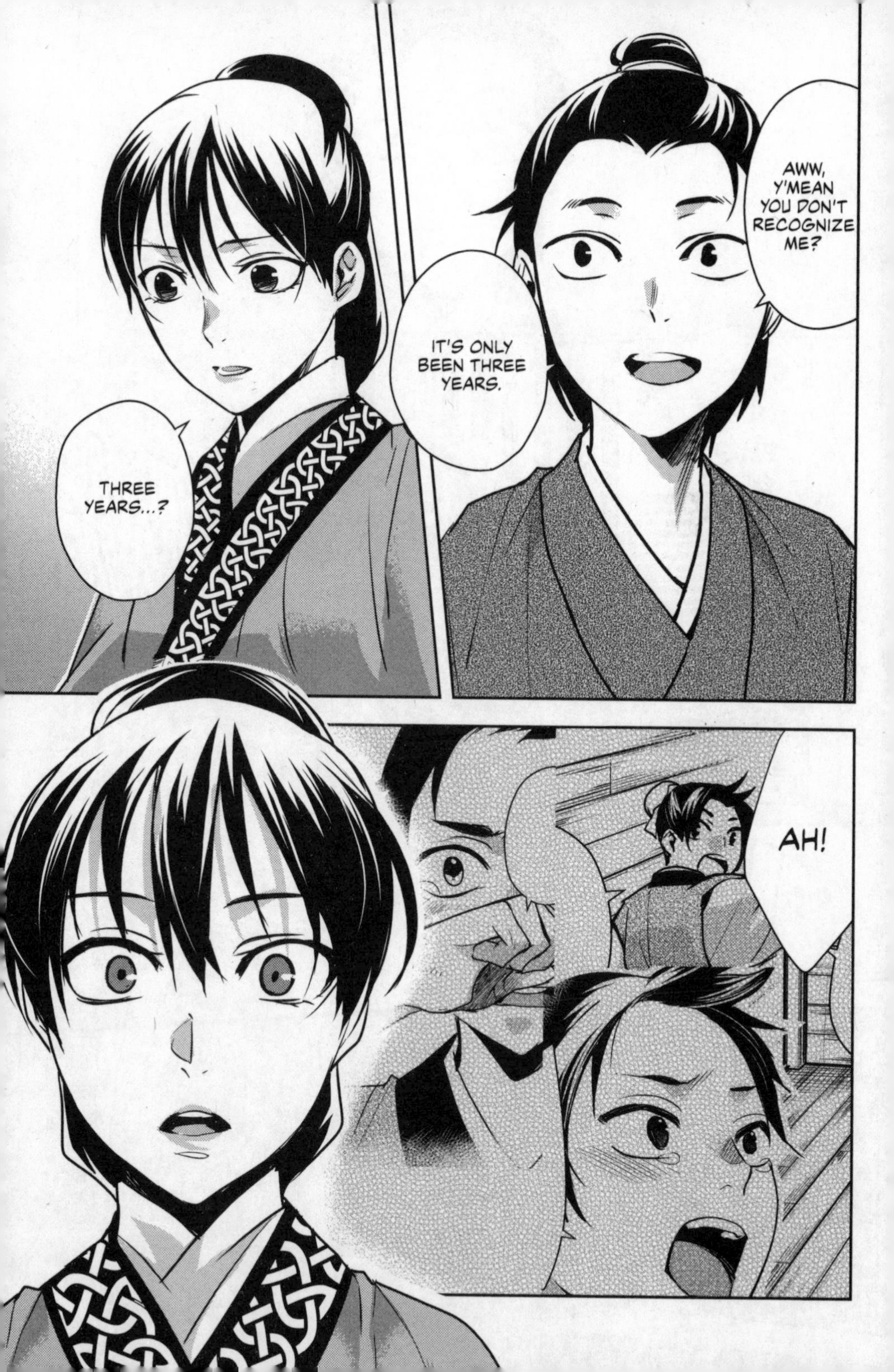
AWW, Y'MEAN YOU DON'T RECOGNIZE ME?
IT'S ONLY BEEN THREE YEARS.
THREE YEARS...?
AH!

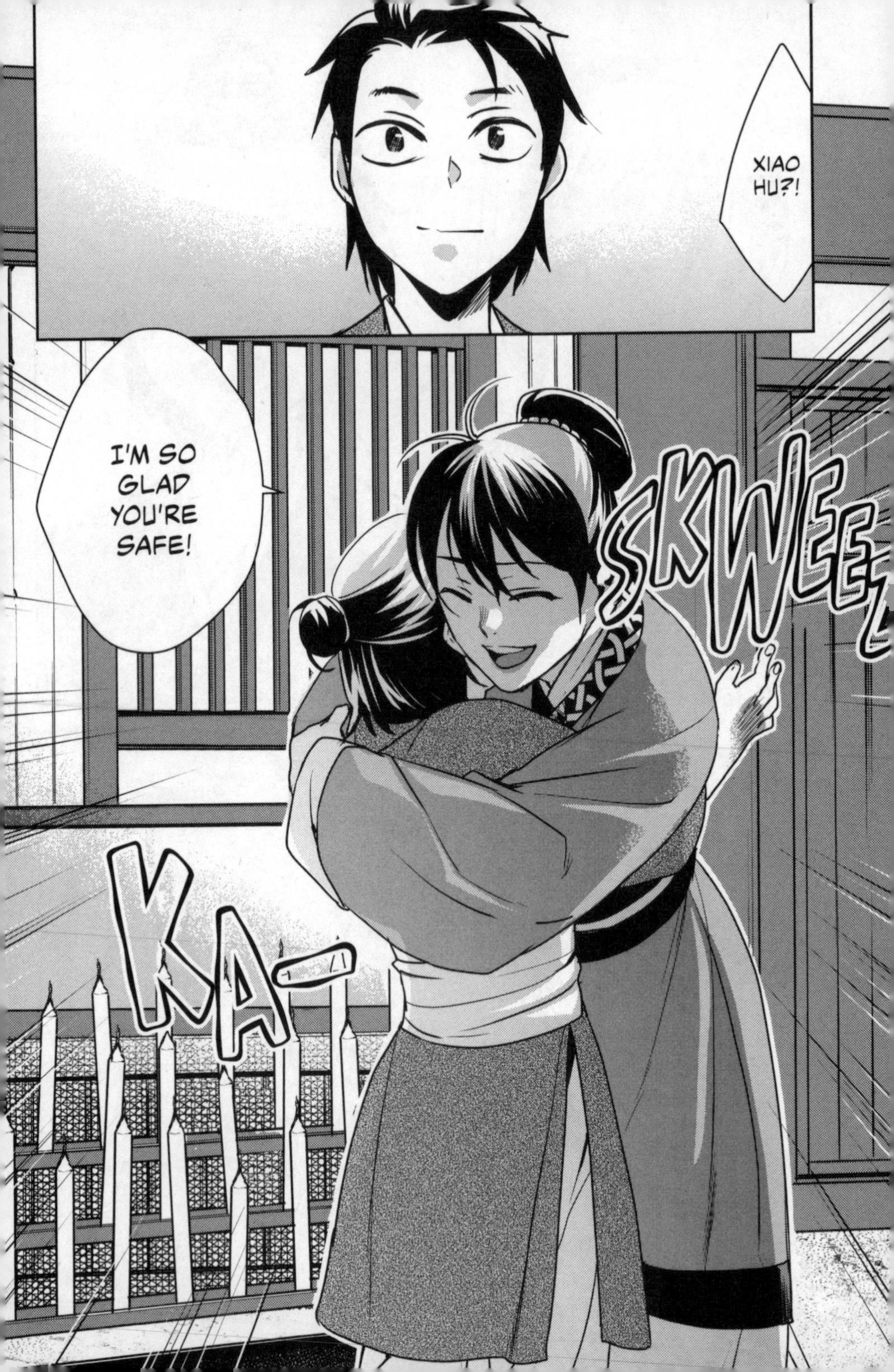
XIAO HU?!
I'M SO GLAD YOU'RE SAFE!
SKWEE
KA-

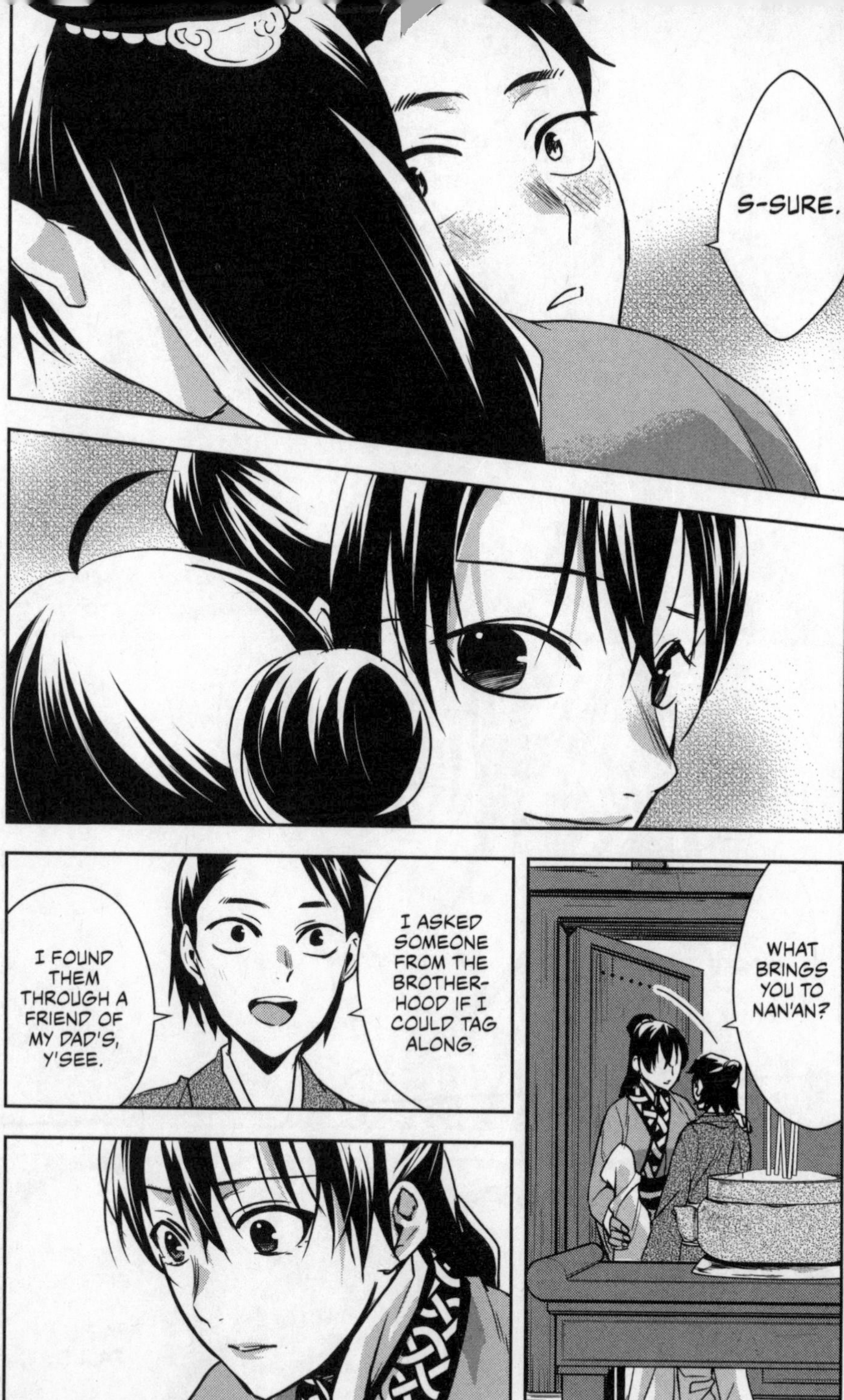
S-SURE.
WHAT BRINGS YOU TO NAN'AN?
I ASKED SOMEONE FROM THE BROTHER-HOOD IF I COULD TAG ALONG.
I FOUND THEM THROUGH A FRIEND OF MY DAD'S, Y'SEE.

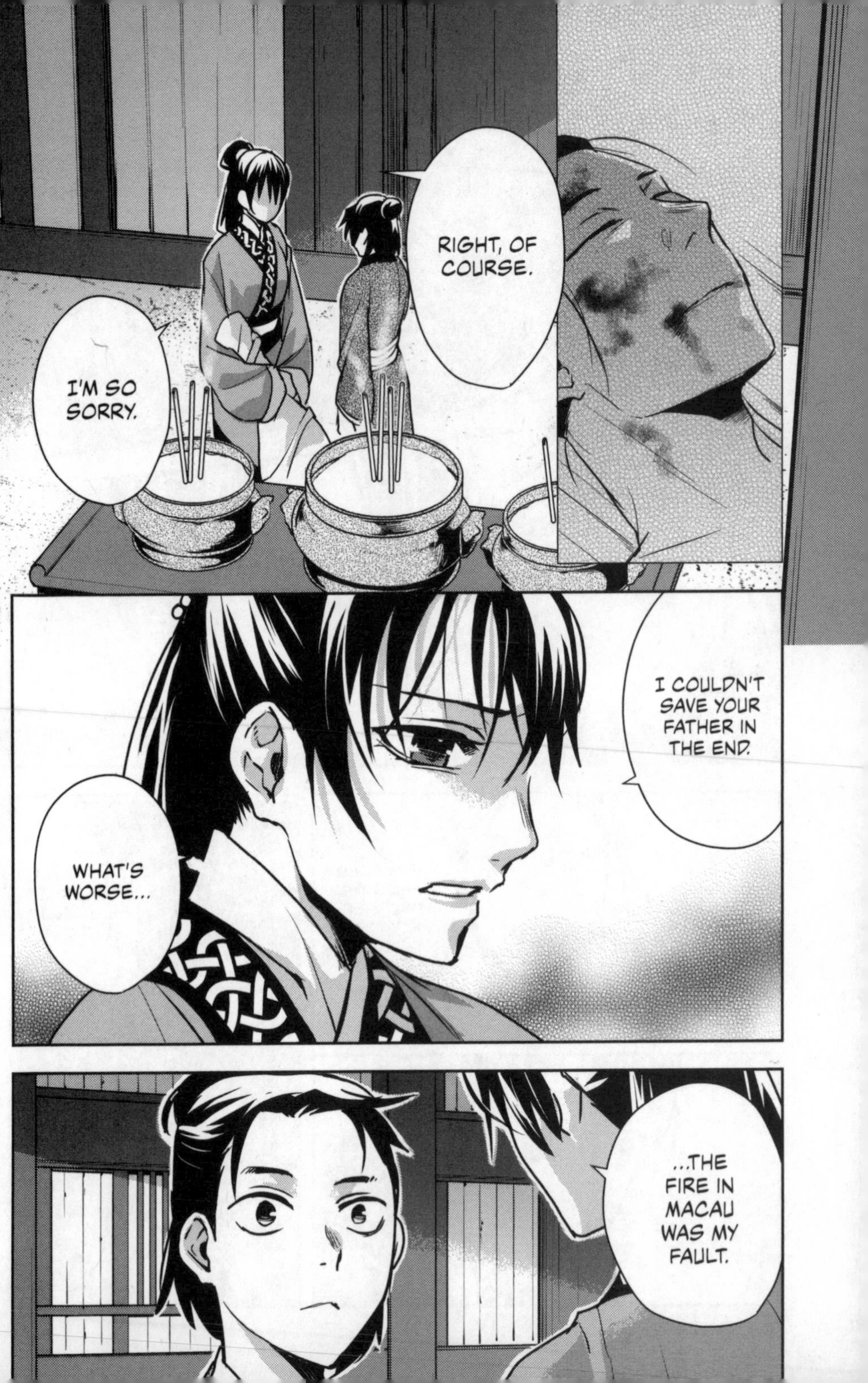
RIGHT, OF COURSE.
I'M SO SORRY.
I COULDN'T SAVE YOUR FATHER IN THE END.
WHAT'S WORSE...
...THE FIRE IN MACAU WAS MY FAULT.

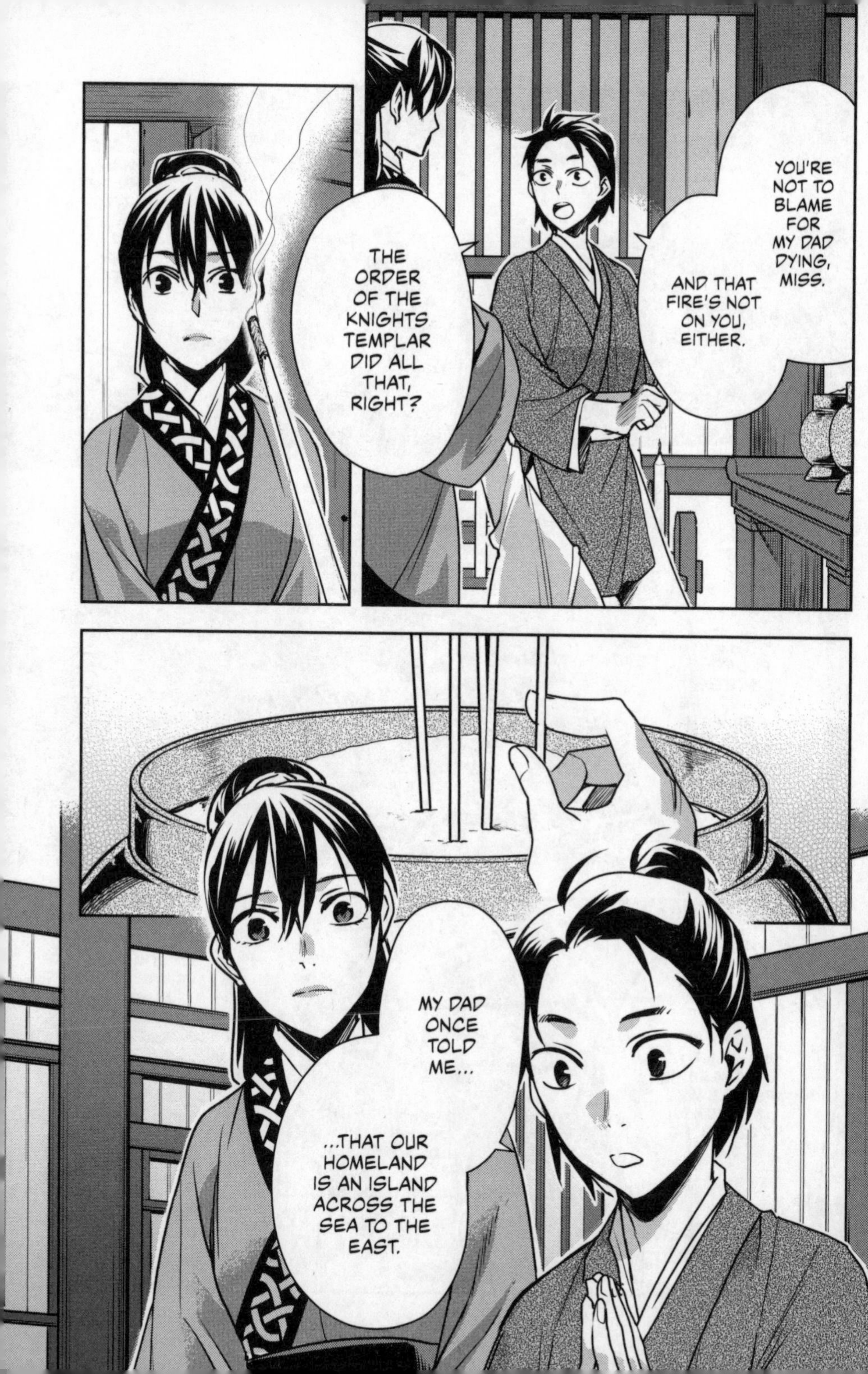
YOU'RE NOT TO BLAME FOR MY DAD DYING, MISS.
AND THAT FIRE'S NOT ON YOU, EITHER.
THE ORDER OF THE KNIGHTS TEMPLAR DID ALL THAT, RIGHT?
MY DAD ONCE TOLD ME...
...THAT OUR HOMELAND IS AN ISLAND ACROSS THE SEA TO THE EAST.

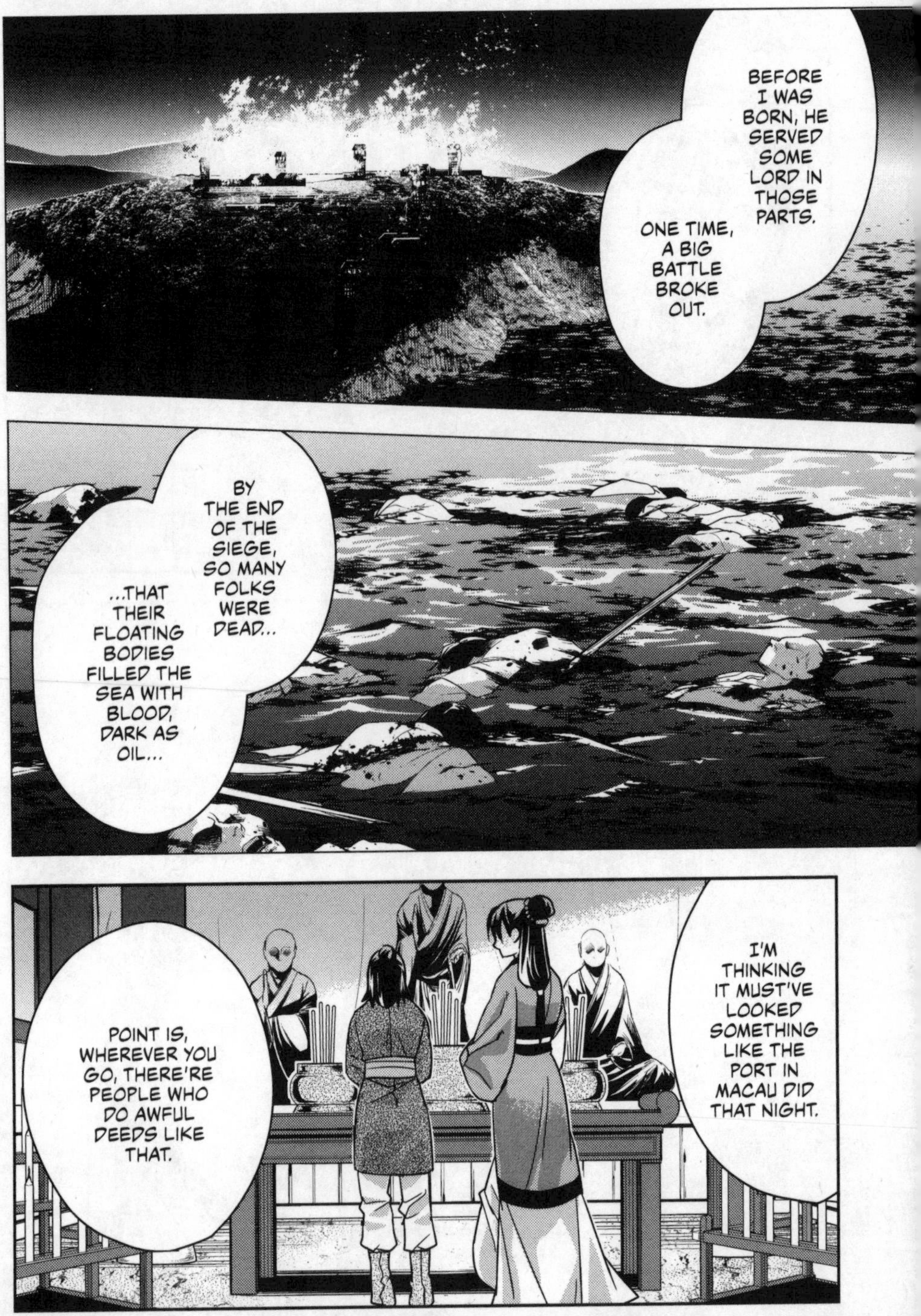
BEFORE I WAS BORN, HE SERVED SOME LORD IN THOSE PARTS.
ONE TIME, A BIG BATTLE BROKE OUT.
BY THE END OF THE SIEGE, SO MANY FOLKS WERE DEAD...
...THAT THEIR FLOATING BODIES FILLED THE SEA WITH BLOOD, DARK AS OIL...
I'M THINKING IT MUST'VE LOOKED SOMETHING LIKE THE PORT IN MACAU DID THAT NIGHT.
POINT IS, WHEREVER YOU GO, THERE'RE PEOPLE WHO DO AWFUL DEEDS LIKE THAT.

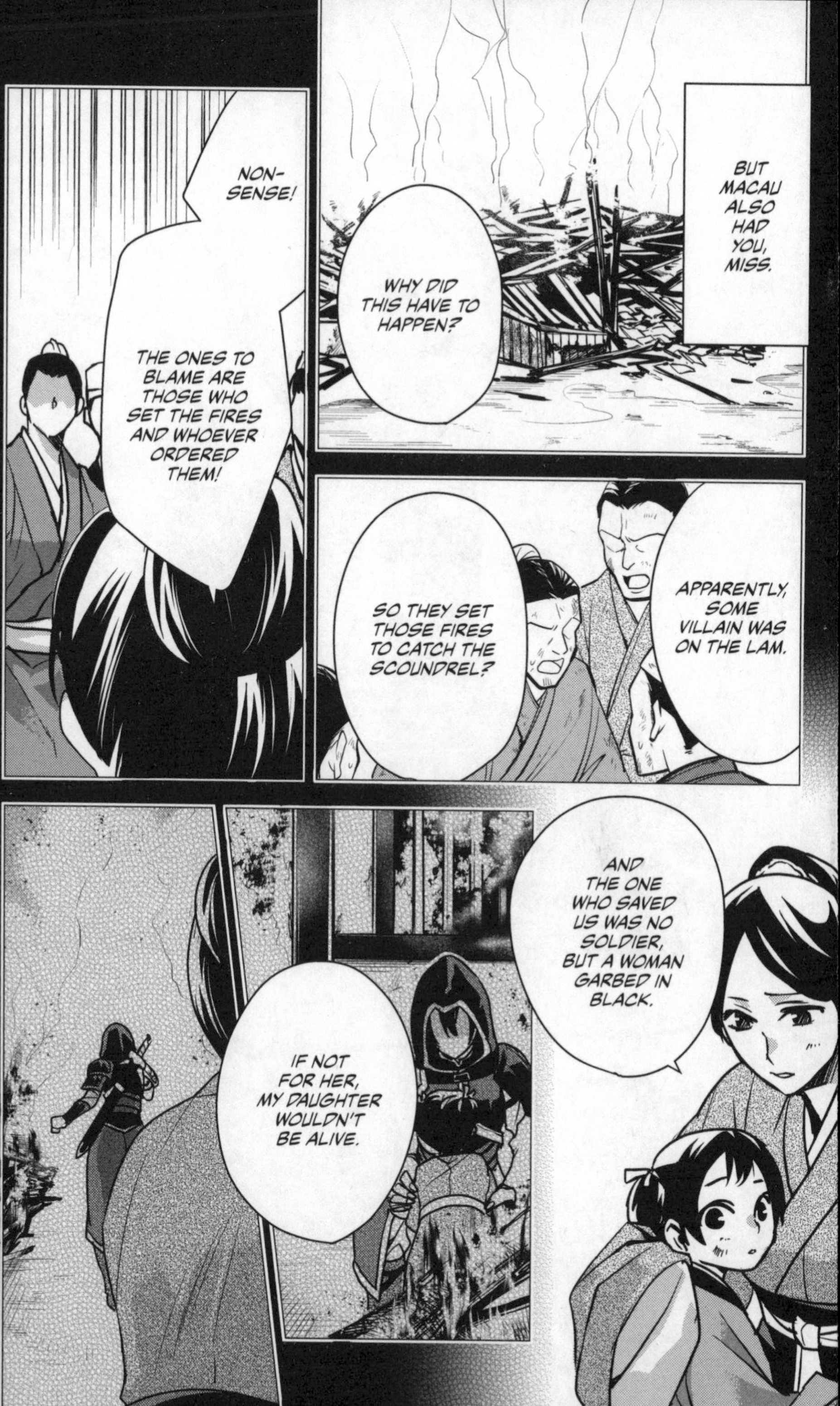
BUT MACAU ALSO HAD YOU, MISS.
WHY DID THIS HAVE TO HAPPEN?
APPARENTLY, SOME VILLAIN WAS ON THE LAM.
SO THEY SET THOSE FIRES TO CATCH THE SCOUNDREL?
NON-SENSE!
THE ONES TO BLAME ARE THOSE WHO SET THE FIRES AND WHOEVER ORDERED THEM!
AND THE ONE WHO SAVED US WAS NO SOLDIER, BUT A WOMAN GARBED IN BLACK.
IF NOT FOR HER, MY DAUGHTER WOULDN'T BE ALIVE.

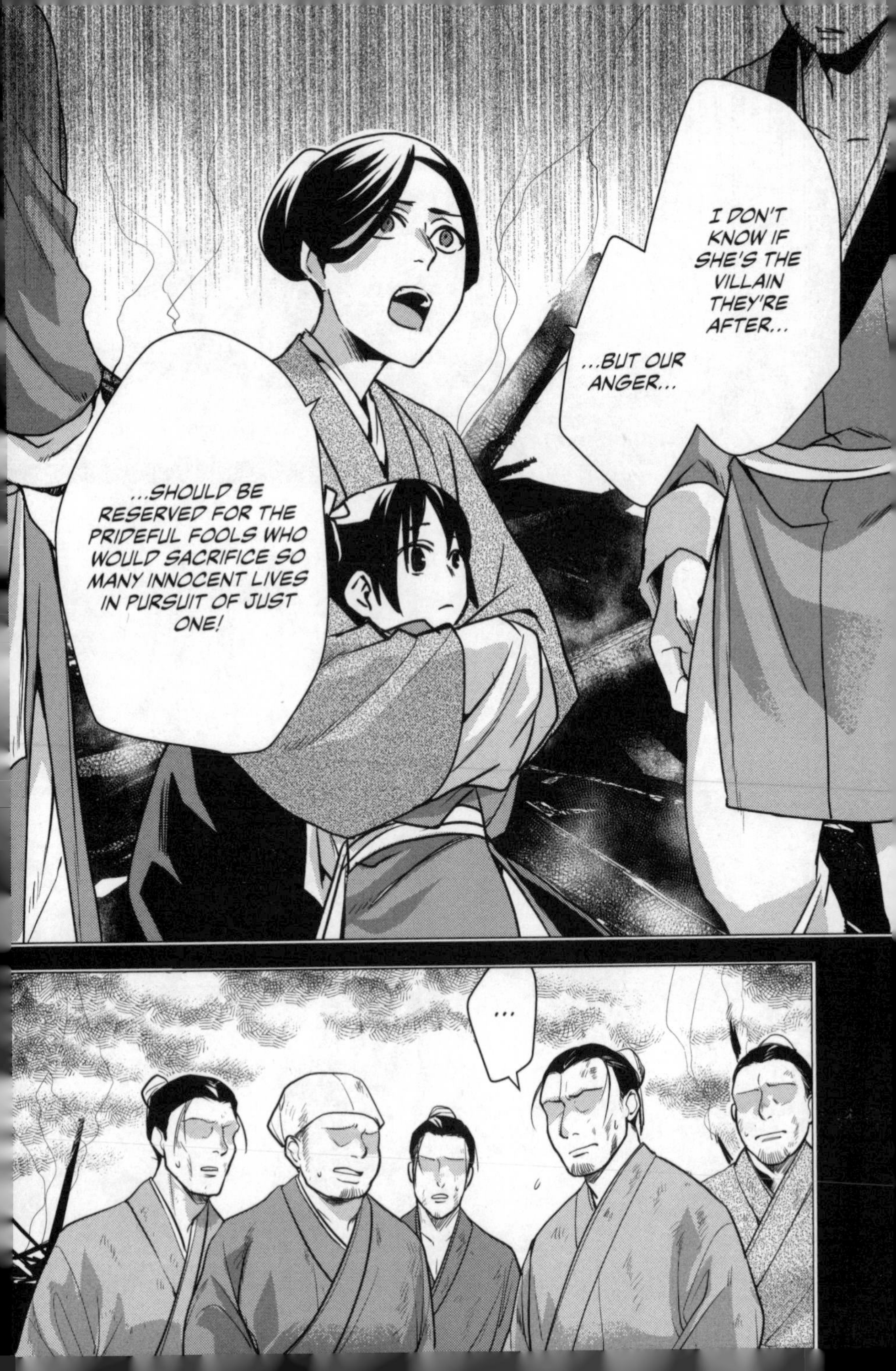
I DON'T KNOW IF SHE'S THE VILLAIN THEY'RE AFTER...
...BUT OUR ANGER...
...SHOULD BE RESERVED FOR THE PRIDEFUL FOOLS WHO WOULD SACRIFICE SO MANY INNOCENT LIVES IN PURSUIT OF JUST ONE!
...

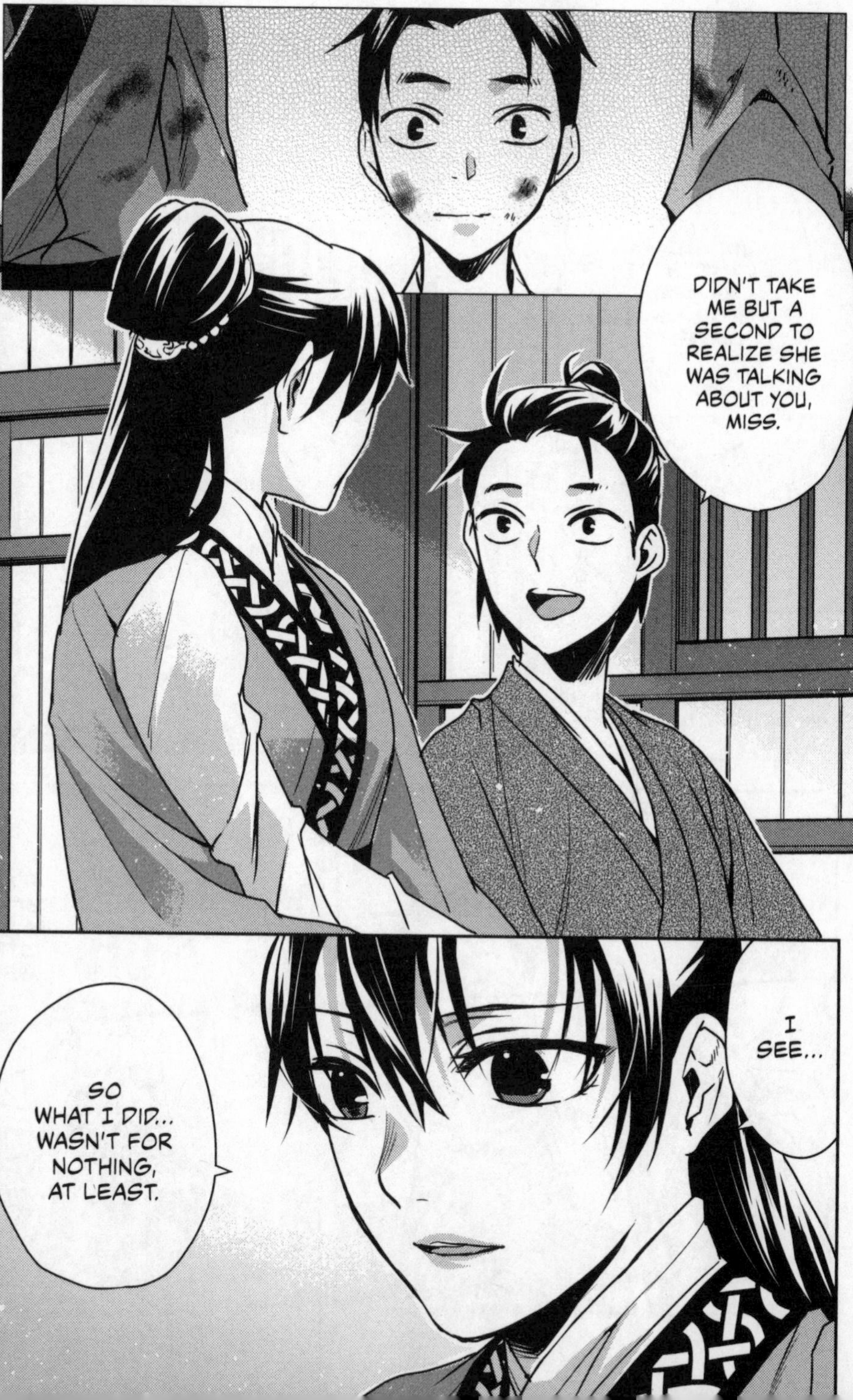
DIDN'T TAKE ME BUT A SECOND TO REALIZE SHE WAS TALKING ABOUT YOU, MISS.
I SEE...
SO WHAT I DID... WASN'T FOR NOTHING, AT LEAST.

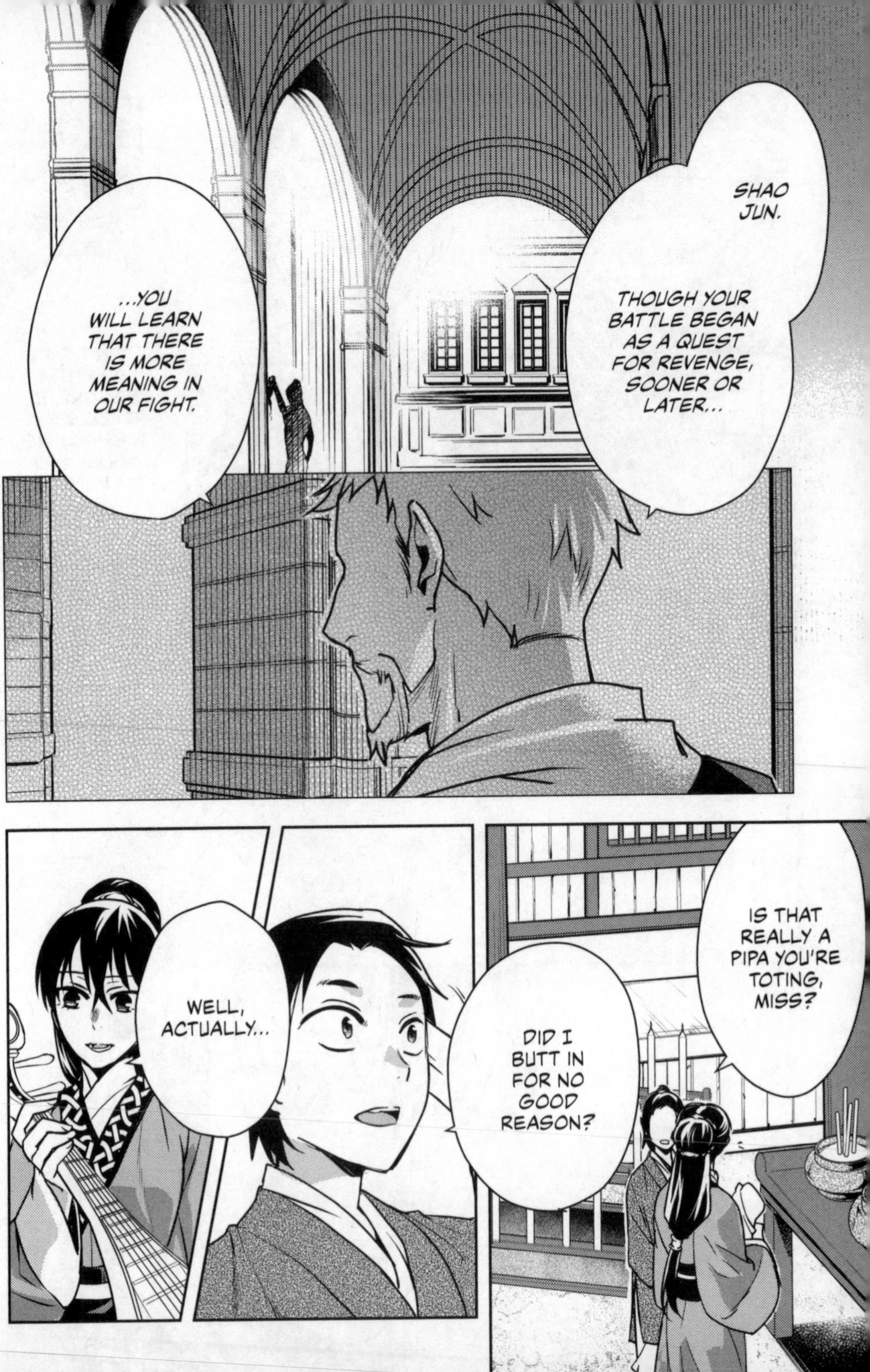
SHAO JUN.
THOUGH YOUR BATTLE BEGAN AS A QUEST FOR REVENGE, SOONER OR LATER...
...YOU WILL LEARN THAT THERE IS MORE MEANING IN OUR FIGHT.
IS THAT REALLY A PIPA YOU'RE TOTING, MISS?
DID I BUTT IN FOR NO GOOD REASON?
WELL, ACTUALLY...

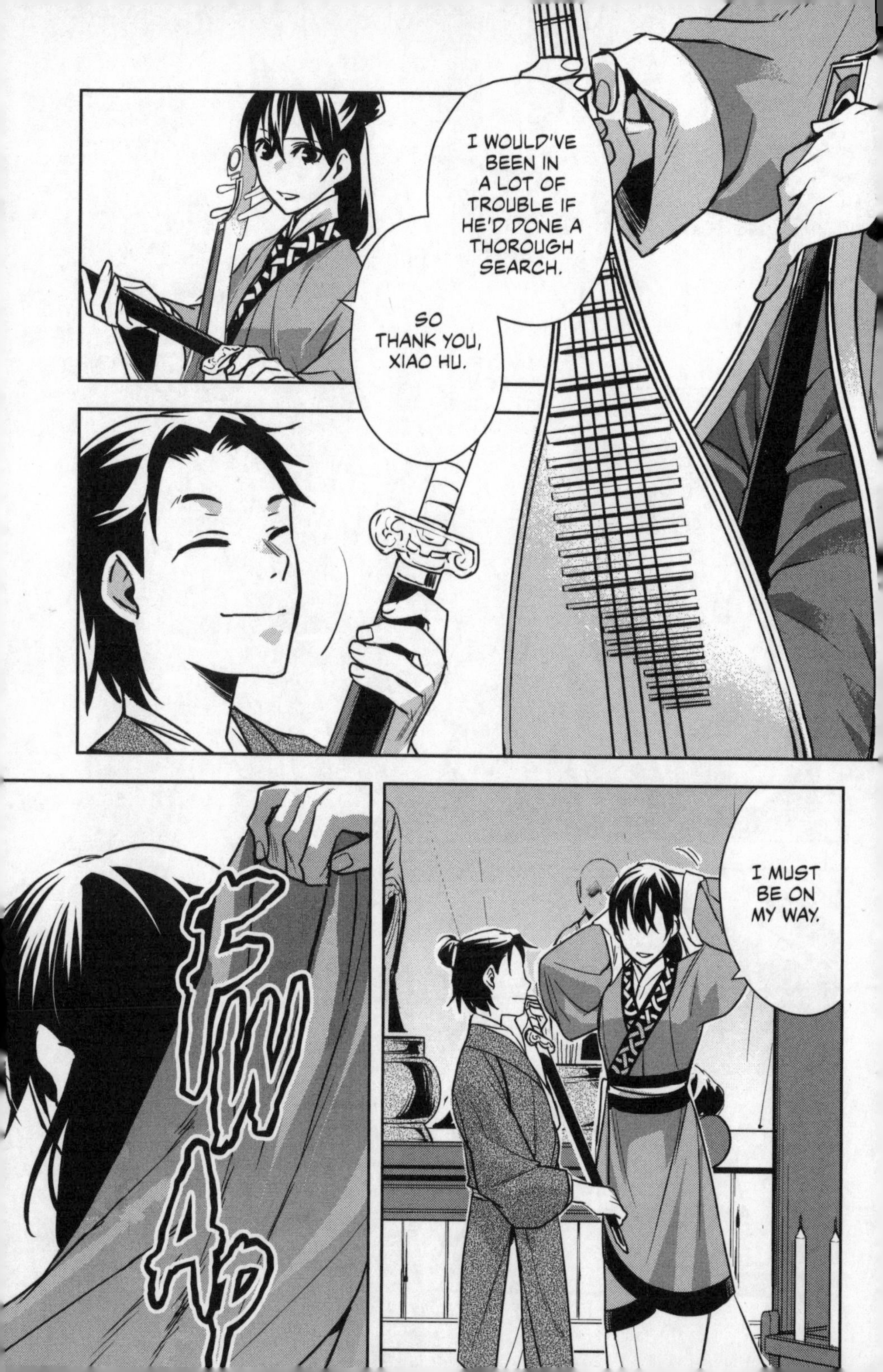
I WOULD'VE BEEN IN A LOT OF TROUBLE IF HE'D DONE A THOROUGH SEARCH.
SO THANK YOU, XIAO HU.
I MUST BE ON MY WAY.
FWAP

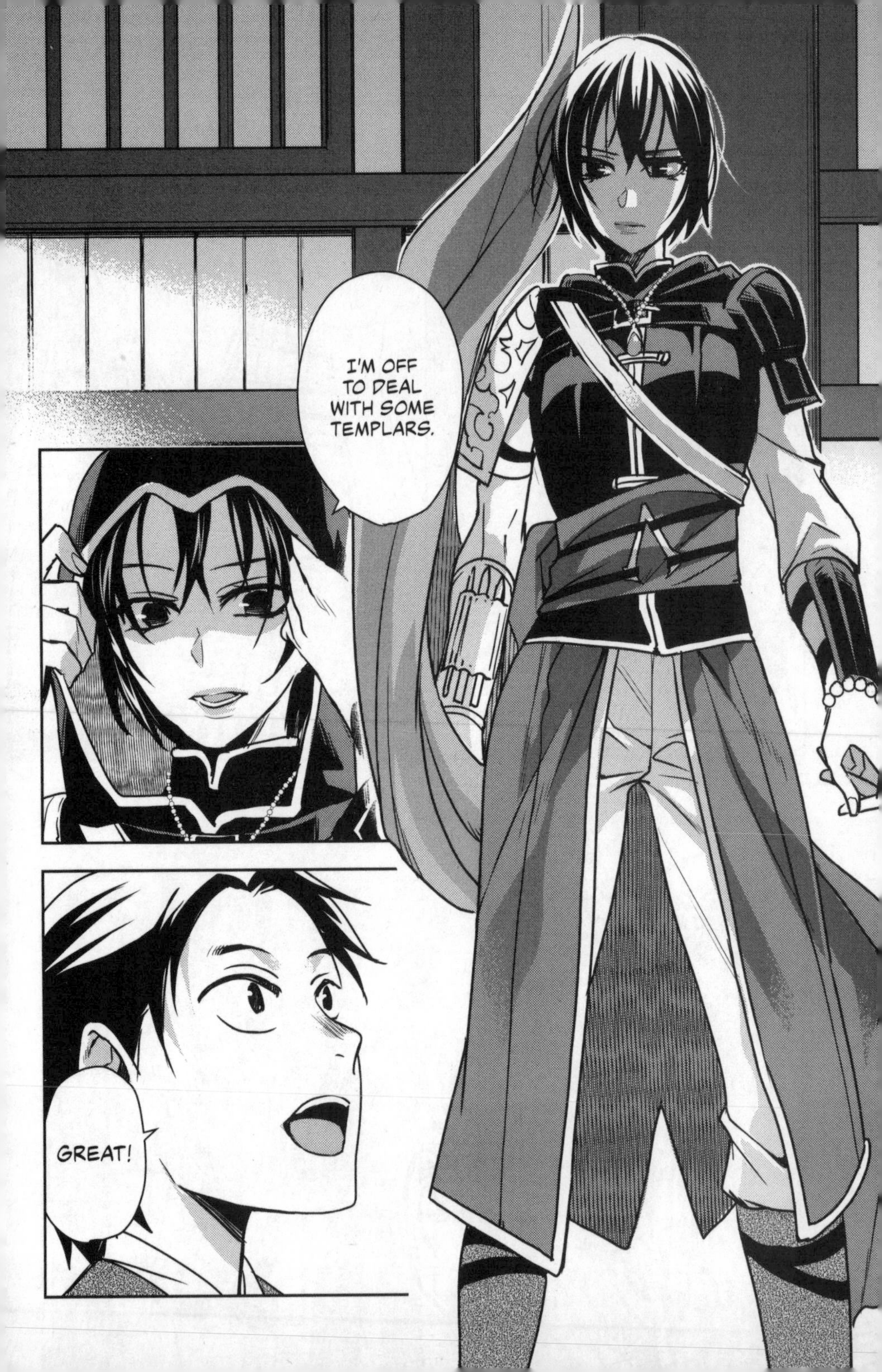
I'M OFF TO DEAL WITH SOME TEMPLARS.
GREAT!

UM, MISS?

?

NAH, I'LL TELL YOU NEXT TIME.

SO YOU'D BETTER COME BACK!

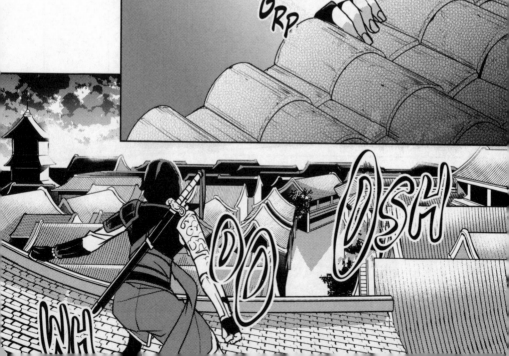

GRP.

OOSH

OO

WH

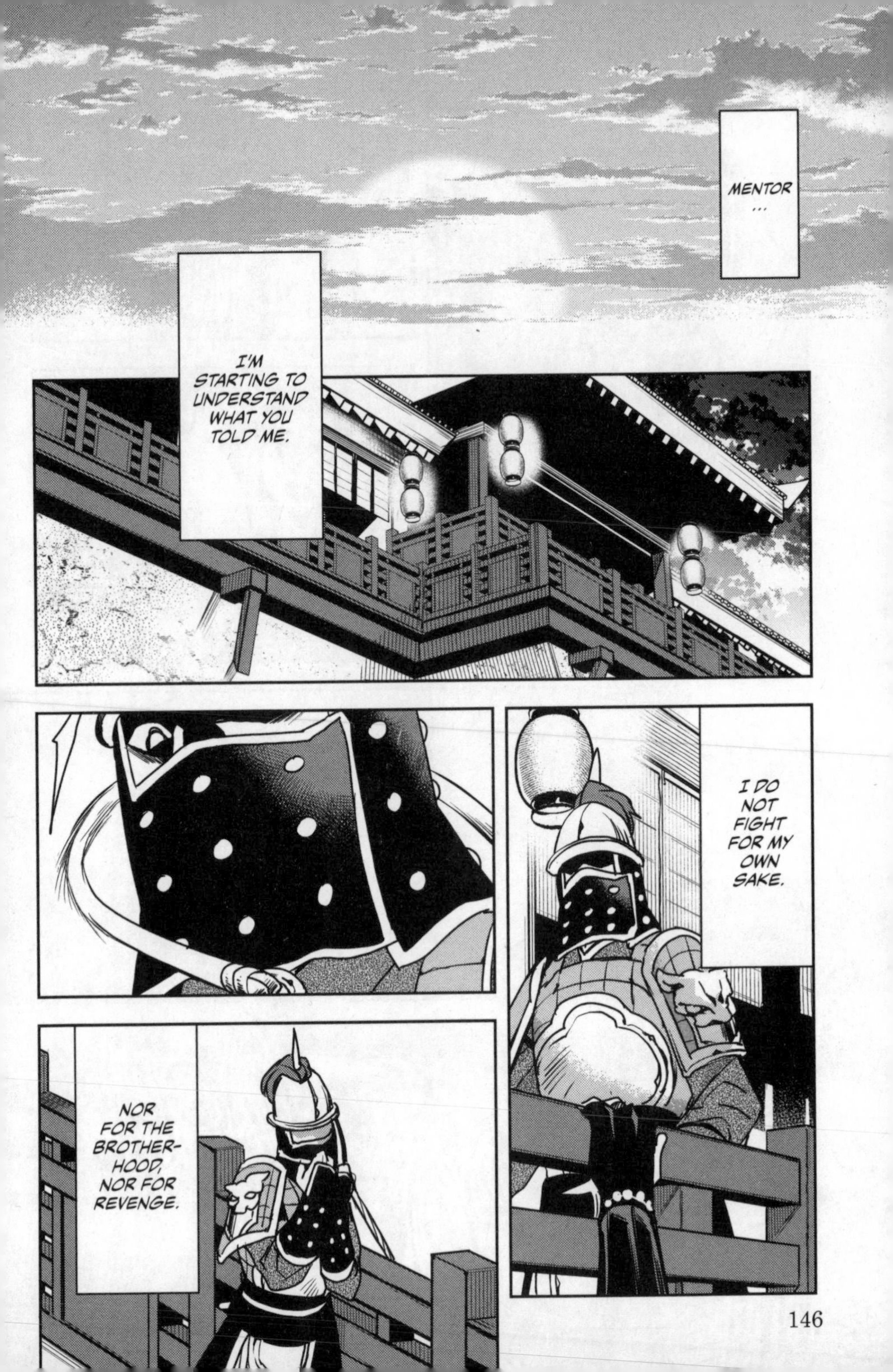
MENTOR ...
I'M STARTING TO UNDERSTAND WHAT YOU TOLD ME.
I DO NOT FIGHT FOR MY OWN SAKE.
NOR FOR THE BROTHER-HOOD, NOR FOR REVENGE.

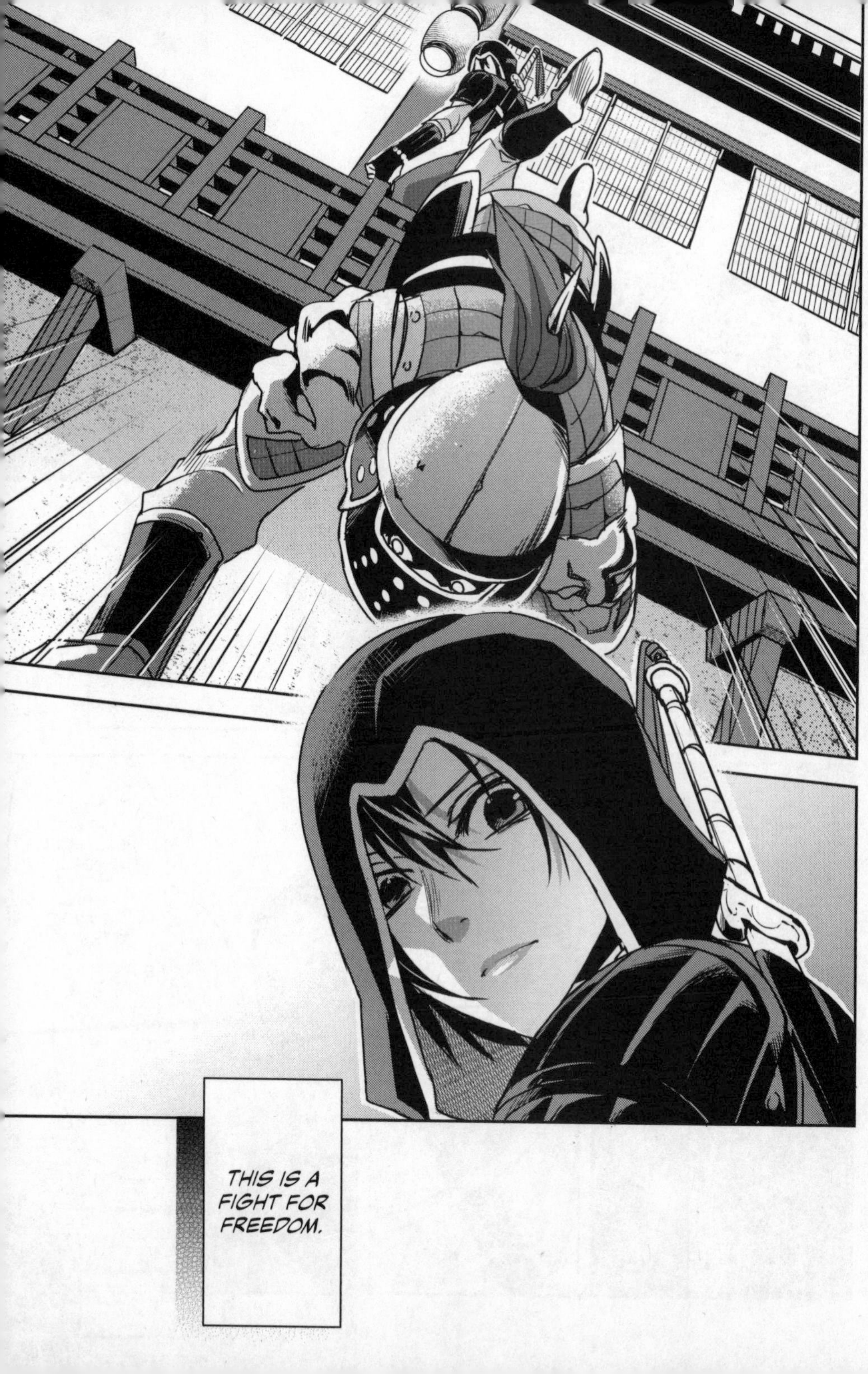
THIS IS A FIGHT FOR FREEDOM.

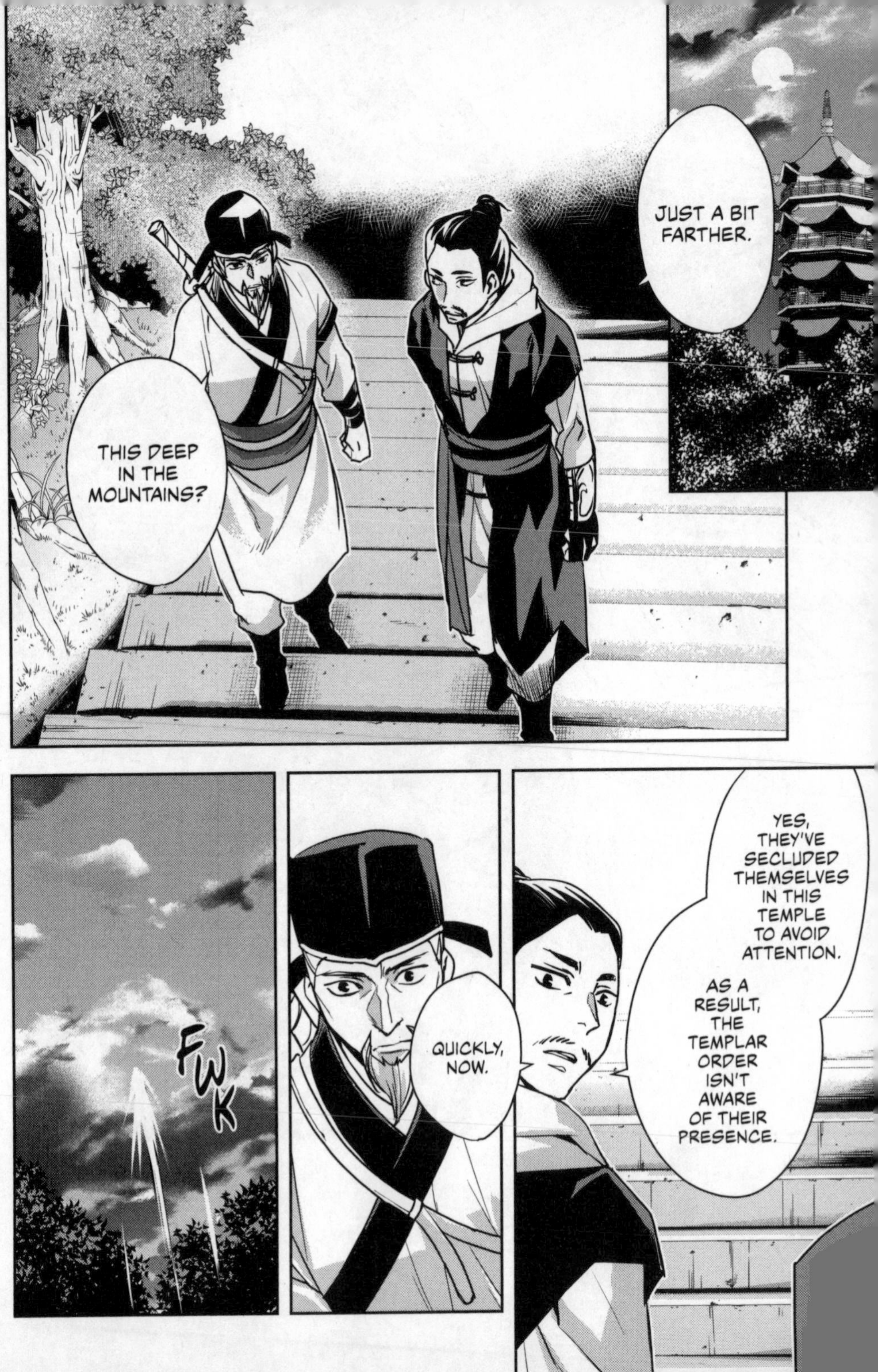
JUST A BIT FARTHER.
THIS DEEP IN THE MOUNTAINS?
YES, THEY'VE SECLUDED THEMSELVES IN THIS TEMPLE TO AVOID ATTENTION.
AS A RESULT, THE TEMPLAR ORDER ISN'T AWARE OF THEIR PRESENCE.
QUICKLY, NOW.
FWK

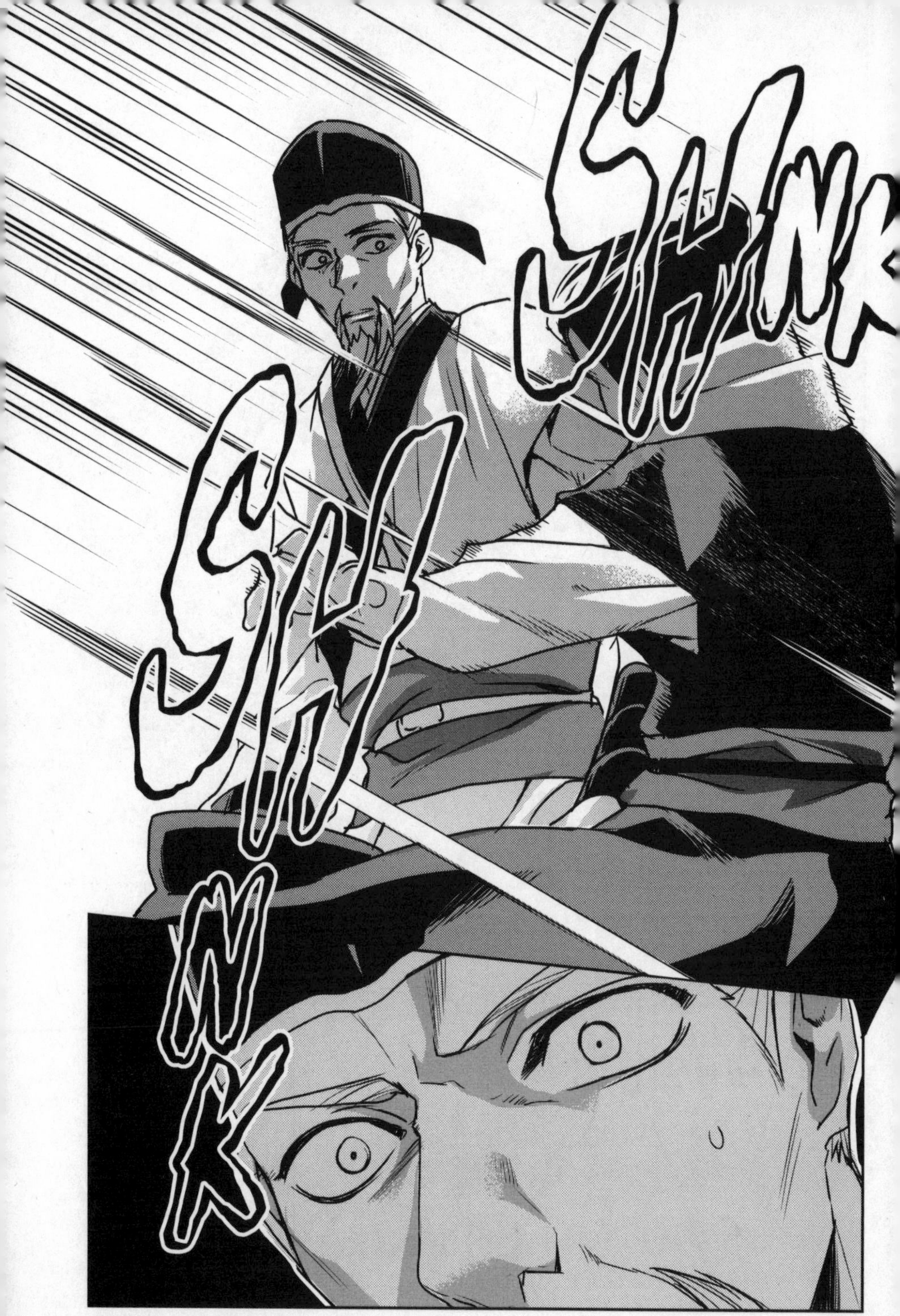
SHNK
SHNK

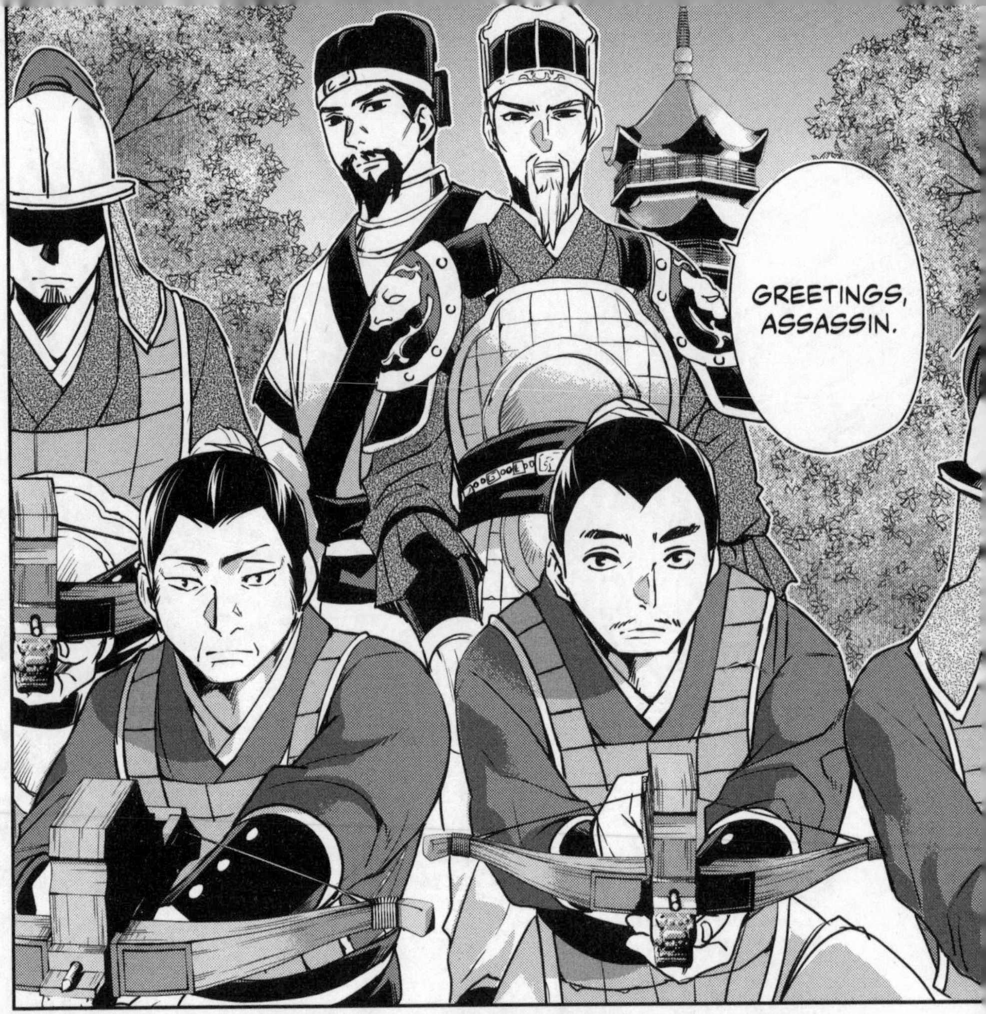
GREETINGS, ASSASSIN.

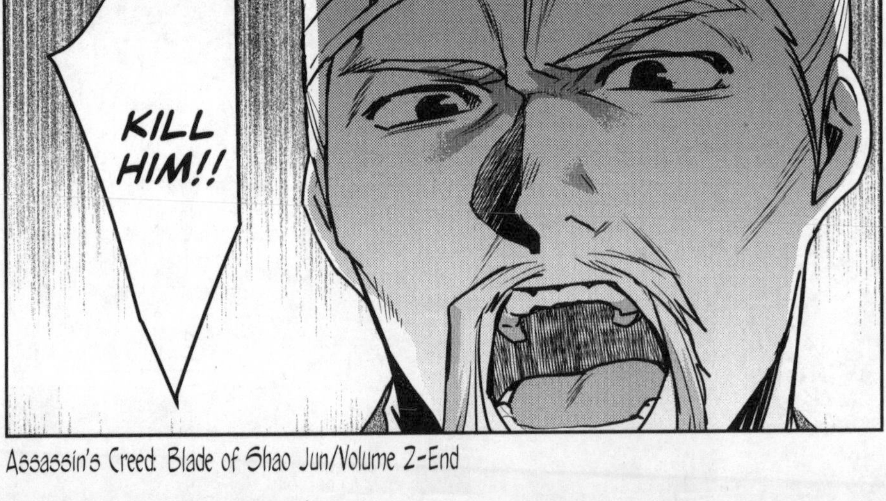
KILL HIM!!

Assassin's Creed: Blade of Shao Jun/Volume 2-End

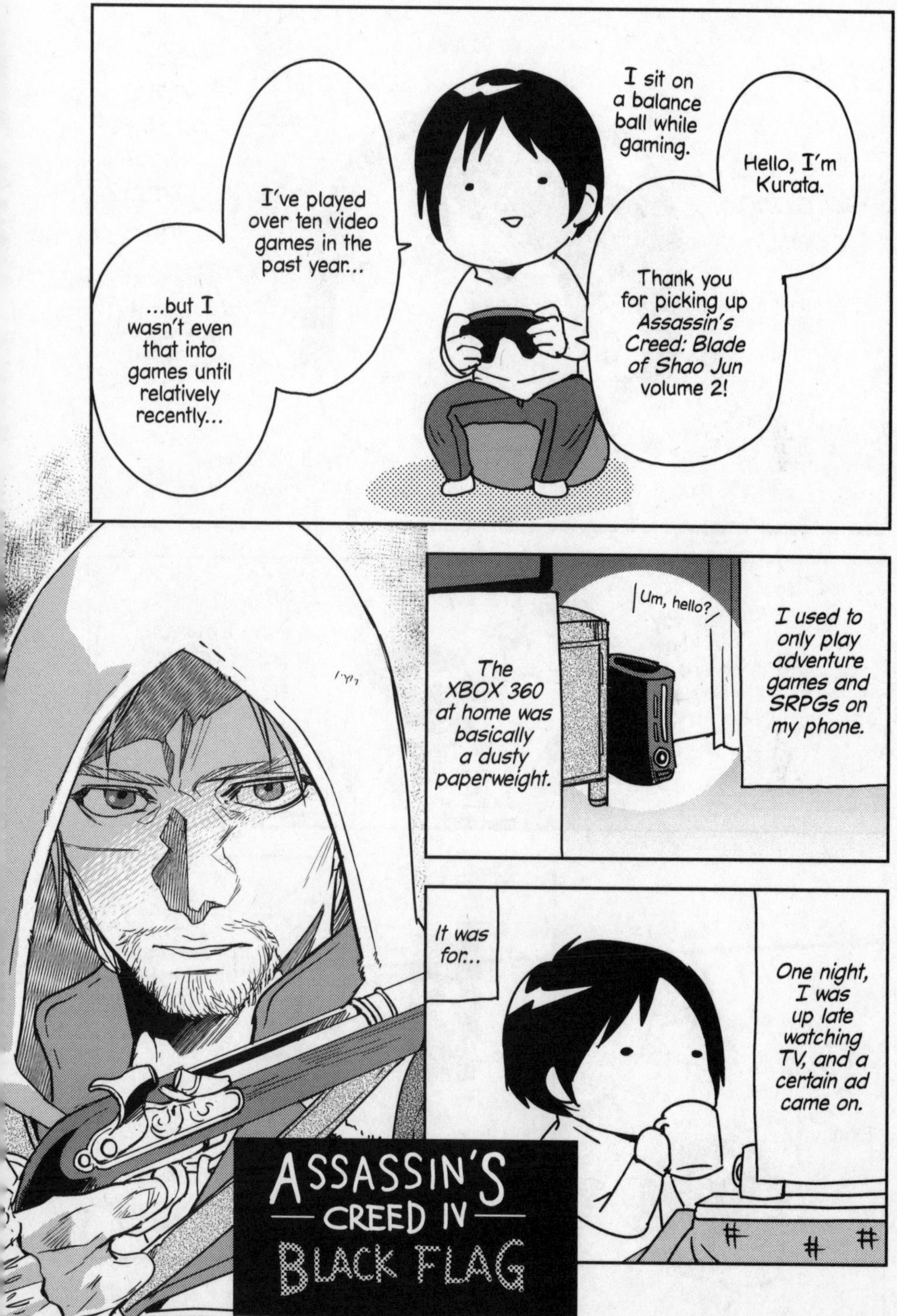
Hello, I'm Kurata.
Thank you for picking up *Assassin's Creed: Blade of Shao Jun* volume 2!
I sit on a balance ball while gaming.
I've played over ten video games in the past year...
...but I wasn't even that into games until relatively recently...
I used to only play adventure games and SRPGs on my phone.
Um, hello?
The XBOX 360 at home was basically a dusty paperweight.
One night, I was up late watching TV, and a certain ad came on.
It was for...
ASSASSIN'S
CREED IV
BLACK FLAG

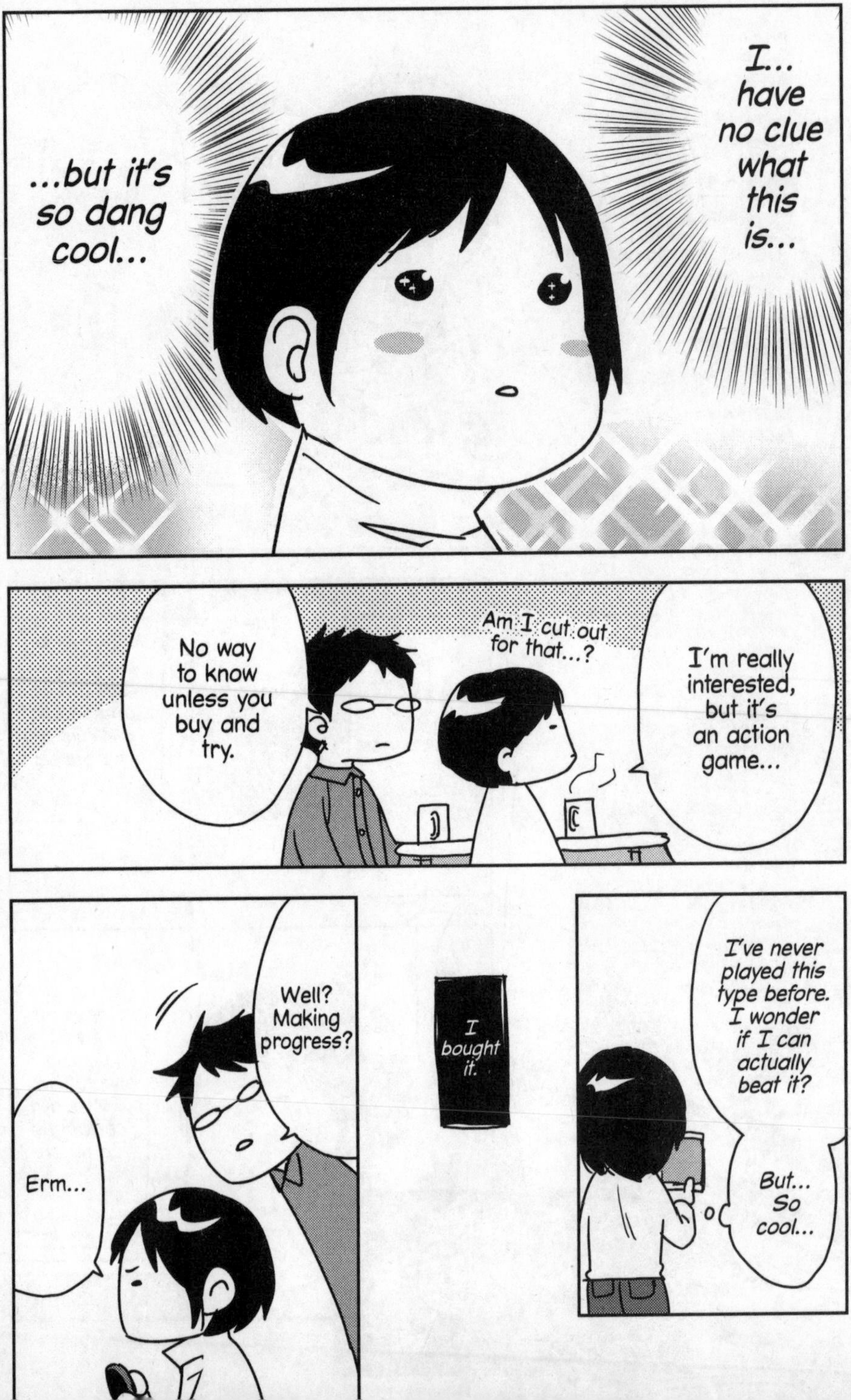
I... have no clue what this is...
...but it's so dang cool...
I'm really interested, but it's an action game...
Am I cut out for that...?
No way to know unless you buy and try.
I've never played this type before. I wonder if I can actually beat it?
But... So cool...
I bought it.
Well? Making progress?
Erm...

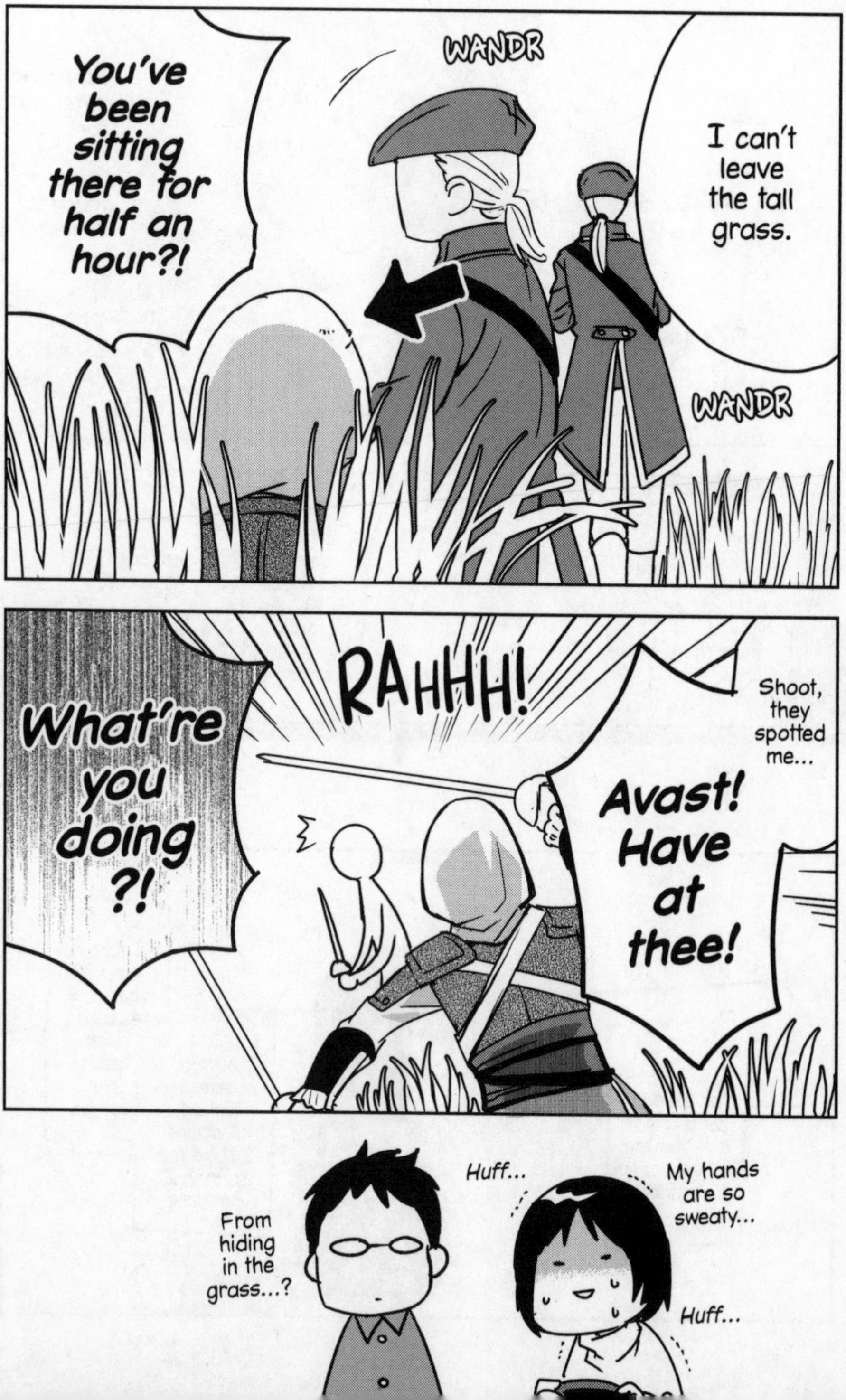
I can't leave the tall grass.
WANDR
WANDR
You've been sitting there for half an hour?!
Shoot, they spotted me...
Avast! Have at thee!
RAHHH!
What're you doing?!
My hands are so sweaty...
Huff...
Huff...
From hiding in the grass...?

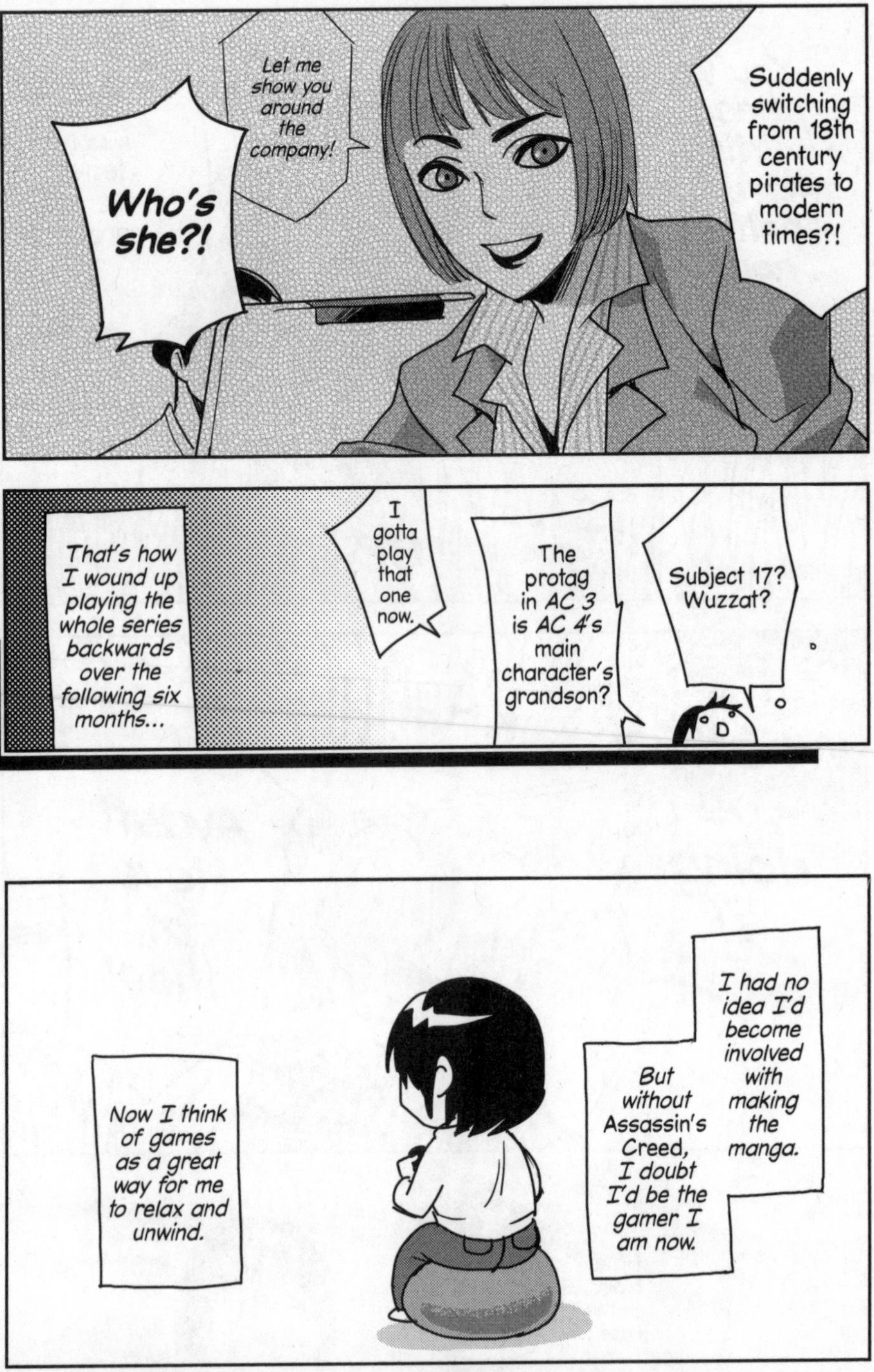
Suddenly switching from 18th century pirates to modern times?!
Let me show you around the company!
Who's she?!
Subject 17? Wuzzat?
The protag in AC 3 is AC 4's main character's grandson?
I gotta play that one now.
That's how I wound up playing the whole series backwards over the following six months...
I had no idea I'd become involved with making the manga.
But without Assassin's Creed, I doubt I'd be the gamer I am now.
Now I think of games as a great way for me to relax and unwind.

EDITORS

**Kikuyoshi Tajima**
**Masayoshi Nihama**

DRAWING ASSISTANCE

**Yumiko Harao**
**Kiri**
**Zero**
**Momo Hachiya**

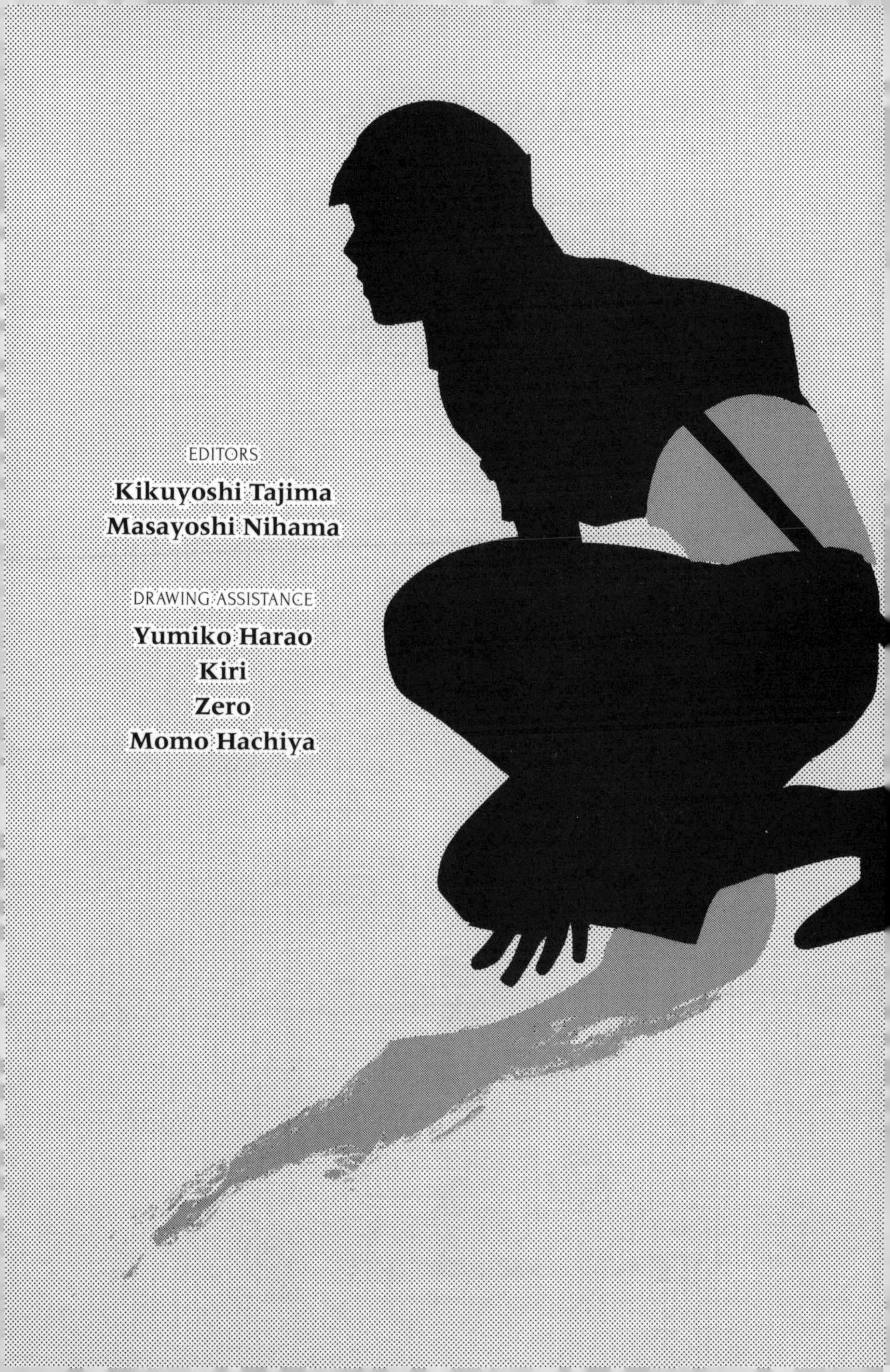

# ASSASSIN'S CREED

## BLADE OF SHAO JUN

VOLUME 2

VIZ SIGNATURE MANGA EDITION

ORIGINAL CONCEPT BY **Ubisoft**

STORY AND ART BY **Minoji Kurata**

TRANSLATION **Caleb Cook**
RETOUCH & LETTERING **Brandon Bovia**
DESIGN **Sten Anderson**
EDITOR **David Brothers**
COVER ILLUSTRATION **Minoji KURATA**
ORIGINAL COVER DESIGN **Junya ARAI + Bay Bridge Studio**



Printed in the U.S.A.

Published by VIZ Media, LLC
P.O. Box 77010 | San Francisco, CA 94107

10 9 8 7 6 5 4 3 2 1
First printing, August 2021

ratings.viz.com RATED T+ OLDER TEEN

**PARENTAL ADVISORY**
ASSASSIN'S CREED: BLADE OF SHAO JUN is rated T+ for Older Teen and is recommended for ages 16 and up. It contains graphic violence.

VIZ MEDIA viz.com VIZ SIGNATURE vizsignature.com UBISOFT

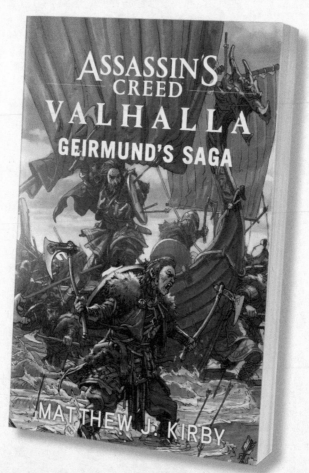

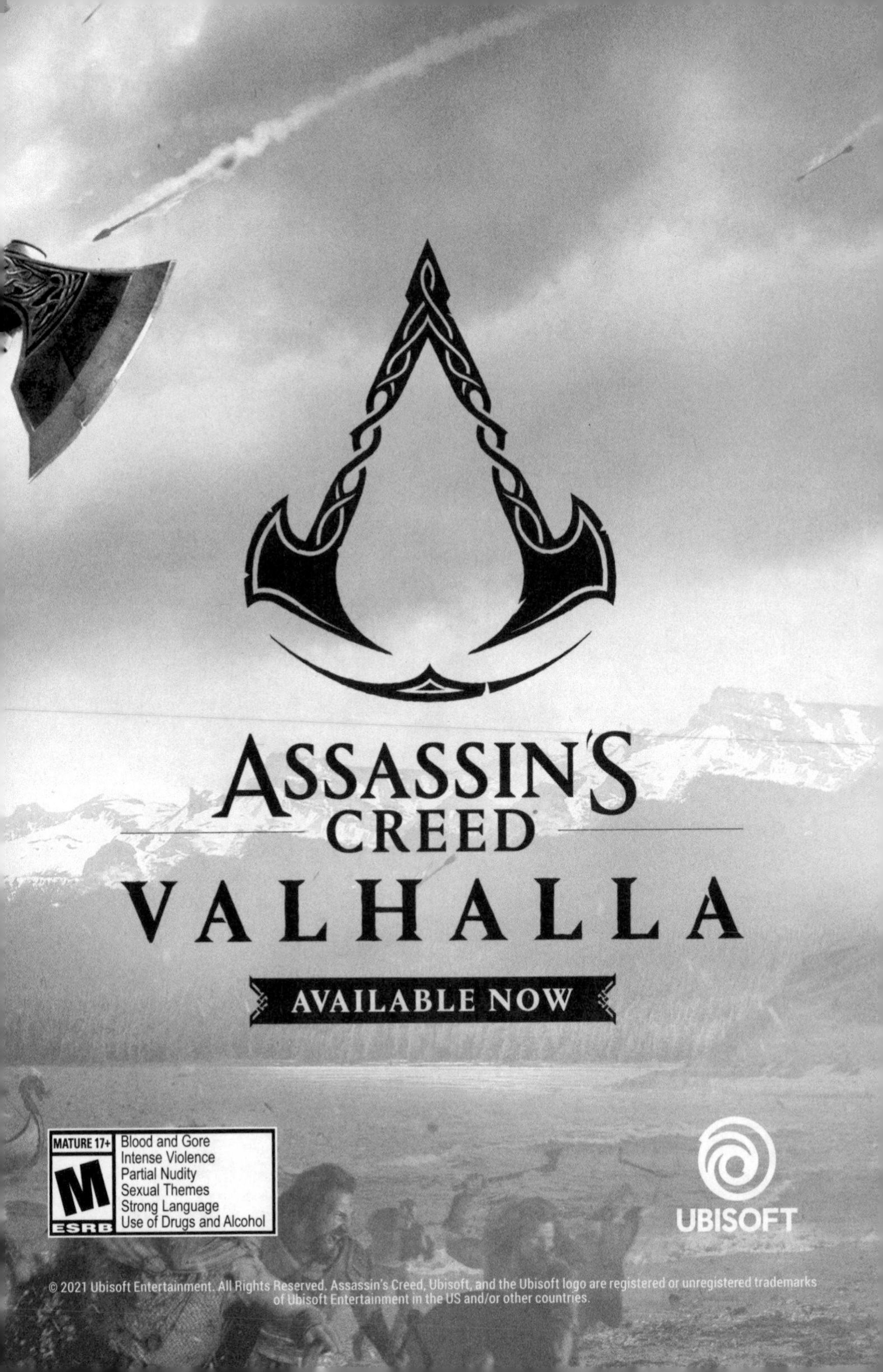
ASSASSIN'S CREED
VALHALLA
AVAILABLE NOW
MATURE 17+
M
ESRB
Blood and Gore
Intense Violence
Partial Nudity
Sexual Themes
Strong Language
Use of Drugs and Alcohol
UBISOFT
© 2021 Ubisoft Entertainment. All Rights Reserved. Assassin's Creed, Ubisoft, and the Ubisoft logo are registered or unregistered trademarks of Ubisoft Entertainment in the US and/or other countries.

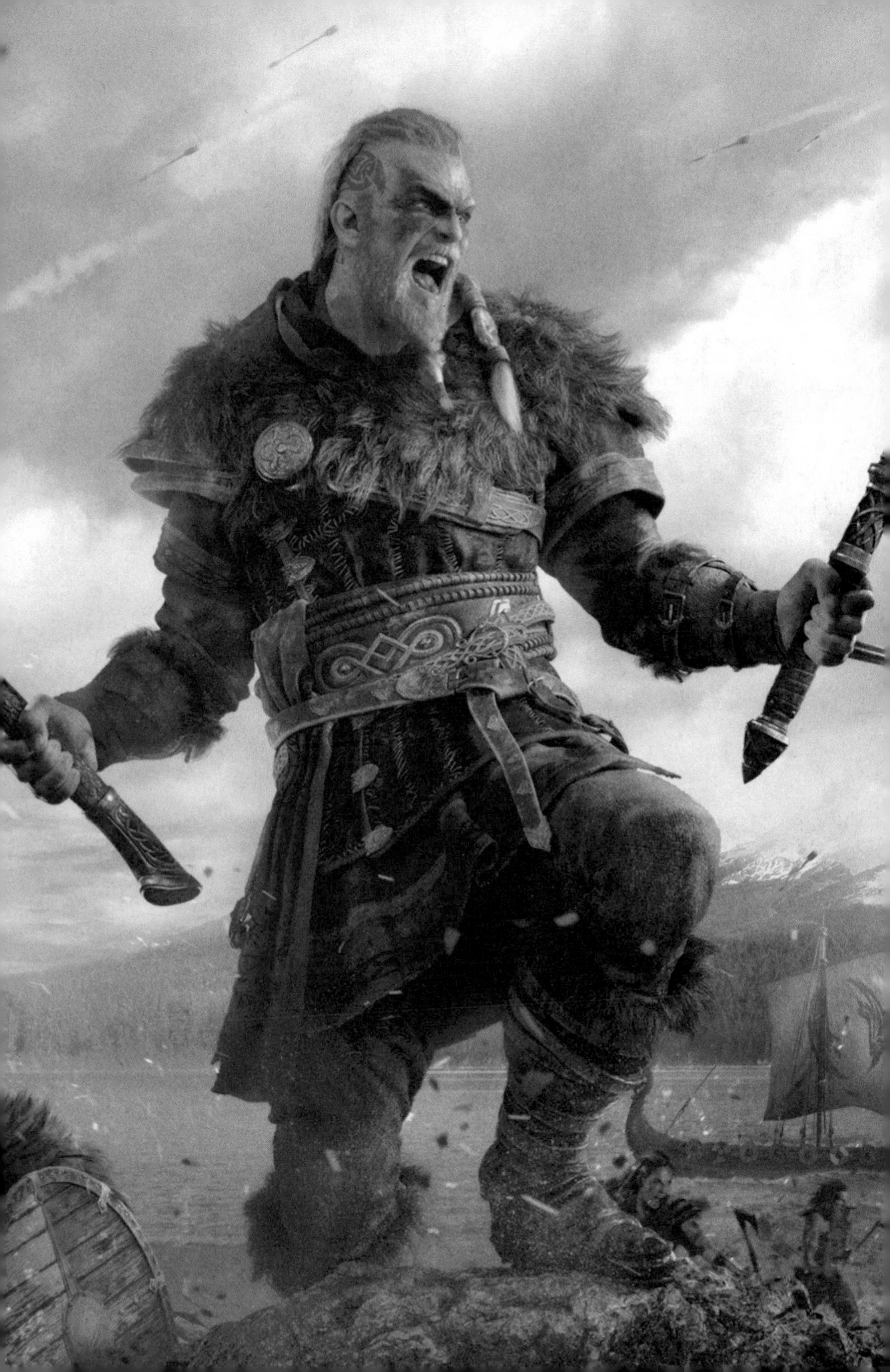

# YOU'RE READING THE WRONG WAY!

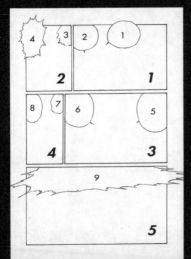

*Assassin's Creed: Blade of Shao Jun* reads from right to left, starting in the upper-right corner. Japanese is read from right to left, meaning that action, sound effects, assassinations, and word balloon reading order are completely reversed from English order.